THE
BISON

DANIIL GRANIN

TRANSLATED BY ANTONINA W. BOUIS

DOUBLEDAY

NEW YORK LONDON TORONTO
SYDNEY AUCKLAND

THE
BISON

A NOVEL
ABOUT THE
SCIENTIST
WHO DEFIED
STALIN

PUBLISHED BY DOUBLEDAY
a division of Bantam Doubleday Dell Publishing Group, Inc.
666 Fifth Avenue, New York, New York 10103

DOUBLEDAY and the portrayal of an anchor with
a dolphin are trademarks of Doubleday,
a division of Bantam Doubleday Dell
Publishing Group, Inc.

Library of Congress Cataloging-in-Publication data applied for

ISBN 0-385-24753-2
Copyright © 1989 by Daniil Granin
All Rights Reserved

Printed in the United States of America
March 1990

First Edition in the United States of America

RRH

CONTENTS

CONTENTS

THE
BISON

1

A CREATURE
FROM ANOTHER
ERA

On opening day of the international scientific congress there was a reception at the Palace of Congresses inside the Kremlin. After the first toasts a thick multilingual flow swirled among the long tables. People moved from group to group, carrying their glasses, making introductions; they drank to the health of some, passed along greetings to others, peered at the name tags glistening on everyone's lapel. This movement, or boiling, which seemed disorderly and meaningless, actually created the greatest satisfaction and, I would even say, the greatest benefit of such international gatherings. The business part, the lectures and reports, was necessary, of course, although most of the participants merely pretended to understand it all. Some didn't even wish to understand, but all wished to socialize, to have the opportunity to chat with someone whom they knew only from his publications, to ask something, tell something, clarify something. This was the important part, dearest to all these people who were separated for most of their lives, scattered throughout universities, institutes, and laboratories in Europe, America, Asia, and even Australia.

Here were the celebrities of the past remembered only by the elderly, those who had once made a splash and had promised new directions; the hopes had not been justified, and very little was left of the promises, but thank God that there was anything at all, at least one mutation, one little article . . . The young people, as a rule, were not interested in the history of their science—genetics. They had the heroes of today, the leaders of new hopes, new promises. There were the celebrities in some very narrow fields— diseases of corn, the hardiness of oaks. There were the general celebrities, who had managed to understand a thing or two in heredity, in the mechanism of evolution. And there were the living classics, of whom even I had heard. Young people who had their futures ahead of them, resounding fame and resounding failures, scurried among the tables and groups.

The reception was good because the meeting and greeting was taking place at the beginning of the congress, you could find out who was who, who was there, who was not.

In this completely chaotic movement, in the din of exclamations, glasses clinking, laughter, and bows, something happened, a light stir, a whisper spread and rustled. An expression of curiosity appeared on the vaguely smiling faces, which had been animated for no specific reason. People began moving to a far corner of the room. Some drifted, others walked with determination and surprise.

In that far corner the Bison sat in a chair. His powerful head was pulled into his shoulders, and his small eyes glittered sharply. They came up to him, bowed, shook his hand carefully. His lower lip protruding, he snorted, roared either in approval or in outrage. His thick mane of gray hair was shaggy. He was old, of course, but his years had not worn him out; on the contrary. He was as heavy and solid as a petrified oak.

A woman, thin and middle-aged, embraced and kissed him. The woman was Charlotte Auerbach, the British geneticist whose books had just been published in Russian translation to great interest and acclaim. Charlotte had come from England. She had escaped there from Nazi Germany. The Bison had helped her get settled in England. It was long ago, in 1933, perhaps he had forgotten about it, but she remembered every detail. Light tears of joy rolled down her cheeks. Forty-five years had elapsed since the day they parted. Eras had passed, the whole world had changed, but the Bison had remained the same for her, still her senior, even though they were the same age.

An American came over, a Nobel Prize winner, awkward, long-armed. He hugged the Bison and sniffled. He behaved as he wished, wiping his nose with his sleeve; he was a hero and could do that. After him came the Greek Kanelis, whom the Bison had saved about thirty-five years ago in Berlin, letting him hide in his cellar until the war ended. The "Ancient Greek" Antosha Kanelis, as the Bison called him, was taciturn, he knew many languages but spoke none, he liked to be silent, and he kept his silence in many tongues. Everyone became convinced through his silence that he was a marvelous man.

Tactfully awaiting his turn, Michael White, the Australian film star, moved toward the Bison. Handsome and usually self-confident, White began an embarrassed recitation, explaining that he was the young man who many years ago had accompanied the Bison and his colleague Feodosy Dobrzhansky around London, or rather, he should have guided them but ended up only accompanying them, because the Bison and Dobrzhansky had talked entirely to each other, kept losing him, then realizing it and shouting, "Where's that fellow?" The Bison chuckled. "Feka Dobrzhansky . . ." Strangely, he remembered White, but London almost not at all. After White came a Dutchman, then a group of Germans, followed by a young Azerbaijani professor, presented by his Moscow co-author. The Bison chatted with Giuseppe Montalenti in Italian. One of the ornaments of the congress, for every congress, symposium, and conference has to have its "excellency," was the Swede Gustafson, who was also pushing through to see the Bison. The other ornament of the congress, the president of a society, a chairman, a representative, an editor in chief, a coordinator, and so on, a worldly, social man who knew how to present himself and was always witty and charming, suddenly got cold feet and kept asking one of the young female assistants whether she could introduce him to the Bison.

Young people huddled at a distance, regarding with curiosity both the Bison himself and this unplanned ceremony—the parade of celebrities paying their respects to the Bison. The Bison accepted the parade as his due. He seemed to enjoy playing the role of marshal or patriarch, he nodded benevolently, hearing out people who worked in the best, most beautiful, and kindest of all sciences. They studied Nature: how and what grows on earth, everything that moves, flies, crawls, why everything that is alive lives and multiplies, develops, changes or does not change, retaining its form. For generation after generation these people had tried to understand the mysterious source that distinguishes the living from the nonliving. As no one else had, they had mastered the soul innate in every worm, in every fly, even though, of course, instead of such unscientific names they used long, hard-to-pronounce terms. But those who had gotten in deep unwittingly bowed to the miracle of perfection of the lowliest organisms. Even on the level of the simplest form, the cell, there was a complexity of behavior that could not be grasped. Proximity to that quivering matter united this multilingual, disparate crowd.

As was to have been expected, a pushy professor gleaning his petty harvest of business cards and handshakes bustled around the Bison, uttering phrases that might have been wise but were lost because nobody paid attention.

The uninitiated whispered, trying not to miss a thing. They sensed that they were observing history in the making. Legends about the Bison, each one more improbable than the next, were recounted in a low voice. Not believed. Gasps in response. It would have been strange if such stories were confirmed. They resembled myths, attempts to explain certain facts in his life. There were also jokes about him; statements, witticisms, and actions were attributed to him that were simply impossible. There were real fairy tales about him, and interestingly, not all were flattering, in fact some were downright malicious. But for the most part the stories were either heroic or roguish, having nothing to do with science.

Now, seeing him in the flesh, everyone unconsciously identified him with the image already held in their minds. And surprisingly enough, they matched. His stocky figure and powerful arms testified to his enormous physical strength. His face was etched with the marks of a stormy and significant life. The traces of past battles, desperate battles, did not disfigure his noble face but somehow improved it. And he behaved differently from the rest—freer, more relaxed. You could see that looking over his shoulder was not in his nature. He could afford to be himself. He had managed to retain that privilege of childhood. He was both refined and crude. Both characteristics corresponded to the legends about his aristocratic forebears and his brawls with criminals.

I once saw a painting in the house of his favorite student, Volodya Ivanov. It was the only thing he took after the Bison's death to remember him by. Ivanov had been given his choice, and he chose the painting. It is called *Three Bisons*. It depicts the Bison, seated, with his hands on a small bison sculpture, and above him on the wall is a photograph of the great Danish physicist Niels Bohr. The photograph is a well-known one, but in conjunction with the other two bisons, Bohr takes on a "bisonness," an oxen stubbornness, the heavy jaw, the concentration and wildness, the untamability of bisons—"a species almost completely wiped out by man." They had a lot in common, the Bison and Bohr, and they became close friends when the Bison came to visit Bohr's research institute in Denmark.

The bison sculpture under the Bison's hands seems to be growing into a rough four-legged, humpbacked creature weighing a ton, with a shaggy mane and a humped nose. Even in game preserves they don't let people come closer than thirty yards to them.

And the Bison himself is in his full glory in the painting. The artist painted him when he was sixty. Or perhaps sixty-five or seventy. He was unchanged in his late years. New wrinkles did not age him. I never met anyone who resembled him. He was one of those people whom you never forget, never confuse with anyone else. I've seen photographs and paintings of him in his youth—naturally, his face was smooth and he had a shock of curly black hair, but you can pick him out immediately in any group. Even in a still picture from a poorly shot documentary film of 1918 you can recognize him in a line of Red Army soldiers. A day of compulsory education in Moscow, May 28, 1918. Red Square. Red Army soldiers in front of the Historical Museum. Velvet banners above them: "Long live the union of workers and peasants!" and others too difficult to make out. The soldiers are in uniform, puttees, caps with patent-leather visors. Among them is our Bison in profile, standing next to a fellow with a mustache. He is thin, but familiarly stoop-shouldered, unmistakably recognizable. The picture was published in 1967 in *Soviet Screen* magazine, and the telephone calls to him began right away: "Did you see it? It's you! We found you right away . . ."

In the portrait the artist had painted him red. I don't know what the Armenian artist wanted to say with the red paint, but the portrait is a success. The brush expresses much better than my pen can the red-hot nature of the man, his "bisonness."

. . . Through my binoculars I saw it come out of the grove. A shaggy torso, unsuited to the preserve. It was cramped in this small forest area, there was nowhere to hide the hulk of its body, nowhere to put its power. Militantly balancing its short horns, it moved almost noiselessly, its damp nostrils quivering. It seemed bulky, excessively heavy, excessively large next to the antelopes, mountain goats, and other livestock in the preserve. You could sense antiquity in it.

I recalled a hospital ward, beds lined up in two rows. There were ten other people in it besides the Bison. I found him right away, because everyone was looking in his direction. He was listening to someone, and from time to time he emitted a low, mighty roar. He was the center of the ward. Wherever he went, he quickly became the center. People always expected something from him, and the more they got, the more they expected.

I sat at the foot of his bed. The strong smells of medicine, carbolic acid, and alcohol, the clink of glass vials, the creak of bedsprings, the moans of ailing bodies—hospital reality just did not go with the Bison. He lay back on his pillows. His broad shaggy chest showed in the opening of his hospital shirt. His forearms, muscular, were flawlessly sculpted. The skin was smooth, white, incongruously delicate. His militantly extended lower lip lent his face both crudeness and pedigree. He was a combination of the rough and the refined. Animal and aristocrat. In that well-washed, faded shirt like everyone else's, wracked by the same cough, subjected to the same procedures as the rest, injections, examinations, there was nothing left, not position, not title, not salary, nothing that was valued out there, beyond the hospital doors. I checked myself: could we be attributing many qualities to him because we know who he was? But even here, in this ward, the patients who had no idea who the Bison was still acknowledged his seniority, his superiority.

I was telling him the latest news when an oblique shaft of winter sunlight illuminated his hairy neck, a corner of his eye, covered with a wrinkled lid, and the gray locks of his hair. The unusual angle and the explosion of light revealed something to me: this wasn't age, this wasn't old age, this was antiquity. A creature from another era, archaic, had miraculously survived to this day. He came from a time when European bison, aurochs, roamed the natural boundaries of the Caucasus and the Harz Mountains. An example of a long-extinct breed, a rarity like a living coelacanth, which everyone thought had died out seventy million years ago.

The Armenian artist had captured that antediluvian aspect, perhaps without realizing it. We had all tried to express it, but he managed it. Artists can be clairvoyants. Leafing through an album of drawings by Leonid Pasternak, I paid particular attention to the portraits of his sons, Alexander and Boris: two nice boys, drawn lovingly by their father, and how clearly Boris stands out, marked by genius!

In this random urban hospital, stripped of privileges, in a common ward, he seemed even more tragic and majestic. A hero of antiquity, a Roman emperor in exile, King Lear in tatters—all sorts of nonsense came to mind.

THE BISON

Including Archpriest Avvakum, whom the Bison esteemed greatly, quoting him and often attributing his own thoughts to him for greater authority. "Let's return to the first place, as Archpriest Avvakum used to say, and see why this is important in the fifth place, and we'll see that in the fifth it's not important at all."

The thin pillows, and the burnt porridge, and the rattle in his chest were not important; what was important was what he had just read in an English book called *Life After Life*, the accounts of people who had returned from the other side, after cardiac arrest, who had been beyond the threshold of existence. The entire power of his mind and his knowledge was helplessly stuck in front of the blank wall that stood at the end of life. What was there? Is there anything there or not? Where will the soul go, my consciousness, my "me"?

. . . The ray of sunlight dimmed, the vision disappeared, and before me once more was a hoarse, coughing patient, who didn't know how to be sick because he was sick so rarely and therefore was having a very difficult time. The sense of mortality, the growing briefness of his stay among us, worried me, perhaps for the first time. Until that moment he had seemed immortal, like the Neva River, like the Urals, like the statues of the Roman consuls in the Hermitage . . . The chain had an end, the other end deep in the twenties and thirties, in the Civil War, in Moscow University in the days of Lebedev and Timiryazev, it stretched further back, to the nineteenth century and even the eighteenth, to the days of Catherine the Great. He was a living, actual link in that chain of time, which had seemed broken forever, but which had been found, still alive.

It was then that I decided to write down his stories, to preserve on tape and on paper at least the remains of what until then had come across in idle chatter around a bonfire or a table, in random questioning. That day I began taking notes.

2

RETURN
TO THE KAZAN
STATION

Quite a few people had come to meet the train at the Kazan Station on a frosty day in 1956. Most of them knew one another, since they were native Muscovites connected through the university, faculties, apartment buildings, mutual friends. Not only biologists had come to meet the Bison, there were also physicists, philologists, and seamen who were his friends by dint of their generation. For some reason they came with their families, with their children, to show them the man about whom they had spoken so often. Everyone felt the solemnity, the history, of the moment.

This was the first time the Bison had been allowed to return to Moscow. He had been gone over thirty years, for he had left Moscow in 1925. He had taken a train from the Belorussian Station to Germany, but he was now returning via the Kazan Station, from the Urals, from the other side of the world.

The year 1956 was a special one, a stormy year of clear vision, a rise of public consciousness, a year of hopes, arguments, and release from old fears. The fears were deep-seated. Even meeting the Bison at the station required a certain amount of civic courage. Everyone was agitated and excited. They could not imagine whom they would see; would he have changed, would they recognize him? Many came back from exile or the camps that year, but this arrival was special. The Bison was not returning but coming to visit them, he seemed to be coming down from his Ural Mountains.

Overheated and happy, the passengers leaped from the train, bustling with their suitcases and bags. At last the greeters saw the Bison and his wife. He was wearing a nobleman's winter coat, with a beaver shawl collar; she, a beauty, a hereditary Muscovite he called Lelka, was half a head taller than he was and was also wearing a high fur hat. They were recognized immediately. The children, who had never seen them, were able to pick them out because of their absolute freedom of manner, their casual movements, a manner that is natural, beautiful, and therefore difficult to achieve. Back in 1956 it stood out particularly. People then were cringing, restrained, especially in public places. Every era has its own gestures, walk, manner of bowing, taking people by the arm, having tea, giving a speech. People behaved differently in the fifties than they did in the thirties or twenties. For instance, everyone was impressed by the fact that the Bison kissed the hands of the women who met him. That was not the custom then. They winced at his loud voice, his careless talk. There was something about the behavior of the visitors that did not belong to that time or place but was vaguely recognizable, as if ancestors had appeared, familiar from family legends. Old-fashioned, obsolete—and lost. Most of the greeters had either gone to high school with Lelka or had studied with him in high school or college. They recognized the youthfulness they had both retained, Lelka and Kolyusha, as his classmates used to call him.

For days and weeks parties alternated with lectures, reports, round tables, endless, delicious arguments, stories, questions. The great names of Soviet science—Kapitsa, Lyapunov, Landau, Tamm, Dubinin, Sukachev—academicians, students, friends of friends, relatives: everyone was curious, and whoever had visited them once tried to come again. The retinue of admirers grew, drawn by . . . what? That was not readily apparent.

But in the meantime . . . Black-bearded Lyapunov, from a family of great mathematicians and a wonderful mathematician himself, was singing the praises of Akademgorodok, the scientific research center just established near Novosibirsk. It would have a school for gifted children, future mathematicians, who would be selected from all over Siberia. Under the aegis of mathematics, the center would advance and support all the other sciences, since mathematics was the science of all sciences. Lyapunov invited scholars in the humanities to move out there, too, promising them a position under the wing of the exact sciences. Mathematicians could use a little humanities polish for their general development. Mathematicians would take charge of music and art. Their main competition came from the physicists, who thought they were more important. After the atom bomb the physicists aroused respect and hope. Perhaps they would be able to create an abundance of energy and with free electricity change life in the remote areas, make life and work easier, solve all problems. People were expecting astounding discoveries from the physicists. And there was cybernetics, everyone was engrossed in Norbert Wiener's books, the fantastic images of the future were getting closer, right here, it seemed—artificial intelligence, robots, automatic learning machines . . . They were building a city for physicists in Dubno, near Moscow; an atomic power station in Obninsk, in the Urals; and institutes in the Siberian Akademgorodok. The entrance examinations for the physics departments were swamped. Movies were made about physicists, you heard words on the stage like "Einstein," "proton," "quantum," and "chain reaction" . . . The physicists were heroes of the day. They were just fellows in checked shirts, casual and rumpled, used to their own secret buzzwords, yet they were crowned with prizes, awards, salaries, and they held condescending and categorical opinions. Scholars in the humanities trembled before them. They were ashamed of their ignorance. Philology, history, linguistics, art history, and philosophy seemed obsolete fields, second-rate. The future belonged to the experimenters and theoreticians. The initiates were mysterious, they were connected to "black boxes," they promised a change in mores, and they offered patronage to artists in disfavor. Social systems, economics, the law—everything would be subject to optimal scientific laws . . .

Newspapermen and lecturers hung on their every pronouncement.

Arguments about physics and lyricism flared in every city and town throughout the land. Some people joked, but others were serious, insisting that art remained only for the sake of amusement, art was nothing but a waste of time if it did not yield information. The artists retreated, heads bowed before the new force.

In the dining rooms of the Lyapunovs and all their friends the conversation was always about where to go, which university center was best, where will we build science, what new rules will we live under there, what principles will we lay down . . . It was a marvelous time!

They promised to reconstruct biology, too, turn it upside down, inside out . . . Young mathematicians, physicists, and chemists rolled up their sleeves to solve ancient problems in biology. They would apply electronics to those bugs and grasses, they would measure and model everything. Technology would open the doors for mathematicians. In the final analysis, all your biology and biochemistry were nothing but physics and mathematics, just various forms of motion of matter. We will establish contacts and learn the essence of life itself, and then we will start controlling processes in organisms and in nature on all levels. Put an end to the centuries at microscopes, counting the number of legs on a beetle.

They considered the Bison one of their allies, but he just laughed at them. The banging of the physics drums did not impress him.

"The first thing I look for on every piece of equipment is the Stop button!"

That was a strange thing to hear from him. But you couldn't disregard it. Who was a better judge of biophysics than he–one of its creators and founders?

The physicists were a little taken aback by the fact that their idols–Niels Bohr, Werner Heisenberg, Erwin Schrödinger–were his colleagues, men he had worked with. Kapitsa himself invited him to give a lecture at the next *kapichnik* he would host, where our best physicists would gather. Appearing at one of these meetings was considered a death-defying feat. The audience was brought up on blood and flesh. They could tear you up, chew you up, and spit out your regalia. They thought fast, got the point in minutes.

But he wasn't afraid of that. Where did he come from, that daring man?

He enjoyed telling where he came from. He had many stories about his ancestors–comic and tragic, obscene and touching.

And how he told them–winking, laughing, roaring! A tape recording is only a blueprint, an account on paper is a copy of a copy, a shadow of the story.

The Bison differed from many fine storytellers in that each of his stories was not merely amusing, it was told for a reason, it explained something about him. But we figured that out only later.

3

ANCESTORS

His childhood was filled with flashes not only of the nineteenth century but also of the eighteenth.

". . . I'm Timofeyev-Resovsky on my father's side. My mother was born Vsevolozhsky. A very old Russian family. They never reached the very top, sometimes getting poorer, sometimes getting richer, but they never lost their estates, so they were never totally bankrupt. One of Ivan the Terrible's wives was a Vsevolozhsky. Peter the Great took a liking to one of the young Vsevolozhskys and sent him abroad to study. When he returned, he worked for the good of the homeland, as he was supposed to. He had a house in St. Petersburg, he did well. However, when Peter's former protégés were being persecuted under the reign of Tsarina Anna, Vsevolozhsky was warned of his impending arrest, and he took off with his family by horse carriage. He went to his unsettled lands along the lower Volga, on the border with the Kirghiz hordes. Since he had been a good master, his peasants gradually moved down to him from his various estates, especially since all his lands had been impounded. And so Vsevolozhsky turned into a private prince. And he set himself a good goal–not just getting fat–he set himself a state goal, you might say: to ensure the safety of the trade routes to Bukhara, Khiva, Central Asia, and then Persia. The Russian merchants were being robbed by the Khivans, the Kokands, all kinds of nomadic tribes. He fought those Asians, as he called them. He put together a large group of Cossacks. He had all the comforts. No authorities around as far as the eye could see, no one bothering him, not a single uniform . . ."

A short laugh, a sympathetic sigh, a proud snort, as if he were talking about family affairs, his own uncle, and not the eighteenth century. His great-great-grandfathers were right behind him, not dusty ancestors, but living relatives. The incongruity between the ancient past and his fervent feelings for it was astonishing.

"A real robber manages without killing. Fear is enough for him. My ancestor really enjoyed one thing: whenever he learned that a German was made governor, commandant, or some other official anywhere along the Volga, he and his Cossacks would storm into the city, horsewhip the German publicly, and then send him off in great shame to complain to the Court. He would gallop back to his secret hideaway. That's how he would satisfy his principles and amuse himself, knowing that merry Tsarina Elizaveta and her mother, Catherine, would never find him. When he was in his eighties he was wounded in the shoulder, but not gravely. He managed to ride home in his saddle, held up on both sides by his loyal Cossacks. He gave orders to be buried in a lovely spot. The Bolshoi Uzen and the Maly Uzen rivers flow there. Neither falls into any body of water, they just go down into the sand. His estate was in the valley of the Maly Uzen. He was buried on one of the slopes.

"I had a relative who seemed quite proper but who became a pirate. Incidentally, Peter the Great had sent him abroad, too, to study land surveying. When he got back, he began working, taking over the lands in Okhota and Kamchatka, in Siberia. He was interested in the formation of rivers, lakes, and other aspects of physical geography. He retired at seventy-five with the rank of brigadier, and settled down on his small estate in Kaluga Province. He had collected a marvelous library in the European languages on geography and mineralogy. What interested him most was the Gulf Stream. He studied the foreign literature on where the waters of the Gulf Stream go. He calculated and calculated and decided that the known branches of the Gulf Stream did not account for all the water, that there had to be yet another branch going east from Grumant, now called Spitsbergen, and from Franz Josef Land. If there were islands there, they had to be green, warm islands, with a mild winter and a bright summer. And he dreamed about it so much it became an obsession, and he organized an expedition. He sold everything, hocked his estate, got together fifty of his Cossacks, and set off for Arkhangelsk. He outfitted three ships and they set off for the Arctic to find the warm islands . . ."

This was the first time I had met a man who knew his ancestors so well. In our times, very few people knew and remembered anyone farther back than a grandfather. There wasn't much interest. Who cared about ancestors? What use were they? "Let's renounce the old world . . ." And at the same time, we renounced our family heritage. Who were they? Either oppressors or the oppressed, illiterate and cowed. We thought we were the beginning of everything. We began everything over again. And again. And once more. In those years, people did not discuss their noble ancestors. The Bison may have mocked his slightly, but he talked about them with pride.

"And so they traveled slowly along the edge of the polar ice. My forefather measured the temperature, the rate of flow, and other indices, and apparently became convinced that he had been wrong—there were no unaccounted-for branches of the Gulf Stream, and there would be no warm islands on the horizon. They reached Grumant, where storms carried them out to the North Atlantic and tossed them on the shores of Normandy. Several people drowned but the rest came out on the French cliffs and headed for Paris. Instead of asking the Russian ambassador to send them home, my forefather came up with a new idea. He didn't want to go back empty-handed. At that time French businessmen were branching out to North Africa, and he offered to join their expedition with his men as bodyguards. They came to terms. They set off for Morocco. They were attacked by Moroccan soldiers, taken prisoner, and sold into slavery. They were brought to market in Egyptian Alexandria. My forefather struck up a friendship with Orthodox Greeks, and they bought some of his men out of slavery and stole others.

"They lived with the Greeks. And one day they saw a Turkish frigate. Only watchmen were on duty. On a moonlit night the Russians and the Greeks rowed over, climbed aboard, tossed the watchmen into the sea (just like in Stevenson's novels!), and set sail in the Turkish ship. They knew that Russia was still at war with the Turkish Porte, and they began privateering. According to custom, a private ship got a percentage of the booty. As the ship turned out to be fast, they were very successful, sharing their booty with the Greeks. The sea was warm and they were as free as birds. The Cossacks liked the work until they came across the Turkish fleet and were taken prisoner. Not as slaves this time but as prisoners of war. They were interned in a camp near Constantinople . . ."

Then followed a story of how their Greek co-religionists helped them escape, bringing them to Asia Minor, until all the men were free and together once more. Then they took up privateering along the coast of Anatolia . . . I heard the story several times, it was always the same, but with variations and new details, the kind that appear when you go through the same station over and over. This story appears in no published sources, and perhaps a historian could find some information about it, but the Bison knew it from oral tradition: it was one of the family legends passed from generation to generation. There were many of them. Each had a plot built around an interesting character at a pivotal point in Russian history. I used to think that our Russian history was too serious and grim because we lacked such heroes as those in *The Three Musketeers, Treasure Island*, or *Captain Blood*. Nothing of the sort, it wasn't a question of the history. The Bison showed me that ours was rich in laughter and in the wild adventures of eccentrics, pirates, dreamers, jokesters, and adventurers; stories that would ornament any picaresque novel.

". . . a new battleship and a frigate under the Turkish flag. The crew was carousing on shore. At night they overpowered the watchmen and set sail to the north. Prince Potemkin was just then forming the Tauride Fleet in the Black Sea. One fine day his sailors saw two Turkish military craft approaching our shores. But they were under the Russian flag. Total confusion. The Russian commanders decided that it was a trick of some sort, but then it was explained to them in their native tongue that these were real Russians on board. They had an enormous feast with much drinking. Runners were sent to Catherine. She gave orders to accept the Turkish ships from the brigadier and to include them in the Russian fleet. The brigadier was elevated, skipping a rank, to lieutenant general and adjutant general in the Court. A good sum of money reimbursed him for the expedition and allowed him to buy back his estate and reward his men . . ."

Apparently they had documents and deeds in those days. The paperwork on the ships was kept in the family archives at Kaluga. They donated the file to the Rumyantsev Library, but did not get a chance to turn it over because of World War I.

". . . It's not that easy to give something to the state. In 1922 the Kaluga authorities finally gave permission to bring out the archives, but by then the director of the *sovkhoz*, or state farm, who had been embezzling, was covering his tracks and started a fire. The house, the furniture, and the archives, which had already been accepted by the Rumyantsev Library and packed for shipment, were destroyed in the flames. I don't care about the rubbish, but I'm sorry about the archives. I should have helped, but I had gone to the front, and when I returned, I would hurry to my zoological museum to see my carp and bullheads . . ."

The archives burned, but memory remained, permanent, duty-bound to preserve the family history. It could be no other way. It didn't matter if he was proud or ashamed of some of his forebears, they all made up his past, his roots in this world, and their blood flowed through his veins, their genes lived in him, he was their continuation.

A family trait on both sides was late marriage. His father, Vladimir Timofeyev, was born in 1850. His mother was born in 1866, and they married in 1895–that is, when his father was forty-five and his mother twenty-nine. Nikolai, or Kolyusha as his friends called him, was born in 1899–that is, still in the nineteenth century. Both grandmothers had been born in the reign of Alexander I. One of them died in Lenin's day–what a slice of history she lived through! Three old men lived on his grandfather's estate: the chef, the gardener, and the bell ringer. His grandfather had pensioned them off; they built themselves three houses and lived out their years. All three were called to Moscow in 1912 for the centennial celebration of the War of 1812 with Napoleon and given bronze medals with the inscription: "Not for us, but in your name!"

". . . Since I was the eldest in my generation, I was the first to get to know them. They loved me, and I always went to have tea with them after lunch. Nadka cooked for them. They considered her a baby, she was eighty, my mother's old nanny. She was also retired. I sat and drank in the stories from the days of Napoleon. They had lived through it all, the entire nineteenth century, so for me it seemed contemporary. History came to me from people, not from books . . ."

In high school he was sharply aware of the difference between his perception of history and that of his classmates. For them the War of 1812 and the Battle of Sevastopol were one and the same, while for him the chef was already an old man at Sevastopol and in that battle served as accountant for the volunteer corps that came from all over the country.

Now I can confess that I checked on the inscription on the bronze medals in the numismatics department of the Hermitage Museum. At first the specialists said that I was mistaken: silver and bronze medals with that inscription were given right after the campaign of 1812, but for the centennial, in 1912, different medals had been made. I was upset: one inaccuracy, then another, and the Bison's stories could turn into tales, the shadow of doubt could fall on many things. I was checking in order to have certainty. I needed certainty. I went back to the Hermitage and asked them to check again. They dug around in some other books and found out that the old soldiers who had fought in the war–that is, the men over a hundred–were given the same medals as those of 1812, specially made from the old stamp, which had been saved at the Mint. "Not for us, but in your name!" The Bison's story was confirmed. I could count not only on his amazing memory but on his scientific scrupulousness.

Naval men abounded in his family: Admiral Senyavnin, who replaced the Dutch scattered battle formation with a wedge column; Admiral Golovnin, who sailed around the world and was imprisoned by the Japanese; and Admiral Nevelskoi, who in the reign of Nicholas I annexed the Far East illegally to the Russian Empire and was demoted by Count Nesselrode.

"Almost demoted! Almost! That 'Kisselvrode,' "jelly-like"–that's what we called him at home–tried to demote him but failed. This is how it happened . . ."

"Disregarding standing instructions, Nevelskoi explored the Amur River and Tatar Bay, established colonies there, and did everything he could to annex the Amur area to Russia. On the insistence of the Ministry of Foreign Affairs, Nesselrode reduced him in rank to sailor for 'unheard of arrogance.' After his demotion he was summoned to the palace. Nicholas said, 'Greetings, sailor Nevelskoi, follow me!' In the next room, the tsar said, 'Hello, midshipman Nevelskoi!' In the next, 'Greetings, Lieutenant Nevelskoi!' And so on, all the way to rear admiral, whereupon the tsar shook his hand and congratulated him. At first the story of Nevelskoi's and Nesselrode's disagreements had been concealed from Nicholas. When he heard about the special committee that had convened on the Amur issue, he called in Nesselrode and wrote on the committee's report, 'Where the Russian flag is raised once, it should never be lowered!'."

I checked this story with N. Zadornov's authoritative documentary novel about Admiral Nevelskoy. The novel has a similar scene, which must have come from the recollections of Nevelskoy's contemporaries or directly from Nevelskoy himself. I was amazed how this oral history had been preserved, passed down through the generations in the family. It was so accurate in the Bison's reminiscences about his forebears.

He had not studied history books, did not like historical novels, but was imbued with Russian history, was part of it. The eighteenth century, the nineteenth, and the twentieth, our own times, appeared equally in his stories, were all part of the flow. He did not need distance to see the historic element in our lives. He treated the present era as a chronicler would. Just as he knew how to find the essential in every problem in genetics, he could distinguish in the present what defined the times. It was never the obvious. As a biologist once said, "Thus, at present, this question is perfectly clear, which bespeaks the fact that no one has studied it."

We have enough historians, but the chronicler is a member of a rare and unpopular profession. It is easier to be a prophet of the past than of the present.

He was grateful for the intellectual curiosity of the young, that is why the past was always with him, did not rot away forgotten somewhere. He did not begrudge the time for his stories and spent it generously, like money.

"This is what happened with my great-uncle, my grandfather's brother. Grandfather was active in the emancipation of the serfs. He served as director of the treasury in Simbirsk. His brother, a naval man, was an eccentric bachelor, but an excellent officer. They blew up not just an ordinary vessel, but a line battleship of the Turkish fleet, hopped into the water in time, climbed out on a spit of land, and were saved. He was awarded the golden sword of St. George and an officer's medal, fourth grade, of the Order of St. George—I remember it well: a heavy white cross. He later became a rear admiral and then a full admiral.

"He was sent with a training flotilla to the Mediterranean. They traveled from port to port as far as Toulon, where they anchored. Not far away were Nice and Monte Carlo. He was drawn there, and once he saw the roulette wheel, that purring ball, he decided to try it. What's good about roulette? It's pure risk. No skills, no calculation. You approach fate, and you have lots of choices: you can come up on any side you want . . . The psychology of roulette players is an interesting thing. In many people the gambling passion is latent. It awoke in my admiral. By the standards of those days he was not a wealthy man, all he had was his salary as an admiral. Even a minister's salary wasn't much. My father, for instance, made twice what a minister made. And a professor got twice or even three times as much as a minister. The admiral took all the gold francs he had, not many, but he couldn't lose them: whatever he bet on, he won. The god of gambling took him by the hand and led him. Gamblers know that moment. You can't be reasonable and you can't stop. The admiral reached a rare plateau: he broke the bank in Monte Carlo. I don't remember exactly how much it was, either three million or five million francs. At any rate, on the day that happens the bank stops making further payments, and the music stops until the next evening. They paid him his money. He sent a long telegram to his brother, my grandfather: find me a good little estate nearby. And he sent several thousand francs for a down payment. He sailed on with his squadron.

"He wasn't a boozer or a partyer, but in every port he headed for a restaurant and opened it to the locals, so that they could eat and drink in honor of the Russian fleet. When I was in Italy as a boy with my father, we still found people in the ports who remembered that a Russian had treated the town. And he made his way to Constantinople. From there he sent another telegram to my grandfather: send me a hundred rubles. He had spent all those millions. That was in the early 1890s. He retired as an Excellency. I saw him in his parade uniform. A dazzling sight! There was an incident with that uniform in '96.

"At that time there was a terrible governor in Kaluga. The landowners did not get along with him. They were trying to set up veterinary stations to keep an eye on the epizoic condition of the dumb brutes on which the speaking brutes fed. The governor blocked their efforts. The admiral heard out their complaints, and he had little respect for these people, and he finally shouted at them, 'Why do you just wag your tongues? How can the governor resist? If this is a righteous cause, then you must force him.' He ordered his carriage hitched to four horses, with a coachman in the box and a former sailor of his behind (he liked to travel the old-fashioned way), and he had a half dozen sheep put in the carriage. And he went into Kaluga. He drove up to the governor's house. They saw a full admiral in full uniform with regalia and ribbons getting out. The governor was informed. He ran out onto the porch to greet him. His Excellency came into the foyer.

" 'I have been informed that you are against veterinary measures,' he said, using the informal second person singular, like a real boss. 'You should set up veterinary stations. But since you're against that, I've brought you a half dozen of my sheep, dear fellow, and you can treat them.'

19

"He clapped his hands and the sailor chased the sheep into the governor's house. The governor was horrified. He babbled that he had been misunderstood.

" 'Well, if you were misunderstood, that's another matter. All that's needed is a piece of paper from you. Send it to the restaurant, I'm lunching there. Will you send it?'

" 'I will.'

"The admiral loaded up his sheep. He went looking for the leading landowners. Took them to the restaurant. They were sitting around drinking when a messenger from the governor showed up with the paper. The men were flabbergasted . . ."

The Bison remembered the admiral well and also his death. After celebrating his eighty-fifth birthday, the admiral put his affairs in order, disclosed his will, and shot himself with a "bulldog" pistol.

The deed is done, the old man is stabbed,
The Danube glistens, silver . . .

He always ended with his favorite lines.

4

TELLER
OF TALES

"In view of this heat, all partici-
pants of the seminar will go neck-deep into the water, and the lecturer up to
the waist," the Bison proposed.

The lecturer, Vladimir Pavlovich, though a former front-line soldier
and not at all elderly in those years, was rather put off by the proposal, took
it for an inappropriate joke, a lack of respect for the lecturer: listening while
standing in the water was clearly unsuitable. This was in Miassovo in 1958.
People weren't used to that sort of thing. At least, biologists weren't. Then in
all seriousness the Bison put the question up for a vote: was it suitable or not?
Naturally, the majority felt that being in the water in that heat was eminently
suitable. After which the audience undressed and got in the water—students
and doctors of science, maidens and old men, and the Bison himself. The
lecturer remained onshore but had to strip to his shorts. He drew his graphs
with chalk on the bottom of a boat.

This lecture was the most memorable of them all. Vladimir Pavlovich
himself remembered it too, despite the fact that it had shocked him a bit. His
information was remembered by all the participants. Because they had been
in the water. Even though it deserved it on its own.

"After the lecture he kissed me. That was an initiation. I felt golden
spurs growing on my heels." He stopped, stunned by his own thoughts, and
then said, "Remember the line in *Faust*, 'You are equal to whomever you

understand'? The Bison was higher than me, because I could not understand him. But the point is *how* I didn't understand him. I didn't understand him so much that he was two heads higher than me."

Vladimir Pavlovich has a sufficiently high opinion of himself. He is a skeptical man, not overawed by people. His descriptions of people are usually caustic, but here . . . I asked what made the Bison hard to understand.

"He had a strategic approach to biology. It's as if I were thinking on the level of a battalion commander and tried to understand the thinking of the commander of the front."

He returned to the kiss, of which he was as proud as of his wartime medals.

In the evenings on the shore of the Mozhaisk Sea they made bonfires and had elaborate talkfests. The ringleader was the Bison. He made old professors, doctors, and other masters speak. Each had his own topic: his travels, Roerich's paintings, female beauty, the poetry of Marina Tsvetaeva.

In the yellow dancing light of the bonfire, transformations took place: famous and honored scientists turned out to be colorless storytellers, long-winded and lacking original thought. They said banal things and were diminished by proximity. Outside the temple of science, the priests became dull men in the street. Not all of them: some grew in interest; some wrote quite good poetry, others were witty, clever raconteurs, knowledgeable in history. Nevertheless, people got tired of it sooner or later, and then they turned to the Bison, asking him to tell something about himself. His life seemed inexhaustible.

5

INFANTRYMAN
OF THE RED
ARMY

It was during the Civil War of 1918-21. The troops were advancing south, he was a rank-and-file Red Army soldier in the 113th Infantry Regiment. Then the fortunes of war switched, and they began retreating before General Denikin's "Wild Division," as they called one of the mammoth White Army units. Kolyusha was made commander of his platoon. He didn't command it long, though, because he picked up spotted fever and had to be left behind on some farm. His regiment was disbanded. He lay sick without care for he didn't know how long. It was still winter. Delirious, he ran outside into the snow. A Red Army unit happened to be passing by. The farmer tried to get rid of him. The orderlies took him and, as they said in those days, "dumped" him at a soldier's field hospital for typhus patients, located at a sugar plant about twelve kilometers from Tula. Officers and soldiers lay about in the main factory building. The windows were shattered. They "dumped" soldiers with spotted fever, enteric fever, recurring fever—with all types of typhoid fever; and also men with concussions or common colds. In the end, they all got some sort of typhoid on top of whatever ailment they came in with. There were about two thousand of them.

Our Kolyusha survived primarily because he was extraordinarily strong. According to his theory, he also survived because he was right by the window, in the cold. There were no doctors, so the medical care came down to soldiers arriving every other day with a sled, bringing fresh patients and taking away the corpses, which they piled up in rows on their sled and hauled away. Along with the patients they brought two pails of "brown eyes" for each room. It was a soup made of the heads and tails of fish. The fish itself was used elsewhere, either by soldiers in combat or perhaps by kindergartens or orphanages, who knew, but the offal was thrown into the soup, to which was added a pinch of *psha,* a wild grain in the Far East resembling millet. In Moscow the only available grain was *psha.* Everyone got so sick of it that they even used to joke: bugs eat grass, rust eats iron, *psha* eats souls.

The pails with "brown eyes" were left by the door, and the problem was in crawling over to them, for he didn't have the strength. When Kolyusha got a little better, he felt hunger, wild hunger, and realized that he had survived, hadn't died. He was terribly weak, he had strength enough only to crawl on his belly, like a crocodile, among the other men. He would crawl over to a corpse, and he knew that a soldier would always have something to eat in his pack. He would feel around and find a crust, suck it. Didn't have the strength to chew. Then he would make it to the pail. He had to raise himself up enough to put his face in it. In the greenish water, boiled fish eyes floated, round and with pupils, and that's why they called the soup "brown eyes." Dried crusts and "brown eyes" were what kept body and soul together. Man's capabilities in terms of hunger are great, he can get by on very little for a long time if he doesn't panic.

A nurse was in charge of this institution. She appeared from time to time, like a fairy, in red rubber boots and a white coat over her fur coat. She would look into a room, cry, and go away. She had no medicine or orderlies. Once she got as far as Kolyusha. He was already able to move his arms. Corpses all around. Naturally, she paid attention to the living.

"Who are you?"

"I'm a volunteer, but I used to be a biology student at Moscow University."

The nurse was glad to see a fellow student; she was studying medicine in Moscow.

"It's horrible here," she said. And tears filled her eyes again.

Kolyusha tried to console her: it could be worse, he said. Of course, it's not so good, it's too bad about all these people, but look, he survived, for example! Now he had to keep from starving to death. He was terribly hungry. He might even be able to get to the food, but he couldn't lift himself up. By the time he got to the bucket, he was exhausted.

"Well, I'll help you with that," she said.

She brought him a bowl of soup and a crust. Kolyusha had a friend, Shura Reformatsky. And his sisters were nursing students, too, so they had mutual friends. The nurse brought him sticky bread made of oil cake, part of her own rations. And Kolyusha began to recover. Only someone with his constitution could have thrived on those rations. He would lean his back against the wall and, using his hands, climb up and stand on trembling legs. The nurse took him under the arm and he would walk a few steps. Then he walked alone, holding on to the wall. One fine day the nurse brought him a paper and a travel warrant: "Soldier so-and-so, having survived a bout of spotted fever, is sent on home leave for six weeks of recuperation."

The nurse had another set of papers, made out for a patient with recurring fever named Sergeyev. He seemed fine, they had discharged him, but he had died during the night.

"Take the papers," she said. "They will come in handy."

And they did.

The next morning, Kolyusha set out at dawn for Tula. For him, covering twelve kilometers was like going to the moon. He stumbled and fell, and whenever he fell he had to crawl to a fence or a tree, because he couldn't stand up without help. He reached Tula by nightfall. It had taken him fifteen hours to cover twelve kilometers.

The only place he knew in Tula was the barracks of the 113th Regiment, where he had once been quartered. That is where he headed.

In his stories of that period, the Bison never avoided anything, never made himself look better than he was. What happened, had happened; he didn't stoop to explaining things away by talking about the times and circumstances. He stole, he conned, he maneuvered—but he never did evil.

He began the war with a rifle manufactured in 1868 and ended up with a cavalry carbine. It was an excellent weapon for those days—a six-shooter, dependable, and very light. He recalled it with a soldier's tenderness. He got it from a soldier in General Denikin's "Wild Division." He kept improving his weapon all through the Civil War. He had owned a Cossack carbine, a German one, and by the end he had the Denikin one, made in Japan. When he lay sick with typhus, he pressed the carbine close to his side, afraid to be left without it. He kept his pockets full of shells.

Nothing changes in people, thank God. A soldier is always a soldier. Thirty years later, in my war, I tried to get myself a submachine gun. I traded my seven-shooter for one. Besides attacking and defending, war is the place for trading, exchanging, for all kinds of dealing. Someone ships a fur jacket, barters underwear for canned goods, tarp boots for leather ones. There was a lot of commercial dealing going on in the marching platoons, in hospitals, and the men always bragged about a successful trade. They boasted about their cleverness, their talent for wheeling and dealing. Just as a brave soldier does not like to talk about an exploit but about how he got scared during a bombing raid. In a ward the most popular stories, and they while away the days and nights telling stories, are about messing up, coming across mines, screwing up, being punished.

Kolyusha never described his brave acts, he liked telling about being taken prisoner by bandits or shooting at a chicken.

He got to Tula somehow, crawled into the snoring fetid barracks and approached the guard, who was dozing by the kerosene lamp. He begged to be allowed to stay the night. The man looked and looked at his papers and let him lie down near him. Kolyusha lay down, but he couldn't sleep. His body ached, his legs hurt. They started talking. Kolyusha told him that he was on leave, going to Moscow. The guard perked up, he wasn't sleepy anymore. He was a native Muscovite, a tailor at the Smolensk market. Kolyusha was happy: they were neighbors! He lived nearby. They smoked. The guard was envious, he was going back home. Kolyusha wasn't so sure about getting there: he didn't know how he could crawl, his legs couldn't hold him, his arms weren't strong enough to pull him up, he didn't know what to do, he'd never make the trip. Then he remembered the extra set of papers, those meant for the late Sergeyev. He showed the documents to the guard. He held them up to the light, turned them this way and that.

"Marvelous documents, worth a lot," the guard concluded. He sighed and wondered how much he would be asked to pay for them. Kolyusha was straight with him.

"Take them for nothing. On one condition—don't abandon me. If I were healthy, I'd walk the two hundred kilometers to Moscow. But I can't even climb up into a freight car by myself. Help me get there."

Kolyusha made him swear, and the man, eyes darting, had to repeat the vow about the mortal fever that would befall all his family, the sepsis of his feet and the shingles he would get if he tricked him and abandoned him . . . The sepsis had the greatest effect on Petya Skachkov, which was the guard's name.

"I won't deceive you. I just want to see my family." Petya struck his chest with his fist. "You gave the papers to me, depriving yourself. You could buy a house in Moscow with documents like these."

"What do I need with a house?" Kolyusha said. "Why don't you get some bread for the road?"

He was confident about the bread, because recently he had been sent from these very barracks to guard the railroad cars loaded with bread. They guarded the cars, all right, but they broke off hunks of crust for themselves and hid them in deep pockets sewn inside their coats. In response to this information, Petya Skachkov opened his own coat and revealed a similar pocket. So this group of men had come to grow the same "organ." Kolyusha was deeply impressed by the ability of future generations to invent exactly the same thing, to acquire the same "organs."

While Skachkov went off to forage, Kolyusha stood guard duty at the barracks with his carbine. About two hours later, before reveille, Skachkov returned with a sack of bread pieces. He had also stolen two slabs of bacon fat and a heavy chunk of salt that had melted down in a fire.

"Let's go now," he suggested. "I've picked out a freight car on the tracks that's not too bad."

They reached the freight station. Skachkov helped Kolyusha along by dragging him by the collar. He hauled him up into a freight car. They settled in the side away from the wind. Skachkov ran off to find a stove: it was a cold spring and the icy puddles crunched in the morning. He swiped a stove somewhere and broke off parts of a fence for kindling. The two soldiers were set up beautifully. They kept the stove fired up, there was a good draft when the train was moving. They could have boiling water anytime at all, and they ate bread and some bacon. They covered about forty kilometers a day. It took them a week to get to Moscow. They came out of their car and the city was still the same: the Kazan Station, the women with baskets sitting in front selling sunflower seeds, baked potatoes, patties in the baskets. Moscow! What joy! There were hackney cabs. Coachmen in top hats, important-looking.

Kolyusha proposed, "Let's hire one. We'll ride into the capital in a carriage."

"And what will we pay with?"

"A piece of bacon."

They chose a carriage with a white horse. Not quite white, it was roan.

"Do you like bacon?"

The cabbie looked down at them.

"Bacon doesn't grow in Moscow."

They showed him a big chunk. "Want it? Take us to the Smolensk market, but at a canter."

Pulled by a cantering roan horse, they drove right up to the house in Nikolsky Alley.

His mother's house was heaven. The central heating worked. Despite the war, there was gas. There was hot water, and Kolyusha spent three days in the bathtub, soaking away the dirt from the hospital, the soot from the train, enjoying the peace and quiet, turning into a bourgeois who had not been bumped off, as he put it.

6

"WE FOUGHT, WE PHILOSOPHIZED, WE GOT OURSELVES SOME FOOD"

The Civil War, War Communism, the New Economic Policy or NEP–those are years we know much less about than the pre-revolutionary times. We have a better understanding of Pushkin's era, or Catherine's, or even, perhaps, of Peter the Great's, than of the paradoxes of the twenties.

"We would fight a bit, chase off the Whites, rest up, fight some more, and when our unit was broken up, return to Moscow, to the university, to our fishes, to the circle we were caught up in then: a logical-philosophical group with a mathematical bent. Then back to the army, rolling off to the front. Because I was ashamed; everyone was at war and I was sitting around. I had to fight! You will never be able to decipher the mosaic of that life. One week you're studying St. Sophia the Wise, the next you're traveling to the front to fight Denikin . . ."

Let us not exaggerate: political considerations were not what brought Kolyusha to the Red Army. That was not it. Politics did not move him deeply, either as a young man or later. He figured that the Communists and the Whites were the ones with political convictions. He wasn't a Communist. Nor a White. He counted up the different ideas the Whites had: absolute monarchy, limited monarchy, dictatorship, a bourgeois-democratic republic of one type, and of another type, and yet a third . . . Kolyusha and his friends had convictions that were patriotic, not political. Why were all these scoundrels getting into Russia–Greens, Whites, Browns, Cossacks, Poles,

Frenchmen, Japanese, Englishmen, and other occupiers? Russia needed national rule. All his life, Kolyusha stubbornly maintained that it was that primal feeling that made it impossible for the Whites and their allies, that whole crowd, to beat them, the sansculottes, the barefoot patriots, armed with old rifles dated circa 1868.

I do not use the word "barefoot" lightly. In the Twelfth Army, Kolyusha was put in a special ski patrol of the 17th Battalion. Not a ski in sight. They were given shoes woven out of bark. And not the customary maple bark, but willow bark, which makes useless shoes, not sturdy and very rough. And that is how his life went: "We fought, we philosophized, and we got ourselves some food."

One summer he got a good job, in terms of food, as a cowherd. And he was happy, for he learned that it was the best profession in the world. First of all, in one season he earned much more than an ordinary professor at Moscow University would in a year. (In those days professors were divided into ordinary and extraordinary ones.) He was paid two sacks of rye. And a sack weighed 350 pounds! Second, he was provided with clothes: a padded jacket with a red lining, which made him quite picturesque, and two pairs of pants, and boots. He had an assistant, a dog. In the morning he gathered the cows with a song. He would walk through the village singing "When I Go Out to the River" and lead the cows along. He had a double-barreled shotgun on his shoulder, to shoot wild geese. He and a friend, the local paramedic, figured out how to turn valerian drops, used as a tranquilizer, into pure alcohol. They had two quarts of the stuff! They distilled it. And they drank it with the roast goose. "What a marvelous life!" It was impossible to get a white-collar job. The value of money was falling catastrophically. People calculated in "lemons"–that is, millions. The only way to earn money was as a laborer.

The heads of their logical-philosophical circle were Gustav Gustavovich Shpet, who confounded their brains with wild paradoxes, rocking the most solid pillars of their world, and Nikolai Nikolayevich Luzin, who was both a major mathematician, and a philosopher. Other members were the philosophers Sergei Bulgakov and Nikolai Berdyaev, whom the circle members called Beliberdyaev, from the Russian word for nonsense.

Semyon Ludvigovich Frank would lecture in his piercing, singsong voice: "Art is always expression. But what is expression? It is the most mysterious word in the human language. Most probably it means an imprint.

THE BISON

The process of imprinting something upon something other. Something invisible and spiritual lies in man's soul; he needs to make it visible, manifest . . . The spiritual takes on flesh. But what is it he wants to express? Not just himself, but something objective. What is that 'something'?"

From a philosopher Kolyusha turned into a conscientious zoologist, prepared to fuss day and night with all kinds of watery denizens, studying them, describing them, taking satisfaction in his modest position as ichthyologist. A natural transformation, but he transformed himself with similar ease into a dashing warrior. Slash, stab, forward in the name of the Soviets! And there was nothing left of the diligent student. You might say it was the boiling blood of his military ancestors.

In order to attend the university he had to earn money, buy food. He had all kinds of jobs.

Once he worked on the loading dock of a printing office. To get a job like that required extraordinary contacts. And he got it through no less than Vladimir Dmitrievich Bonch-Bruyevich, head of the office of the Council of People's Commissars. During the Revolution of 1905 one of Kolyusha's aunts hid Bonch-Bruyevich from the police. And in gratitude, he got her nephew a cushy job. The crew packed newsprint, loaded books and brochures. They were publishing very actively then: Bukharin's *The ABCs of Communism,* *Engel's Anti-Dühring,* political primers, the Soviet Constitution–printing shops were working full speed, there was a lot of paper, and they shipped books all over the country. District and provincial commissars came to pick up the loads. The loaders received additional ration cards, a quarter pound of bread. Each worker was allowed three lunches at the Council's third canteen, which was located at the Hotel Metropole. Three lunches of those days were not enough for a young loader, but still it was an important supplement to the ration cards. So being a dock loader was a good position, the best a young scholar could hope for. The crew found other ways of getting food. While they loaded–and they didn't knock themselves out hurrying either– one of them would siphon some fuel from the tank of the truck they were loading. In those days trucks in Moscow ran on a mixture of gasoline and alcohol called "autocognac." There was a truck drivers' bar on Sretenka, which coach drivers also frequented, as did chauffeurs, though there were not very many cars in Moscow then. And the whole crew of loaders, about twelve people, went there, too. They would give the owner their keg of "autocognac." He sold it by the shot to drunkards. In return the loaders got a bowl of cabbage soup with meat and a piece of real bread. After eating, Kolyusha went off to the university to check on his work or to the circle, where Andrei Bely might be lecturing. Or he would catch a class by Grabar on art history, then go from Grabar to Muratov's class and from Muratov to hear Trenev lecture on old Russian art, on frescoes. Kolyusha wanted to know everything. He was attracted by the beauty of words, by their elusive meanings, by friable forms. He got rather deeply involved in those things. He gnawed on philosophy and art history until he became convinced that it was "empty muttering" and that he could not trade in his precious piscatorial projects for idle chatter.

That is why he became a biologist and not an art historian. Nonetheless, he kept an interest in art, in descriptive art history without fancy talk which helped you learn what happened when, which artist did what, what was good about him, what he invented.

7

"TEN RANKS
OF ANGELS . . ."

Here there is a break in the author's notes, and for some reason the story about denatured alcohol follows. Why this was told, it is now hard to establish. The author—that is, I—wrote things down haphazardly, hurriedly, recording some things and not others, listening intently, for my own pleasure, forgetting my responsibilities. I argued with the Bison, trying to show off, instead of doing what a writer should—listen, remember, record. Here the author wants to complain about himself and to share with the reader his belated sadness. If the author had modestly written down everything about the Bison he had heard and seen for just a few years, it would have been worth many of his own works. The author has never come across similar diaries. The few people who keep diaries usually record the things worth mentioning, events that are more or less significant from their point of view. They don't consider it worthwhile to record the conversation of women in a store, or a lunch in a coffee shop, or a parent-teacher meeting at school, or the prices at the market . . . But how are we to know what is worth recording and what is not?

"The denatured alcohol was green, Kerensky green . . ." This sentence is interesting in that it belongs totally to that period. None of us knew that denatured alcohol used to be green or that the money issued by Kerensky's Provisional Government was also green.

They used to add an emetic to denatured alcohol. During the war Russia had a dry law. Vodka, raw alcohol, and denatured alcohol were stockpiled in

33

warehouses. There were warehouses like that in Kashino, not far from the state farm where Kolyusha herded cows. When they began attacking the warehouses in Kashino, the villagers sent Ivan Ivanovich, an old worker and activist, and cowherd Kolyusha. They outfitted them with a cart and some pitchers. Kashino was a madhouse. At first the Red Army unit tried to pour the vodka out onto the ground. They opened the faucets, but the vodka poured out into the street. Drunkards dove into the vodka puddles. Women lay down and scooped up the dirty liquid into bowls. Kolyusha acted in a scientific manner here, too: he convinced Ivan Ivanovich that there wasn't much point in trying to get at the vodka, they should try for the alcohol. They couldn't get through. So they turned to the denatured alcohol reserves; after all, that was alcohol, too. They filled their pitchers with the "green serpent." They had to fight their way out. It was a fight to the death: they fought with picks and spades. It's a good thing they got out before the Latvian troops arrived. Kolyusha was almost killed. He could have been squashed like a fly over a stupid thing like that. Later he taught the villagers how to purify the alcohol. Naturally the still he made worked slowly. So you could say he saved them from total drunkenness.

He demanded immersion in all kinds of things before he settled down in the quiet of a laboratory. It was as if he knew what lay ahead. His youth did not resemble the youth of a scientist.

He could have become a professional singer. That temptation came his way several times.

When he returned to Moscow after his bout of typhus, a family was moved into their apartment. The father, Egert, used to be a church choirmaster and was director of the Red Army Chorus. When he heard Kolyusha singing in the tub, Egert tried to persuade him to sing first bass with them. Kolyusha had sung in high school, in the church choir, and at the university for Tatyana's Day, January 25, a favorite college holiday. Kolyusha loved choir singing. Whenever he could, he joined the amateur choir in Kaluga. He didn't want to be a soloist, he liked the unity of choral music. He was an individual in everything, but here—and this was curious—he was drawn by the communality of the choir, where you are inseparable from the rest, where you cannot hear yourself in the mighty unity of voices, where there is no you, just us.

The Red Army Chorus was an all-male one, without altos and sopranos.

The singers received two Red Army rations, which equaled a front-line ration, enough for his mother and two sisters.

His sick leave was over. Kolyusha went to headquarters with his Japanese carbine and bag of shells to request transfer to the regional Red Army Chorus. He stood in the entryway a long time, patting the carbine and pressing it against his cheek. Even the gratitude of the authorities did not help, although he was taken to meet the Commander of Moscow as a model soldier who held on to his weapon even when delirious with typhus.

"Why did you turn in your carbine if it meant so much to you? You could have held on to it."

"I could have, but the orders were to turn it in."

Orders were orders, the law was law, right or wrong, but you had to obey. A strange obedience in a rebel.

His voice was incredibly beautiful. I don't know how he would have done as a soloist, but in the chorus Kolyusha was considered indispensable. His voice and musical talent helped him out more than once in life, occasionally even saved him. He used his voice in his youth. In 1916 Grabar and Muratov persuaded him to collect "bagels." That was their word for the icons of religious dissidents. A new wave of persecution of the Raskolniki began in the reign of Nicholas II and the order went out to take away their icons. A hole was drilled in the corner of each icon, and they were threaded on a rope, just the way bagels are sold. This chain of "bagels" was turned in to the church chancellery. Kolyusha was instructed to travel around Karelia and collect these "bagels" in monasteries and churches. He was financed, and the expedition went up Lake Ladoga and then the Onega River to Kandalaksha in boats and then traveled on foot. They would enter a village, have tea, and he would sing something from the repertoire of wandering cripples.

If the priest's daughter played the guitar, he would sing love songs and she would give him "bagels."

As a child he had pleaded with his parents to be taken to Masalsk Monastery, where twice a year, for Trinity and before the autumn fasts, priests came from all over Russia to elect deep-voiced protodeacons. The classic deacon singers were at Novozybovsk Monastery and Masalsk Monastery, near the Timofeyevs'. He also listened to the pilgrims who passed by on their way to the Solovetsk fathers in the north and the Kievo-Pechersky fathers in the south. They sang religious songs.

Kolyusha knew many religious songs, and there was nothing more interesting than hearing him around a campfire on the Mozhaisk Sea or at Miassovo in the southern Urals, singing the ancient songs instead of the usual tourist fare.

He would start out with prayers in his deep voice and then switch to a buffoonish chant:

> *Ten ranks of angels*
> *And as many archangels.*
> *Three aspects of one God,*
> *Who rules in heaven*
> *And on earth,*
> *King of us all.*
> *Give to a blind man, for the sake of Christ!*

Mikhail Vasilyevich Nesterov and Ivan Florovich Ognyev took him, as a young boy, to listen to good deacons at vespers. When a deacon started singing, Ivan Florovich checked where he started the "Apostle." If it wasn't from the lowest C, then he was just a kid. A good deacon could handle two and half octaves and had to reach E flat, even F.

Who were they, those old men? Nesterov, Mikhail Vasilyevich? Not the artist? I think of that just now, and check the name and patronymic. And it is he, the artist, one of my favorites. And Ognyev, Ivan Florovich? According to the encyclopedia, he was a famous Russian histologist, fired in 1914 from Moscow University by the reactionary Minister of Education, L.A. Kasso. So, therefore, they must have been friends, Nesterov and Ognyev, and somehow fate brought them together with Kolyusha. The three of them went around Moscow churches together. What did they see in that young man? And what, besides the singing of deacons, united them? After all, in those days Nesterov was a famous artist. . . . Dozens of questions arise. When I listened to the Bison, I had not stopped him, did not ask questions. I realized it too late. The more deeply I get into his life, the more omissions of mine I find.

8

A POWERFUL CALLING

"**W**hy did you go into science when you have such a marvelous voice?"

"Because in those days there weren't many of those parasites, scientific workers, and they weren't wreaking great damage upon the country."

The Bison laughs. You could never get the expected answer from him.

"In 1921, 1922, I didn't have much time. We didn't consider it proper to earn money through science, so we did manual labor."

What did he do? He repaired mowers, reapers, and other farm machinery for the villagers. That was in the summer. In the winter he gave lectures. He was talked into teaching zoology at the Prichistensky Workers' Courses, which had just been set up. It was one of the first educational projects of the Moscow intelligentsia, which was just regaining its strength after the famine and was trying to aid the Revolution. The department was enormous, almost twenty-five thousand people assigned to prepare workers and demobilized soldiers for college entrance. Kolyusha was paid a small salary and given a small food ration. The salary was worthless because it was equivalent to approximately the price of a trolley ticket, and the trolleys weren't running.

In 1920-21 life in Moscow had not yet returned to normal. The Smolensk market, not far from the Timofeyev house, was empty. Only recently a noisy and bustling place, it was now row upon empty row of closed stands. Old women and men in pince-nez wandered through the square littered with sunflower seed shells, papers, and manure, offering with embarrassment to sell things of little practical use—coffee grinders, black gauzy evening gowns with bugles and beads, yellow paper roses, uniforms with the insignia and galloons torn off. Sometimes you could find crusts of rough rationed bread, pieces of soap, gray lumps of refined sugar wrapped in blue paper, and one-ounce bags and more often half-ounce bags of homegrown shag tobacco.

To earn more money for food, Kolyusha began giving lectures on the club circuit—zoology with a revolutionary twist. That paid a soldier's food ration. Once he was taken to the Central Club of the Red Army. A big audience awaited him, about fifteen hundred people, commanders and their wives. It turned out that a lecture on the French Revolution had been announced. The authorities had made a mistake. Kolyusha said he was a staff lecturer on biology, he knew nothing about the Bastille, the Convention, and all those Jacobins. The club director clutched his head: "What can I do? For Christ's sake, help me out of this mess!" Kolyusha refused.

Someone remembered that the club had a collection of slides on art and architecture history. What if they selected slides on the French Revolution?

"That's another matter," Kolyusha said with animation. "I know a bit about art, I used to be interested in styles, rococo and the Baroque. Let's call the lecture 'Changes of Style in the Architecture and Art of Europe During the French Revolution.' "

Who would have thought what his compassion for the club director would bring? The lecture was a success. He went through the styles, correlating them with the French Revolution with enthusiasm and inspiration. And that led to his appointment as chairman of the Cultural Education Commission of the Central Procurement Directorate of the Red Army. Besides getting another food ration, he was given a carriage, two horses, and a coachman, which was fully the equivalent of an automobile.

It was a comical sight: Kolyusha getting into the carriage with his briefcase, first going to the university, where he worked with his little fishes and attended lectures, and then being taken to the office, where he gave lectures himself.

Of all possible work, science was the worst paid. Scientific work did not produce food rations, money, or fame. Few people entered science in those days. It was not enough to be uninterested in money, you also had to be eccentric. Or crazy. And that just reinforced the cliché of the mad scientist completely engrossed in his work, in his bugs, test tubes, and formulas.

People went into science solely for the sake of science, obeying the ancient instinct to pursue knowledge. So the Bison's response to my question of why he went into science was not as sarcastic as it sounded.

Let us note that doors leading to promising offices with comfortable chairs were flying open before Kolyusha. He was young, just back from front-line service with the Red Army, educated but not a tsarist specialist, still a graduate student. And in those days "student" still had an honorable ring, so that he could have moved up into higher ranks easily and quickly. His carriage drove him lightly down that road, with good shock absorbers. He had excellent connections and his parents were tolerable to the new regime: even though his father was a nobleman, he was a railway engineer and not a factory owner, not a bourgeois capitalist; people like him supported the Revolution. Kolyusha was a relative of Kropotkin. He had a good tongue, and in that period oratorical gifts were essential. It was the time of the young, the silver-tongued, the brazen. It had to be a powerful calling that kept him from temptation. Especially since it was neither sin nor the devil that was tempting him; rather, he was beckoned by the national surge toward culture, toward literacy. The Revolution had just thundered by, and the clear air of hope intoxicated people much more experienced than Kolyusha. But he took his carriage every morning to his university laboratory, shamelessly rolling up to the entrance to which important professors and academicians walked.

But let me state it right away: he suffered no torment. We cannot count overcoming temptation among his good points. He did not make a choice, he did not seek his path, because after every zigzag and detour he calmly returned to it, the way you go home.

9

THE SCIENTIFIC
LINEAGE;
LELKA

H is teacher was the famous
Nikolai Konstantinovich Koltsov, who developed certain fundamental postulates of modern genetics and experimental zoology, who created, presented,
founded, and so on and so forth; the list of his achievements is great and
indisputable. Koltsov's own teacher was also an outstanding scientist, the
zoologist Mikhail Alexandrovich Mensbir, the founder of Russian ornithology and zoogeography and a vigorous advocate of Darwinism. Mensbir in
turn had his own teachers, of whom the most important was Nikolai Alexeyevich Severtsov, the founder of the ecology of animals, a science he
developed with his teacher, Karl Frantsevich Roulie. Severtsov is known as
"a marvelous zoologist, an outstanding theoretician of biology, the creator
of the first Russian school of evolutionary zoologists." You can follow this
chain far back through the generations, from one outstanding scientist to
another equally outstanding, for we have come upon a lucky chance. Not
every scientist has such a noble lineage. The Bison's scientific family tree is
broad, majestic, and honorable, no less glorious than his family tree, and
assured him good heredity and first-class traditions. The Revolution did not
interrupt or destroy this scientific lineage. Professors were still professors,
carp were still carp, and mollusks behaved the way they had under the
Romanovs.

To tell the truth, Kolyusha liked to brag about his ancestors, on his
mother's as well as his father's side. But his stories about them paled in

comparison with those about Koltsov and Mensbir, who was rector of Moscow University when Kolyusha attended it.

Descriptions of Koltsov generally agree that he was talented, extremely hardworking, and incredibly decent. After that, opinions diverge. For Kolyusha, the most essential point was that Koltsov was a brilliant zoologist. There are not many good zoologists. There are enough good mathematicians, physicists, chemists. But zoologists, especially good ones, you can count on one hand; we need more of them, the way we need good people, since as a rule they really are good men. Kolyusha's deep conviction was that zoologists differed from the rest of educated humanity in that they were better on the average.

Koltsov started out as a comparative anatomist. His first student work was on the frog. And his first adult work was on the head of the lamprey. So, like the Bison, he was a "wet" zoologist. His work on the lamprey head became an instant classic. From the multitude of marine fauna Koltsov moved on to the shapes of animals—why animals have some shapes and not others—and then to the shapes of cells.

Koltsov's significance goes beyond genetics. His school was broader than is now understood. G. G. Vinberg explained this to me: "Koltsov started experimental biology, organizing an institute by that name. That seems obvious now, but then, in 1917, it was unusual, even strange. All nineteenth-century biology was descriptive. Koltsov's experimental direction elicited irony among his professors. He began by applying physical chemistry to biology. You could study the live cell, put it in various media, and so on. This new approach aroused many hopes."

Vinberg himself was not a student of Koltsov, but he had seen Koltsov, had known him, and he spoke of him without the awe I had come to expect. His dry and creaky voice was sometimes enlivened with a giggle that had nothing to do with his words. Apparently, he was recalling something beyond the story. For now he told me nice details of Koltsov's drawings on the blackboard with colored chalks.

"Scientists did not receive grants then, they lived only on teaching salaries." Georgi Georgievich Vinberg is about to sigh over their lot, but snorts instead. "The golden age of science . . . At the beginning of the Revolution, Koltsov was suspected of something, arrested, and sentenced to be shot. But his case was quickly cleared up and he was released. In the first issue of the *Proceedings of the Institute of Experimental Biology* he printed a scientific article on the influence of psychological suffering on a man's weight. Speaking of his own case, he said that he had been condemned to death at such and such time and had eaten such and such. The calories were such and such, adequate, but he lost such and such. Even when waiting to be shot, he made observations as a scientist. Looks? Striking. Tolstoy jacket, big bow, elegance." Vinberg pauses and adds drily, "Like the cat in Maeterlinck's *Blue Bird*." And without changing intonation: "White mustache, always in a gruffly good-humored mood. A liberal, so liberal that he couldn't fit in with the Moscow professors."

The comparison with the cat from *The Blue Bird* is probably more than just physical. Vinberg is our major hybridologist, a corresponding member of the Academy of Sciences, and has a reputation for not throwing his words around carelessly.

"He had a very primitive concept of the cell. He often got fascinated with unimportant things. For instance, in rejuvenation. Or publishing an article on thinking horses."

For Georgi Georgievich these things are inexcusable. Hence the cat. But then I realize that there is more behind the comparison.

He recalls Koltsov's wife. He begins mockingly, with condescension.

"A hysterical 'lady,' stupid, spoiled, who loved to prattle about her love for her husband to the grave, that she would not outlive him. Everyone laughed at this. When Koltsov died—and he died unexpectedly, in Leningrad—one of his co-workers rushed to her side. Just in case, you never know. He found her so apathetic that he stopped worrying and hurried off to take care of the funeral. When he came back, she was dead."

His voice is just as dry and creaky. But that doesn't matter to me anymore.

As soon as you understand his manner of narrative, the feigned irony, both he and Koltsov's wife become different. The tragedy of love alters all incorrect and superficial judgments upon this woman. In those ever more dangerous years for Koltsov, her hysteria seems different. What kind of a person must you be to instill such love? What a pure and wonderful heart you must have to love this way! Maria Koltsova was worthy of her husband.

Each of Koltsov's students builds his own image, creates his own portrait. If you superimpose them, the picture will not become more accurate, but the image will blur and the liveliness will vanish. Approximately the same thing is happening to the Bison now. Listening to his students, you can no longer tell what he had been like: one considers him farseeing, another naïve, a third secretive. One considers him an idealist, another a materialist. Some maintain that he was religious, others that he began thinking about God only in his later years, still others insist that he was always an atheist.

Koltsov was Kolyusha's teacher, and Kolyusha was Koltsov's student. When Koltsov was Mensbir's student, he was like Kolyusha—a headstrong fellow with extreme left radical views. And because of that he had a major confrontation with Mikhail Alexandrovich Mensbir. The event made a strong impression on Kolyusha.

Koltsov, who had ties to liberal circles, kept revolutionary literature in his lab. Those were the reactionary years, just before the outbreak of World War I, and Mensbir, learning about the literature, shouted at Koltsov. He didn't listen. Then Mensbir simply took away the lab from Koltsov with a strict warning: if you've been given the opportunity to do science, don't get sidetracked. People recalled the conflict in different ways and interpreted it differently. But later, in the twenties, Koltsov himself grumbled through his thick drooping mustache that the young assistant professor had been stupid, he could have gotten his innocent colleagues into trouble by setting up practically a warehouse of illegal literature in the lab. "Mikhail Alexandrovich dealt with me and my silly brochures correctly." And Mensbir explained, drawling and nodding his gray head: ". . . a dangerous age, when they think that political ambiguities are the most important things, without realizing that normal scientific work is much more useful. I couldn't let him endanger the laboratory, set up with such difficulty. Not for anything. Thank God, Nikolai Konstantinovich understands that now."

Kolyusha's Red Army background argued against those conclusions. He knew how valuable and how necessary the truth found in those brochures could be, and it upset him that Koltsov agreed with Mensbir, confirming from the heights of his life experience that science was superior to the flurry of political passions, to the brochures that contain agitation rather than truth, today one thing, tomorrow another. The teachers he respected were not afraid to say so, even though they were surrounded by a blaze of rallies, deluged by a shower of brochures and posters; everything was imbued with politics, it seemed that it could be enough to turn Russia to a new life. But the old men held their ground. They maintained that sooner or later comprehension would come: the only worthwhile goal was serving science, which would not deceive or disillusion you. Science, laboratory work, unraveling the secrets of nature—it was beautiful, clear, and protected you from other responsibilities. And if it would come sooner or later anyway, then it would be better to see this sooner, without wasting young blood.

Let us not reproach these men, it would be too primitive to consider them fanatics possessed by science. The word "possessed" does not suit them. They served science faithfully and with love, but many things were higher than science for them, for instance the rules of honor and decency. In 1911, during the events at Moscow University, the same Mensbir quit his position of prorector of the university and left the department he headed as a protest against the repressive moves of the tsarist government. Many other professors retired with him—K. A. Timiryazev, P. N. Lebedev, V. I. Vernadsky, S. A. Chaplygin, and N. D. Zelinsky.

Koltsov was called in and asked to take over Mensbir's department. The answer to a young assistant professor's dream. Koltsov refused without any hesitation. He was offended that they thought him capable of such a vile act. They looked for another candidate. They offered it to Alexei Nikolayevich Severtsov, who was at Kiev University. He accepted. He came from Kiev and took over his teacher's department. The ticklishness of the situation lay in the fact that Alexei Nikolayevich Severtsov was the son of Nikolai Alexeyevich Severtsov—Mensbir's famous teacher. Mensbir held the memory of his teacher in high esteem. The father had the reputation of a most honest and universally respected man. People joked about his absentmindedness, but they loved him and were proud of his achievements. And suddenly, his son acted this way! This upset everyone bitterly and they could not forgive him. He was roundly condemned for this act.

A sentence handed down by public opinion is much graver than a court sentence. You can't appeal. You can't bribe your way out. Public opinion judged according to the unwritten laws of decency. According to those laws, the younger Severtsov's act was considered indecent, and no matter what Severtsov did later, no matter how hard he worked to organize the lab, to create a major school of morphologists, he was avoided and blackballed. He wrote good monographs, he elaborated a theory of the appearance of new characteristics and their changes, he did a lot of fine work. Nevertheless that business lay like a shadow upon him.

Public opinion in those years was intolerant of sucking up to authorities and was suspicious of state prizes; it was ruthless in condemning lies, in condemning falsifying data . . . Koltsov's act was the norm and Severtsov's act was a violation of the norm. Mensbir's older students–Sushkin and Koltsov–and his younger ones mellowed with the years and, seeing how hard being an outcast was on Severtsov, said to him: all right, then, Alexei Nikolayevich, you have to go beg Mensbir's pardon, otherwise it's no go. Severtsov tried to wriggle out of it, but he had been wrong, and admitting it would do no harm. Finally, he did it, he went to Mensbir, in sackcloth and ashes, and repented.

Sometimes Koltsov is considered the founder of molecular biology. Being categorical in these matters is risky. It is enough to say that he was one of the founders. But Koltsov said nothing about evolutionary development. It was Kolyusha who worked out the evolutionary genetic idea on a molecular basis. But that was far in the future. First he had to pass through a great amount of practical work at the university, and most of all, study under his great teacher.

Koltsov's students did their practical work with great thoroughness. Kolyusha was part of the middle generation of students. Serebrovsky, Skadovsky, Astaurov, Frolova, and Zhivago were among those who passed through Koltsov's department. This generation helped organize the practical work in a new way. No matter where Kolyusha went later–universities in Germany, Italy, England, and America–he never saw its equal. The practicum lasted two years. First the students fussed with ringworms and then with arthropods, then lower vertebrates, and it all ended with the lancet. Since each student had to earn enough for his board, by lecturing, doing carpentry or repair work, soldering, whatever one could, Koltsov kept the lab open around the clock. People came to work whenever they could. Morning, noon, and night. Once a week, on a day convenient for all, usually a Wednesday, everyone gathered and the teacher gave a lecture on the materials to be handed out for the next week's work. Koltsov did some of the work with them himself, especially on topics he liked or where he had made new discoveries. This lasted for two years, from Wednesday to Wednesday. They learned to determine species, did live culturing. Everyone had his own cultured amoebas, flagellates. Every stage of division and multiplication had to be fixed, compared, drawn. Then the same with sponges. All this was done independently. They dissected all kinds of bugs and beetles, observed regenerations and transplantation in guppies and tritons. Everyone did his own research, made discoveries, gasped, made mistakes, asked questions, and felt like a real researcher.

They had special sessions. Sergei Nikolayevich Skadovsky taught the course on hydrophysiology, Dmitri Petrovich Filatov on experimental embryology, Petr Ivanovich Zhivago on cytology. Each of these names has entered the history of biology. It just so happened that the Bison was surrounded from his youth by extraordinary people.

There were six or eight special courses. And no enforcement. Go if you wish, don't go if you don't want to, it's up to you. As class monitor, Kolyusha kept no attendance records. The freedom offered by the practicum bound them closer to it than any orders could have. They gave all their energy to the practicum, their young enthusiasm went into competition, into the thirst to comprehend, to keep up. No one asked what languages you read. If Koltsov or Chetverikov gave you an article to read in French, then you had better start learning French; dictionaries were invented a long time ago. Kolyusha had a funny story about his first assignment: he was given a monograph in Italian. Two months to familiarize himself with it. He had to read it. He worked almost around the clock. Once he was at the theater and fell asleep. He slept sitting up. Then there was a ruckus. Turned out that two girls sitting next to him had drawn a clown face on him with lipstick.

All those who took part in the practicum in the ten years between 1917 and 1927 consider themselves among the luckiest people in the world; it was the best time of their lives.

When a new person arrived wishing to work with Koltsov, Kolyusha as monitor met with him and reported to Koltsov. It was usually his job to keep an eye on the newcomer for a while. Elena Alexandrovna Fidler appeared this way. She had started studying with Koltsov back at Shanyavsky University. She was a tall young woman with gentle features and a flawless figure. She came from the famous Moscow Fidlers, the ones who operated a private girls' high school which was quite popular at the time. She had to take a lot of ribbing, that fair maiden, that mama's girl, with her aristocratic manners.

One of the teachers working under Koltsov was M. M. Zavadovsky. He organized a field trip to the nature preserve in Askania-Nova. He got together a group from Shanyavsky University, where most of the students were female, and took them to the nature preserve. But the Civil War was fierce in the Ukraine—there were gangs of Makhnovites, Petlyuravites, hetmanites, and anarchists. The road to Moscow was cut off, they couldn't go back, they could only head toward the Crimea, and the young women scattered. There were adventures galore. Elena Alexandrovna had a few wild experiences, was miraculously saved, and made her way back to Moscow in the winter of 1920. Lena, or Lelka as Kolyusha called her, had been transformed—she had matured and blossomed. Kolyusha, who was having an affair with her girlfriend, suddenly turned things around and in two weeks announced their engagement. They were married in the spring, in May.

The affair was stormy and unexpected for all those who had tried to set him up with girls whom they thought more suitable in temperament, position, or height. Lelka was half a head taller than Kolyusha and his complete opposite in character. No one thought they would be compatible. Superstition considers May a bad month for marriages.

But their real affair started only after the wedding, when they began to get to know each other better. They did seem incompatible. She was calm and rational, he was fiercely explosive; she was steady, controlled, able to deal with the most different people and yet keep them at a distance, whereas he shouted, screamed, dove easily into any company, where he was immediately surrounded by interesting people. Lelka was a homebody, she needed order, and it seemed that she created order so that he could disturb it. She got a fix on people better than he did, she was punctilious, responsible, and managed to live within their meager budget. She was always well groomed, dressed carefully, her quiet green eyes glowing; his shirttails were always hanging out, his trousers were sometimes torn, and on occasion he showed up barefoot. He did not control his intake of food, cigarettes, or alcohol, while she merely sipped from a glass . . .

As a biologist she was an impeccable practitioner. She knew how to set up a sensitive, long-term experiment, and could guarantee success whenever patience, precision, and the ability to take thousands of repeated observations were required. She could examine one hundred twenty thousand flies and find the twelve light-eyed ones among them. In another experiment, she radiated fruit flies and selected three red-eyed flies among the ninety thousand descendants.

Their common work joined them solidly, as did the foreign country in which they later found themselves. With the years he needed her more than she did him, but she took ever-greater pride in him; other men just couldn't hold a candle to him. They were boring, they lacked his fire and courage.

Neither he nor she ever told me the story of their relationship and I am not about to make it up. I never saw them argue or bicker in the ordinary way. Their mutual respect kept them from that. They did have conflicts, of course, there were hurts and tiffs, but on a different level; they never insulted or humiliated each other. I met them in the period when Lelka took care of their correspondence, read articles and books aloud for him, because after certain events the Bison did not see well.

Apparently, he had had many affairs, fleeting ones, women were drawn to him, but not one could replace Lelka, not one could be more important to him than his wife.

Of course, judging by certain recollections, I am oversimplifying; their love developed in a much more complex way, he lost her and regained her love over and over. And perhaps it is for the best that we don't know for certain.

10

A ROBBER
BROTHERHOOD

In those years study was not enough to exhaust his energy. Rolling up his sleeves, he got involved in the organization of the Practical Institute. They wanted to create an institution of a completely new type, with three departments—biotechnical, agronomical, and economic. He wanted to bring biology closer to the needs of the people, to the agricultural concerns of the country. Creating a new institute, especially along those lines, was amusing, unheard of—and much simpler than it would be now. The main wealth of the new Soviet authorities was trust. The other asset was buildings. The institute was given a large empty building, a former commercial school, on Ostozhenka in Moscow. Get the rest yourself, find what you need. Soon they got permission to use the stores of the Russian Red Cross, which got all kinds of laboratory equipment during the war. Kolyusha would put on his military uniform, get into a two-horse buggy with a soldier in the coach box, and in that awe-inspiring way, drive up to the necessary establishment. He would demand. Procure. Convincingly and meaningfully. He would discover new microscopes, binocular loupes, monocular loupes, microtomes, thermostats, crates of chemical glassware . . .

By 1923 the institute was better equipped than the biological laboratories of the university.

There was one more source. It wasn't very honest, but what can you do? You had to make do. They had to use "secondhand" what P. P. Lazarev used

49

first. The physicist and academician, whom the students called "Pepelaza," had more authority than the "red belly in the carriage," as they called Kolyusha going on his rounds. Lazarev had support from Lenin to realize the dream of a generation of Russian physicists and geologists–to penetrate the secrets of the Kursk magnetic anomaly. He visited various institutions–in a car!–"arm in arm" with his magnetic anomaly and requisitioned anything he needed for the anomaly. He didn't have time to inventory. If they had glassware, he took it, and sometimes along with laboratory glassware he got kitchen glassware; along with lab coats and towels he got bed linens, even underwear. "Pepelaza" cleared out the stocks of organizations that had survived the war, brought things out for his biophysics institute, which was still under construction; he piled up crates in the courtyard behind a high fence.

Winter came. Kolyusha and two of his friends got a sleigh. Under cover of darkness, they drove up to the fence of the Lazarev institute. Two of them climbed over into the yard, checked out the crates, and passed them over the fence, the third loaded up the sleigh, and then they drove off. They would open a crate and find a Chinese tea service. They would swear–they didn't need a tea service, they needed lab dishes, which were not manufactured in the Soviet Union. What to do with the tea service? Trade it for towels. Their activity wasn't particularly moral; theft is theft, no matter what justifications are used. But this was their justification: first of all, they weren't stealing for themselves; second, they were risking their lives, the militia could easily shoot them on the spot. The thieves weren't overly burdened with logic, they prided themselves on not telling Koltsov, so as not to overburden his conscience.

Student years . . . Nothing like pre-revolutionary student years, and also different from later generations. These first Soviet graduates were distinguished by their talents.

There were no wunderkinder. Kolyusha was twenty-one and still a student. This didn't bother him in the least. He wanted only to work in the practicums which interested him and to take the courses he needed. When he did that, he decided he was done with the university and he didn't bother taking any state examinations. He wasn't the only one to behave this way. Many considered a diploma an unnecessary formality, a remnant of the past, a bureaucratic blip. Paper had no force, no one depended on it in science, the rare inhabitants of science were pure enthusiasts, seekers of truth, lovers of adventure in thought, knights of the idea or of some vague innate strivings. They would have done science for nothing, as long as they got some food. They weren't fanatics or men possessed, they were romantics.

When Kolyusha went abroad, no one asked for his diploma there either. As a result, he made his career without paperwork. When he returned from his long odyssey, in the fifties, he realized that he was no one. And in the course of their stormy life Lelka did not manage to save his high school diploma, and the Bison turned out to be a man without a higher education. With difficulty, they arranged a salary for him as a senior laboratory assistant.

But that didn't happen right away. For a start he began working in one of Koltsov's laboratories for the Commission on the Study of Russia's Natural Resources. There were many committees and institutions then, some dying, new ones springing up. Scientific life flourished despite famine and ruin. Lazarev's institute was being built, Koltsov's grew stronger, Martsinovsky's and the Institute of National Health appeared. They didn't build tall buildings, the institutes moved into old mansions, very small by today's standards, and they were staffed by just a few people—but things went well. It was also important that during World War I and the Civil War many ideas had accumulated. They were acted upon at the first opportunity, leading to an upsurge of Russian science in the twenties.

11

ANARCHIST
BANDS AND
CAVALRY RAIDS

When Kolyusha was returning from the southwestern front, he was taken prisoner by a band of anarchists. They were considered Greens, they fought on their own with the Germans who were advancing on the Ukraine, and as Greens, and anarchists at that, they obeyed no one, recognized no authorities, and felt that in Russia order could be born only out of anarchy. The leader of this band was a certain Gavrilenko, who called himself "a student of Prince Kropotkin himself." Gavrilenko interrogated Kolyusha and who knows what sentence he might have meted out to this Red Army soldier, suspiciously literate, making his way to Moscow for reasons unknown. The study of carp could not be considered a weighty reason at the height of the Civil War. Something was wrong here. It would have been simpler just to get rid of the fellow. Or at least give him a good crack on the ribs. With Kolyusha's fiery character, I hate to think what might have happened, but out of curiosity he asked, "You're a student of Kropotkin, but have you ever seen him?" Gavrilenko, naturally, had not seen him and wasn't ashamed of it. Who could have seen Kropotkin himself?

"I've seen him!" Kolyusha announced. "Since I'm a relative!" And he told him that Petr Alexeyevich Kropotkin was his grandmother's cousin, so that Kolyusha was his cousin twice removed.

"Grandmother and I visited him several times and we talked about revolutionary problems. He gave us raspberry jam, which, by the way, was a gift from Lenin. Lenin respected him, paid a call, and he took a liking to Lenin."

Of course, Kolyusha then told him that he had argued heatedly with Kropotkin. Not about anarchism, he had no interest in anarchism. The argument was over Kropotkin's evolutionary views, and he had been wrong to argue, he hadn't understood his views then. Later he had read his book *Reciprocal Aid as a Factor in the Struggle for Survival*—an excellent work–and admitted that Kropotkin was smart, even though he was a real master of the manor. Besides which, he had created a geological theory of the formation of the ice age.

"How did you dare argue with Kropotkin himself!" Gavrilenko shouted.

But he developed great respect for Kolyusha, this representative of Kropotkin, and began taking him along on raids against the German troops, whom he had sworn to drive from Ukrainian soil. On one such raid a German trooper hit Kolyusha on the head with a sword, luckily with the flat of the blade, and he fell unconscious from his horse. He regained consciousness during the night. The horse was there. His hat was gone. He mounted the horse, and feeling hurt that he had been abandoned, went off in search of the Red army unit of his Twelfth Army . . .

Fate could not spare him the events of the times. It was his nature to live the moment, tasting the day. But fate took care to get him out of desperate situations, dragging him back from the brink by his hair . . . Sometimes it seems to me that it was no miracle but providence which nurtured him and kept him alive, a scarred example of the period.

The adventures of his life came out at random, tangentially, in conversation, repeated but different. Like a kaleidoscope. I should have put them together and come up with the complete, full version, but I didn't dare.

. . . In the next story of Kolyusha's he explained how they were taught in the cavalry to use their sabers.

"There are two important points: when you move your hand forward, be sure not to cut off the horse's ear, and then when you swing, be sure not to chop off a piece of its haunch. So you have to keep your hand turned at an angle, which requires accuracy and practice. Chop what you want, but remember not to harm the horse's ear or ass!"

And in passing I learned that Gavrilenko's band was ambushed returning from a raid. The band traveled with carts: women and children, sacks, samovars, pots, goats—a nomadic republic. The column moved into a bottle-neck, the river on one side, thick impassable brush on the other. A German squadron came at them. Gavrilenko ordered: "Forward!" It was a question of who would have the luck. Kolyusha rushed forward, leaning low on his horse's neck: get me out of this, dear one! He wasn't a very good cavalryman, but he had a good seat, the horse understood him, animals understood him, and he understood them, that's why he was a real zoologist. He rushed, then there was the blow, and then the starry sky and his horse standing next to him . . .

You would think a scientist didn't need to be a good storyteller, but it was somehow part of his scientific talent. The famous mathematician A. M. Molchanov described his art this way: "The Bison had this manner: hold on to the main idea. Digress as much as you like, but get back to it. Small details could vary, but the main idea was always preserved. Preludes, digressions—he was a master. But the main thought came through step by iron step. Lectures like that are harder to do than writing many volumes. When the Bison died and Academician Keldysh died, I said sadly, 'I have no one to fear anymore.' I was afraid only of those two. For many reasons. Both were much quicker thinkers than I and could make me look like a fool in my own eyes. Both were very strong and could subjugate you, which is also not very pleasant. Yet they weren't the same at all, you could say they were complete opposites. For instance, I've noticed that when I speak, I imitate the Bison."

12

KIDNAPPING
A COMMISSAR

In 1924 Oskar Vogt asked the People's Commissar of Health, N. A. Semashko, to recommend a young Russian geneticist for the Berlin Institute, for the new division of genetics and biophysics.

Professor Vogt was director of the Berlin Brain Institute. He had been invited to Moscow as a consultant when V. I. Lenin fell ill. After Lenin's death, in 1924, the Soviet government asked him to take part in the study of Lenin's brain and help them found a brain institute in Russia.

Semashko talked with Koltsov. After some thought, Koltsov recommended Kolyusha.

"What Timofeyev is this?" the commissar asked. "You don't mean that brave young fellow who attacked me with a cudgel?"

"The very one," confirmed Koltsov.

"Hmm." Semashko scratched his head expressively. "You're recommending a highway robber?"

"Most assuredly."

Semashko laughed and asked that Kolyusha be brought in.

Before their meeting takes place I have to explain how Semashko knew Kolyusha and why he scratched his head.

A year earlier Koltsov had persuaded the commissar to visit both of his biostations, one in Anikova, where the colleagues of A. S. Serebrovsky worked, and the other nearby, in Zvenigorod, where Kolyusha and his friends worked.

Serebrovsky, Koltsov's senior student, ran a famous genetics station where population genetics was studied in chickens. They had good results, useful for the agriculture department.

The Zvenigorod station was less prestigious, because they studied flies, which seemed ridiculous to outsiders. Once Kolyusha was the butt of many jokes, when a friend, Reformatsky, organized a hunting party and Kolyusha begged off because he had to watch his flies. Flies, how valuable, ho-ho! It was silly to miss a good time because of some stupid flies. He could not explain, at least not then, that those flies were revealing hitherto unknown processes of the development of life. Two-winged flies for many years served as the source of his joys, his disappointments, his fame, and his troubles . . .

The fly was called Drosophila. A three-millimeter fly with a tiger belly. If I were writing a popular science book I would praise the fly, compose an ode to this insect, faithful assistant of thousands of geneticists since 1909. An ode to its frankness. Or its chattiness. A chatty subject is good because it keeps nature's secrets so badly. It is hard to appreciate just what a fine job the Drosophila has done for science. If it was deemed suitable to erect a monument to Pavlov's dog, then we should eternalize our gratitude for the fruit fly . . .

One of the Bison's students, Nikolai Viktorovich Luchnik, recorded his teacher's speech praising the Drosophila: "Irreplaceable subject! Reproduces quickly. Has many offspring. Clear hereditary signs. Can't confuse a mutation with a normal individual. Red eyes, white eyes. All serious laboratories around the world work with the Drosophila. Ignoramuses like to talk about the fact that the Drosophila has no economic significance. But no one is trying to develop a strain of dairy and meat fruit flies. Drosophila is needed to study the laws of heredity. The laws are the same for elephants and fruit flies. You'll get the same results with elephants. But a generation of fruit flies grows in two weeks. Instead of making an elephant out of a fly [the Russian equivalent of a mountain out of a molehill], we are making flies out of elephants!"

They had begun working with fruit flies in Russia not long before, and there were no authoritative works on the subject. Actually, the fly was still in disrepute in the forties and even in the fifties. It was attacked, rebuked, mocked, used as an example of science removed from reality, it was considered dangerous to deal with it—a criminal fly!

Thus, they found out at the Zvenigorod station that the commissar was coming, but after visiting the station in Anikova. They were crestfallen. They pictured the feast the better-equipped station would throw, with their hens and with alcohol. It was quite possible that the commissar might not even bother coming to their station, and if he did, he certainly wouldn't hurry over. What should they do? Kolyusha suggested hijacking the commissar. They decided to kidnap him at a fork in the road about five kilometers away: left to Anikovo, right to Zvenigorod.

They were very casual at the station in those days. Kolyusha was usually barefoot. He wore striped pants and a gray shirt. Dmitri Petrovich Filatov and Boris Lvovich Astaurov looked the same, but they wore shoes. They decided to lie in wait in the bushes at the fork. They were armed with cudgels.

In those days commissars traveled simply. Semashko took the train as far as Kubinka, where he was met and taken further by carriage. He was always accompanied by his assistant, an incredibly fat doctor.

The troika jogged down the road carrying the commissar, his assistant, and the people who had met them at the train station. And then, just as in a real highway robbery, young fellows with cudgels leaped out of the bushes. Shaggy and bearded fellows who didn't waste time shaving.

"Stop!" They waved their cudgels.

Semashko's assistant got scared and kept trying to get at the pistol in his back pocket, but he couldn't reach it.

The young men said, "You'll be unharmed, we don't need your money, but you will go where we take you."

They turned the horse toward Zvenigorod, they made the coachman get down. Kolyusha took the reins and the rest ran alongside with cudgels like an escort. Semashko quickly understood what was happening, and he liked the kidnapping very much. Ever since then they have been friends.

The Bison liked telling the story of the commissar's kidnapping, but he made it sound like another prank, nothing serious, he didn't load it with any justifications. It was only later that his colleague and friend N. N. Vorontsov got at the reasons. The kidnapping was the blood call of Kolyusha's ancestors. There was something of the robber in Kolyusha, and that call was stronger than his scientific passions, his nature often ruined his plans. He would make a scene for no good reason. For instance, once he talked his friends into carrying off the young women of Anikovo. Steal them so that they could court them, dance and frolic at their station, where there weren't enough women. It ended badly. They grabbed one girl and stuffed her in a sack. She lay very still, it was easy to carry her—she was fat and soft. When they got her home and shook her out, she wasn't breathing! She had fainted in the sack. She just lay there white and with her eyes shut. Kolyusha and Astaurov got scared. It's a good thing that their colleague Minna Savich didn't lose her head, she brought the young woman back to consciousness, sprinkled her with water, calmed her down. After that, they stopped kidnapping young women.

Olya Chernova was the youngest person working at the station, but even sixty years later she remembers all the details of their summer life and repeats the Bison's stories word for word. A born leader, he solidified his position through the game he popularized at the university. Volleyball didn't exist then, he had been tired of soccer ever since high school, and that left *gorodki,* or Russian skittles. He soon became a champion. Actually, he could never settle for being just a player. He had to be a champion. He reached the top of whatever he did, otherwise he wouldn't even try. In the university courtyard he set up games between the zoologists and the chemists. The chemists' best player was Nesmeyanov, the zoologists' was Kolyusha. At the station they played until nightfall. They placed white pieces of paper near the goals.

He recalled the time that Koltsov brought Hermann Muller, the famous American geneticist, to their Zvenigorod station. Muller brought them some Drosophila flies. After that Chetverikov developed plates with agar, flies, red-eyed mutations, crossovers, and at last, the Drozsoor.

None of the non-initiates could explain to me what the Drozsoor was. Something like a seminar or circle to discuss work with the fly.

Did the word come first or the act? That's always the quandary. That's what philosophers argued about. And will continue to argue about. Because even in things that happen before our very eyes we don't always notice which came first—word or deed.

How did the Drozsoor begin, Chetverikov's creation, so dear to his heart, that boiling, roiling cauldron from which came, one after the other, like thirty-three heroes, the founders of original directions in genetics?

It began, apparently, from the need to communicate. But to communicate without any customary forms of meetings. To propose and discuss the thinkable and the unthinkable without looking over their shoulders.

But something preceded that.

After graduation from the university you were supposed to do science. But the Bison did not graduate and did not take the state exams. Without finishing his studies, he took up science. Everyone knew it, and the university knew it, and that was enough. Then, in the early twenties, paperwork was not so important in scientific life. A man was valued for his work, a student for his abilities. Paradise, when everyone was naked, not covering up with diplomas and titles. When Kolyusha was going abroad to work, his teacher Koltsov gave him a letter of recommendation. That replaced all reports and mandates. The important thing was that he was his student and that he had been taught.

And when Kolyusha organized the Practical Institute in Moscow, he had no special papers, he just had the desire to create something necessary and practical in biology.

Fortunate era! He recalled it with a blissful smile: all the enemies surrounding Russia were beaten, and he could take up his beloved work.

One of the stories of those years he began this way: "How well the Lord was disposed toward me! Once I was convinced of that, I took up experimental biology."

13

A MISSION TO ENLIGHTEN THE TEUTONIC TRIBES

Oskar Vogt was a neurologist, a neuropathologist, who did much for the study of the architectonics of the hemispheres of the brain and was a great specialist in wasps. He had the largest collection of wasps in the world. Vogt wanted to investigate the changes in wasps genetically. There was no suitable geneticist available in Germany. So Vogt's work promised to be interesting. However, Kolyusha refused it categorically and did not go to see Semashko, there was no point. He did not want to hear any inducements. Why go to Berlin if he was happy here? But Koltsov insisted. You have to give him his due: he knew how to handle people who argued with him.

Why had Koltsov chosen Kolyusha? He had plenty of talented young people in his lab. Every one of Koltsov's students later became an outstanding geneticist. But he considered Kolyusha the most independent of the young people. Kolyusha already had his works published, one of them a major work. When did he have the time? His work ability was unique. We know that he continued teaching because he needed the money and Lelka had given birth to a healthy bawling son, Dmitri, whom everyone called Foma for some reason. The new father would say, "Yell, go ahead and yell, it'll make your face wider."

When he had time to say this, I don't know, just as I don't know when he had time to play skittles. Teaching took up to fifty-eight hours a week, more than nine hours a day, just talking, month after month. No other instructor had such a heavy load. Some tried to keep up and quickly faded. He mocked them: Sissies!

Naturally, he no longer sang in the choir. The front-line food rations had been stopped, so there wasn't any point anymore. He jumped up every morning to the clatter of a huge alarm clock hung on the wall. He had bought it in seventh grade, when he realized that he didn't have enough time and the only free hours were at night. It was silly to spend eight hours, a third of your life, on sleep. He set his alarm clock for seven once and for all and started going to bed later and later, until in college he got down to two-thirty in the morning. It was hard at first. In order to get to sleep right away, he would run around the block several times and then fall into a deep and sudden sleep. He never had any dreams. No time, he had to rest. Gradually he got used to it and he didn't feel sleepy during the day. When he was at the Koltsov institute, he usually slept four and a half or five hours. He stopped at that. That's how he slept the rest of his life. Some might think that he deprived himself of the pleasure of a good sleep, but he felt that living was a greater pleasure than sleeping. He was helped by a rule that the children had to obey: if you're awake, get up! No lolling around in bed. (There were two other rules just as strict: don't leave anything on your plate and don't tattle!)

The alarm clock would shake and jump overhead. A half hour later Kolyusha was running to the trolley stop. His classes started at nine at the Prichistensky Workers' School, with breaks to give him time to get to the medical-pedagogic institute and back again. Nine to ten hours of talking, two hours for travel. He came home at nine in the evening, ate like an Australian, once a day, everything that he could, and then went off to the Koltsov institute, which luckily was nearby. He played there till one in the morning with his beloved freshwater creatures and, after the year 1922, with his fruit flies.

It was back then that he developed his house specialty: dump everything in the cupboard and refrigerator into a pot—meat, sausage, yogurt, boiled potatoes, eggs, maybe cheese and tomatoes—heat it up and ladle it out, without wasting time for courses and hors d'oeuvres.

When he got home, he read. He devoured the Russian philosophy that was then popular with students—Ferodov, Solovyev, Konstantin Leontiev, Shestov.

He was cautioned: a life like that would lead to brain overload and death. He said that was for ordinary intellectuals. Apparently, he didn't get overloaded, either mentally or physically. And he didn't die. He ran around tirelessly and assured everyone that, compared to the feet, the head was not an important organ. The head is rarely needed, while the feet and hands are needed for everyday life. And that's how he lived: with his feet and rarely with his head.

In 1923 Koltsov took Kolyusha into his medical-pedagogic institute to run a small practicum and gave him a small salary. For Kolyusha it was astonishing, the first time he earned money through science.

The practical institute still drew him. There were interesting students there, ones whose education but not their love of science had been interrupted by the war. They applied to the institute that gave them a clear specialty and offered cycles of courses: forestry, animal husbandry, water resources—everything which could be obtained from natural resources that replenish themselves. That was the point. They studied the theory of exploitation and reestablishment. Zoology professor M. N. Rimsky-Korsakov, son of the composer, got him into the creation of a new biostation, maintaining that Kolyusha was a marvelous lecturer and a talented teacher and organizer.

Koltsov and Kolyusha's friends, however, were seriously worried about his health. An overload like that could end badly.

I haven't described the Drozsoor yet or the main passion of its participants. A new idea in evolutionary teaching was born and grew in the Drozsoor—to join modern genetics with classical Darwinism. The idea entranced all the Drosophiliacs. Koltsov did not attend the Drozsoor, so as not to overwhelm them with his authority or confine them. He was nearby, up above, on his peak, and they shouted at the foothills.

Drozsoor can be decoded as joint shouting about the Drosophila. Kolyusha's mighty bass rose above the joint shout. Surely the "shouting" was thanks to Kolyusha, who was a master at it, a real shouter, yeller, screamer. It's quite possible that he came up with the name, though he didn't admit it. The shouting also meant work for them, plowing, hoeing, clearing . . . The name stuck and even entered the official history of world genetics.

Their shouting had its own rules of order, which boiled down to the "rule of the red thread": you can be interrupted and sidetracked by others' shouting, but you have to follow the "red thread" of your point to the end.

Koltsov neither helped nor hindered them. He was a difficult person to get to know. He was equally polite with everyone, no pleasantries. They were proud of him. At the most difficult time, not one of them turned away from him. He did not teach them decency, but it turned out that all his students, from oldest to youngest–Rapoport, Sakharov, Frizen–were all meticulously decent and proper.

Now it becomes clear why Kolyusha did not want to go to Berlin. What did he need with Berlin, when he was up to his ears in work here, when genetics in the Soviet Union was on the upswing, when a scientist as famous as Hermann Muller was thinking about moving from the United States to Moscow to do his work? No, he wasn't going to that institute of Vogt's in Berlin, where there was more medicine than biology.

Nonetheless, Koltsov dragged him to see the commissar. Semashko spoke of the need to raise the level of the authority of the young Soviet Republic. This was such a convenient opportunity: organize a joint German-Soviet scientific center in Europe. It would be a sin not to take advantage of it.

"You have to think of more than your own scientific interest," Koltsov said.

"Ordinary Russian scientists travel abroad to study," Semashko went on, "to work with some celebrity, master some method, or familiarize themselves with new equipment. But here they are asking a Russian geneticist to come and create a genetics laboratory, basically to teach–and not Zulus, but Germans."

The situation was, of course, flatteringly rare: a young Russian scientist of twenty-five going to Germany, a country from which the Russians had always imported "scientific fruits" in order later to export them.

Koltsov had another motive as well.

"You won't have to rush around to lectures there, you will have a good salary, you can devote yourself to research, to genetics–that is, to science and nothing else. As for the organizational period–these are Germans, they'll have *Ordnung*, everything under control. Once you say it, it's done, and once it's done, it doesn't have to be redone. The new work will free you from overwork, from cares and worries. So what if they're foreigners, you speak German."

He knew German well, German and French. The teachers in high school and the home tutors had done their job. As for teaching foreigners, Semashko was not quite correct: Russians had gone abroad in the past to teach.

Take Kolyusha's father, Vladimir Nikolayevich Timofeyev-Resovsky.

His father graduated from the physics and mathematics department of St. Petersburg University. In 1871 he went to Central Asia to observe an eclipse. But instead of studying the eclipse he looked around and was horrified by the conditions on the land. Like Radishchev, "his soul was wounded," not by human suffering, however, but by the state of the roads, the primitive conditions that led to illiteracy, xenophobia, lack of culture, and immorality. No means of transportation for thousands of kilometers! This affected him so much that he gave up his career in astronomy. He had just defended his dissertation brilliantly and then, astonishing and saddening his family and friends, he joined the newly reorganized Institute of Transportation Engineering. He studied engineering, finished the course in two years, and went off to build railroads. He laid mile after mile of track, a road to Russia's future. To him the railroad was the means to overcome Russia's backwardness and poverty.

His first railroad was in Siberia, from Ekaterinburg to Tyumen. And his last road was the Odessa-Bakhmach line, with its daring and famous engineering feat, a bridge over the Dnepr River.

He died just after that on Christmas Day 1913. In between he had built almost sixteen thousand kilometers of railroad, including the Elton-Baskunchak road leading to the Volga wharf, not a major line, but because it traversed salt desert it entailed special construction difficulties. After that project an Anglo-French company asked him to build a road from Morocco to the edge of the Sahara, so Timofeyev-Resovsky went off to teach the foreigners how to build in the desert. It wasn't often that a Russian engineer was invited by the British or French to head a construction project. Vladimir Nikolayevich turned down the directorship and agreed to be a consultant. He said, "I'm used to our own crooks, I know how to deal with them, and I have no intention of learning about foreign crooks." It's too bad that Kolyusha was little interested in his father's affairs; perhaps it stemmed from the fact that his father was often away and he saw him rarely. Kolyusha was born when his father was fifty. What he remembered well were his father's stories about hunting in Africa for elephants, antelopes, and leopards.

So going abroad to teach was a Timofeyev tradition. Lelka joined Koltsov and Semashko in persuading Kolyusha.

"If you don't do anything substantial in science by the time you're twenty-eight, you never will." He later repeated that ruthless dictum to his young students, not sparing them. In 1925 he still had some time left. Besides, he had already done a few worthwhile things. But were they substantial? He knew that he was about to grasp something, he was right in the middle of things. Perhaps he would have more time to concentrate in Germany. That decided it for him. He agreed.

The assignment was the envy of all. But he sighed. Most of all he regretted missing Chetverikov's Drozsoor.

Talking about those days, he always returned to the Drozsoor.

"You know, the last time I didn't tell you about Alexander Nikolayevich Promptov. He was also in the Drozsoor . . ."

"You mentioned him."

"But is mentioning the point? He was not only a geneticist, he was an ornithologist and lover of birdcalls. Birdcalls require a separate science. Promptov could imitate all the passerine calls of Central Russia. They didn't have tape recorders in those days, there was no way to record the songs and warbles. He memorized them. He spent all his spare time birdwatching in fields and groves. To tell the truth, he really could speak with birds, at least with passerines. He was hunchbacked and lame, pathetic-looking, but he was king of the birds! And he also produced several first-class works on the genetics of bird skeletons . . . And did I tell you about Astaurov?"

Nothing gave him as much pleasure as talking about talented people. Delight in other people's talents is rare in science and in art. He seemed to have no envy. Talking about S. S. Chetverikov, N. I. Vavilov, V. I. Vernadsky, he took off his hat and bowed before them with all respect. They belonged to his order, where three qualities were required: talent, decency, and hard work. He had respect for scientists who weren't in the first rank, too. He dragged out of oblivion zoologists, ichthyologists, a botanist named Zverev, giving due credit to their work and their human qualities. He knew the value of his words: his praise was like an award, his appraisals put everything in its right place, casting official fame aside. If he said, for instance, that Takhtadzhyan was our best botanist, then he was, and no one was worried that Takhtadzhyan was not going to be elevated to the rank of academician soon.

He was equally ruthless and fearless in exposing mediocrity at all levels, especially among the pretentious. During the period of the Drozsoor there was a man named Vendrovsky, who was bemedaled and wore a semi-military uniform. Kolyusha always sang the Gilbert and Sullivan line about him,

"When I was young, I loved a uniform." Vendrovsky got hot under the collar, took offense, and finally filed a complaint against Kolyusha.

The Timofeyevs realized that they were poor only when they began packing for Germany. They had nothing to travel in. No shoes, no clothes. Kolyusha had his old jodhpurs, once navy blue, now of uneven hue, dark gray in some places, an indescribable light color in others. He did have his "tanks" —his British-made dress military boots that laced all the way up. The laces had torn ages ago and they were replaced with hemp twine, inked black. Kolyusha rubbed castor oil into his "tanks" every week, because he knew that it prevented mildew. His "tanks" didn't rot and became absolutely waterproof. He also had what remained of his soldier's field shirt, a pair of canvas summer trousers, and five shirts. In the summer he went barefoot and toward winter he would put on a pair of woolen slippers knitted for him by old women, with twine soles, like espadrilles. With such a wardrobe it was impossible to go abroad, where everyone was elegant and formal. Buy new clothes? Vogt had offered to pay for their trip, to give them some spending money. But Kolyusha declined. Why should he take unearned money from the Germans and be in their debt? He behaved like a big shot, he had all his life. He also refused Vogt's offer to rent him a furnished apartment in Berlin. We'll find one ourselves! He wouldn't take anything free. His pride wouldn't let him— rather, his honor. People shouldn't think he was accepting handouts because he was poor.

Lelka's aunt made her nice dresses from some silk drapes. They found him a gray shirt with several changes of collar, two pairs of underpants, and a tailor who agreed to make a three-piece suit for him out of Lelka's uncle's old rain cape. He measured carefully and had just enough for trousers, jacket, and vest. There was nothing else, because they had sold their pre-revolutionary wardrobe to buy food. Of course, they did find his father's parade university uniform—white with gold buttons, a standing collar, and slits in the trousers for his sword. But they decided that it wasn't a twentieth-century suit and it was impossible to retailor it into something suitable. They borrowed from friends and got a pair of shoes and two pairs of spare laces. The suit started acting up during their voyage: it ballooned at the elbows and knees, and no amount of ironing could smooth it out. It must have been the nature of the fabric—who knows. The one thing that saved Kolyusha was his innate dignity. He did not look funny no matter what he wore, and he certainly didn't look like a country bumpkin. The ballooning fabric wasn't handsome, but he didn't notice and therefore he was perceived independently of it. All the more so because the intelligentsia of the period was not ashamed of poverty.

The train carried them through the shimmering July heat. Ripening fields, villages sparkling with new whitewashed houses . . . It was 1925. The height of the New Economic Policy, the NEP. At every station platform people were doing a brisk business selling fried chicken, baked milk, luxurious pies filled with fish backbones, home-cured hams. Kolyusha ate and drank a lot throughout the trip. Piles of rusted metal lay along the sides of the road. Dray horses pulled carts with the remains of aircraft, armored cars, and artillery to the stations—the rubble of famous battles; swearing and cursing, people cleared it from the fields. What would they do with this trash? No one imagined that it would have to be recast for new cannons. Germany, at least, would never fight again. Then they traveled through ruined, impoverished Polish settlements, destroyed churches, stone crucifixes at the crossroads. Who had won this war? The weeds filling the fields? The bubble of imperial pride had burst with a stench and with blood.

It amused him to recall that he had traveled to Germany without any anxiety, almost with missionary zeal, to teach, to implant the science of genetics, to create a staff of trained personnel, to enlighten the poor Teutonic tribes. He worried a bit to himself, knowing that the Russians were hopelessly ignorant, but he still felt superior.

He took no documents or identity papers with him, he had no diploma, all he had was Koltsov's letter, which said that Timofeyev-Resovsky had been his student, he was trained, and he was highly recommended.

Wheezing into his mustache, Koltsov said in parting, "Turning your life around, not letting it lie still—that's a good thing in itself."

You might think that he envied Kolyusha. At least, Vogt's needs concerned him much less than the fortuitous opportunity he wanted to use to the advantage of his student.

14

"THE RUSSIANS' BULLDOG": DECODING NATURE

The institute was in Buch, a suburb of Berlin. They took up residence there, too. And the first thing Kolyusha did was start a laboratory discussion group like the Moscow Drozsoor. They gathered at Timofeyev's house. What was wrong with the laboratory? They had to wait for the cleaning women to leave. It was good at home. They drank tea and had talkfests. The Germans weren't used to domestic gatherings like this. They usually met in beer halls.

"We got them used to sitting around the samovar. They came willynilly. They were innocent about genetics, I had to teach them to think. And that's very hard. To force an adult who considers himself a scientist to think! It's easier to train a cat."

The sessions followed the tried-and-true Moscow model. In Moscow they met at Chetverikov's, or the Romashovs', or at the Timofeyevs' house—conversation flowed better at home than at the lab. But the Germans didn't invite people to their homes, so all the meetings took place in the cramped Timofeyev apartment.

Buch was twenty-five kilometers from downtown Berlin. Now Buch is part of Berlin, but then the city limits were about ten kilometers away. So they lived and worked in an out-of-the-way place. Buch had enormous hospital buildings with forty-five hundred beds, a tuberculosis clinic with twenty-five hundred beds, and many other clinics, for a total of fifteen thousand beds serving the staff and the institutes.

What luck to work without distractions. Work from morning till night—nothing could be sweeter.

First of all, he finished his work on phenogenetics, the action of genes and their interrelationships in the course of an individual's development, an excellent piece of work; then in 1927 produced two good studies with Lelka on population genetics.

He expanded the scope of his research, feeling his powers growing. He involved the physicists Max Delbrück and Karl Günther Zimmer. The latter's nickname was K.G. (Everyone had a nickname; Kolyusha was called Tim.) K.G. was phlegmatic, slow, calm, and methodical, and he managed to construct all the necessary equipment for various types of radiation; he created a method for studying radiation dosage which is used to this day. As Nikolai Viktorovich Luchnik recounts, Tim and K.G. were complementary: Tim was heated, impatient, and noisy, and K.G. was slow, careful, puffing his pipe over a cup of black coffee . . . You would think they would be incompatible. But they worked together for many years. Opposites don't repel. "K.G. was practical," Luchnik recounts. "Timofeyev had other friends for discussing wild ideas: the theoretical physicist Max Delbrück, Pasquale Jordan, John Bernal." (Here, referring to Bernal's political involvement in the fifties and sixties, the Bison always boomed, "The peace dove.")

Germany and the Soviet Union had very friendly relations in the twenties. After the Pact of Rapallo in 1922, Germany was the first country to establish diplomatic relations with the Soviet Union, setting up trade arrangements and then signing an agreement on friendship and neutrality. They created publishing houses and joint-stock companies. Conferences were held for Soviet and German physicists, electricians, and chemists. German-Russian magazines were published.

The Russian geneticist working in Germany quickly acquired authority. The Germans and the scientific milieu of the times must be given their due. They were not put off either by his nationality or by his youth.

Besides, one's self-image has an effect on what others think, and Kolyusha had a high opinion of himself.

In 1926 S. S. Chetverikov wrote a theoretical work that became a classic: "On Certain Moments in the Evolutionary Process from the Point of View of Genetics." He demonstrated that natural populations are affected by external factors and that therefore it was to be expected that populations would contain many mutations. They absorb them like sponges. Kolyusha experimentally confirmed this conclusion. Working with several hundred flies, he got a new generation and found twenty-five mutations. In 1927 he published "A Genetic Analysis of National Populations of the Drosophila." That same year Chetverikov came to Berlin for the Fifth International Genetics Congress and gave a paper on that theme. The greatest dream in science had come to pass: your discovery on the tip of your pen becomes visible and tangible through an experiment. The dream comes true!

The publication created a stir in many countries. Geneticists rushed to apply the discovery to other subjects. Kolyusha, however, unhurriedly continued the experiments. Why? The prospects were great. He could keep it up and keep it up . . .

"A scientist has to be lazy," the Bison explained to me. "The English have a wonderful rule for this: don't bother doing what the Germans will do anyway."

He took up reverse mutations: would the mutant flies return to normal? There was a hypothesis then that any mutation destroyed the gene. He didn't believe it. If it destroys the gene, then there couldn't be reverse mutations, and he did get some. You can put on a glove and smash a windowpane, but another blow like that won't put the glass back in. There are examples and comparisons that are more effective than scientific conclusions.

Simultaneously he determined how selection and external conditions affected various manifestations of a certain mutation. Year after year passed in the examination of thousands, tens of thousands of flies. Generation after generation, action, check, calculation. His work took seven years. In 1934 he published his results. At first he published a long article. Then, when the problem became clearer, he printed a short article which summed up his work and remained the last word for a long time. You can state the point of any work briefly, if, of course, you understand it yourself. Reducing something to its simplest form—that is real science.

He came to the conclusion that determined much for him: every starting point has to be simple.

Once he heard Niels Bohr say that if a man doesn't understand the problem, he writes a lot of formulas, but by the time he realizes what is really involved, he will have only one or two formulas left.

At the same time he worked on radiation genetics—powerful doses, harsh radiation, and so on. As a result, the famous *Green Notebook* was published in Göttingen, written in collaboration with Delbrück and Zimmer.

"Have you heard about the *Green Notebook?*" he asked me.

"I haven't," I confessed.

The less I knew, the more elaborately he explained things, without jumping around, beating elementary information into my empty head. Sometimes I provoked him simply for the pleasure of hearing him, but I really didn't know anything about the *Green Notebook*. He was astonished by my ignorance, as if I hadn't heard about the Decembrists' "Green Lamp" or the green revolution in agriculture . . .

I do not intend to describe his scientific achievements, that is not my business. I'm not writing about that, I am telling about one human life, which, it seems to me, deserves attention and thought.

He chided me for my grayness, he was ashamed of me for not knowing things every cultured person should know. I thought about how self-centered scientists were. They think that the thunderclap of the discovery of DNA, the chromosomes, the double helix resounds in every heart. Humanity exults—one more mystery of life uncovered! A universal holiday marked with twenty-one gun salutes, for nothing is more important than these events, everything else is just so-so.

Instead, the ungrateful citizen of the world erects monuments to Churchill, reads books about Marilyn Monroe, buys postcards of the Beatles, and demands the autograph of chess master Karpov. What kind of a world is it where high jumpers and generals are better known than the geniuses who are decoding Nature!

He decided to study evolution in sea gulls. He ran experiments on the vitality of certain mutations. Gradually qualitative studies were done on the starting mechanisms of evolution. He determined the minimum and maximum populations. The difference could be colossal. Sometimes in one year a population can multiply to gigantic numbers. For instance, with bloodsucking insects in the north, fluctuations overnight can reach tens of millions. The changes over a single season can be myriad, unimaginable. Or, for instance, so many gypsy moths can develop that the trees are all stripped bare. And then an unnoticed mutation can suddenly be given gigantic distribution, skipping stages that would require thousands of years. In developing Chetverikov's ideas, Kolyusha sought the mechanism of the waves of life. What was their point? What role did these life waves play in evolution? He studied these phenomena for many years. In 1938 he gave a sensational lecture, "Genetics and Evolution from the Point of View of a Zoologist," at the annual meeting of the Genetics Society; in 1940 he contributed to *New Systematics*, a book compiled by Julian Huxley devoted to genetics and evolution. All the major geneticists of the world contributed a chapter. The Bison wrote the third chapter, and Vavilov the last. Julian Huxley was the brother of the outstanding English writer Aldous Huxley. The Bison thought of it in just the reverse terms—Aldous was the brother of the famous biologists Julian and Andrew, grandsons of Thomas Huxley, "Darwin's bulldog," who propagandized and defended Darwin's theory.

By then his friendship with physicists had grown. He attended Bohr's colloquia in Copenhagen and began attracting physicists who were interested in problems of biology. They decided to separate from Bohr and create their own international discussion forum on biology.

But before that, in the late twenties and early thirties, he had an insight.

"Max Delbrück and I, and later Paul Dirac as well, saw that wherever any elementary creatures multiplied, they built identical creatures next to themselves—doubling molecules, replication . . . One of the main manifestations of life is not that the mass of living things grows but that the number of elementary creatures grows. An elementary creature builds one like itself and pushes it away from itself, giving rise to a new individual."

They got money for the colloquium from the Rockefeller Foundation. Fourteen people gathered, all stars of the first magnitude. The physicist Delbrück; the cytologist Casperson; the biologists Bauer, Stubbe, Efrussi, and Darlington; the physicists Heisenberg, Jordan, Dirac, Bernal, Lee, Auger, Perren, and Aston. They would meet at some elegant resort in the off-season, when the rooms were cheap.

At all these seminars, colloquia, and meetings, in all his talks he referred to the works of Koltsov, Chetverikov, Vernadsky, and other Russians. If Thomas Huxley had earned the nickname "Darwin's bulldog," then Kolyusha could have been called "the Russians' bulldog." Much of the information in the West on the achievements of Russian scientists in biology came through him. Their contributions turned out to be—unexpectedly for the West—significant and, most important, productive, leading to many new ideas.

The young scientists whom the Bison persuaded to join him did not resemble office recluses in the least. They could be compared to today's young physicists and cyberneticists—scuba divers, mountain climbers, disco dancers, ladies' men, connoisseurs of poetry and of Buddhism. There were not many of them then and few people knew them or how they spent their time. They knew how to live happily and merrily, without worrying a whit about their reputations.

They began drawing isolines at these meetings. Weiskopf and Gamov developed so-called isocals, graphs of feminine beauty, like isotherms. They drew them on a map of Europe. Every scientist had to rate the local beauties wherever he traveled. The goal was to determine the distribution of beauties throughout Europe. The data came from everywhere: Rosetti sent them in from Italy, Chadwick from England, Auger from France. Most of the observations were done in the street. They rated the women they saw on a five-point system. The observer strolled with friends, who helped him keep the tally and retain his objectivity. A "four" was given to women whom the observer singled out for his friends' attention; a "five" to those he *didn't* point out to his friends; a "three" to women who paid attention to *them*. When they had data on, say, a thousand women, they did a statistical analysis and drew the isocals. The greatest number of beautiful women lived in Dalmatia, Serbia, and in Bologna and Tuscany, Italy. There were no peaks of beauty in Central Europe. Rosetti had a large map with the isocals showing several years of energetic observations.

People started coming from other cities to the chats in Buch, they had to move the sessions to Saturdays. The department grew to as many as eighty people, an enormous number for the times. Cooperative work with physicists attracted people because of its fundamental newness.

Max Delbrück, a student of Bohr and Born and the grandson of one of the founders of organic chemistry, was young, confident, and arrogant.

"We treated him arrogantly too. That shaped him up fast enough!"

Delbrück had worked for Bohr in Copenhagen, along with Gamov, and in 1932 he went back to Berlin and became assistant to Otto Hahn and Lise Meitner at the Kaiser Wilhelm Institute. One of his main interests was the secret of the gene's nature. By then genetic analysis of Drosophilas had allowed the Bison to measure the gene, whose size turned out to be comparable with that of a molecule. Similar data had been gathered by the Vavilov Institute in Moscow.

The gene was a special form of molecule, and it was also clear that it was an element of life. They had finally gotten hold of something . . .

All that was in their joint article. It attracted no particular attention then; the soil wasn't ready for it; it had appeared a bit too soon. A discovery has to appear at the right time, otherwise it is forgotten. A small gap is necessary, just like shooting at a flying bird.

Later, however, Schrödinger referred to the article in his book *What Is Life from a Physicist's Point of View?* and then the Bison's discovery became a sensation.

Biology, genetics, radiation genetics moved forward in Europe and the United States, through laboratories in England, France, Sweden, Germany, Russia, and Italy, but the sector in Buch was noticeably ahead. Why? Did its superiority derive from that Russian? Yes, and also from the fact that he managed to gather together a good group, he did not act alone with lab assistants and helpers but with colleagues. He was not a lone hunter, he was the leader of a group, and his gift was joined with the gifts of other vibrant and unique scientists. He could inspire them as no one else could, set fires even in the most nonvolatile natures. The Drozsoor that began in Russia had been a discovery, and he, Kolyusha and now also Tim, inculcated it, held on to it, and loved that form of work–noisy, merry, companionable.

The Timofeyev's youngest son, Andrei, recalled, "None of our furniture ever matched: the oak wardrobe, painted black, was beside Father's small desk. We lived poorly, more poorly than any German burgher. I once dropped by the house of a gardener in Buch, who lived across the way, and I remember being astonished by the mirrors and armchairs. But we had a lot of guests on Saturdays and Sundays. We went mushroom hunting. Father had trained everyone to do that. A lot of people slept over Saturday nights. We set up wooden cots in all the rooms. Our windows faced the park. We lived on the first floor. On Sunday morning many people climbed out the windows, instead of using the door. That was the style then. The Russians came on their own; the Germans we invited. People would bring food and help Mother prepare it. Father and I made oxtail soup."

15

RUSSIAN FRIENDS;
A WHIRLPOOL OF
ENTHUSIASMS

Most of all, of course, I was interested in the Bison's Russian friends. Who were they? Berlin in the twenties and thirties was a Russian émigré center. Whom did they see? The Bison told me a few things, the rest came from Andrei's stories. The life of the Russian post-revolutionary emigration had interested me for many years. I had met these people abroad, and the meetings had left me with an impression of a special bitterness, comparable to nothing else, that permeated the lives of these people and also with the impression that the Russian emigration had contributed enormously to European culture and science. In our country we know little about this and we underestimate this contribution, as do people in the West. I could name hundreds of people in the emigration working in physics, chemistry, philosophy, literature, biology, painting, sculpture, people who created entire directions and schools, exhibiting great genius.

The Timofeyevs spent little time with the Russian émigré community; they were too absorbed in their work, and in turn they were regarded with suspicion by the émigrés.

The Bison did develop a friendship with Sergei Zharov. Zharov had graduated from the Synod Gymnasium during the war and he was evacuated with some Cossack units. He tried here and there, but he couldn't return. He did odd jobs and then in 1922 in Vienna he organized a male choir. He was an extraordinarily gifted musician and a brilliant organizer. He had thirty-six people in the choir. Thirty singers, four dancers, the manager, and himself.

75

No soloists. He and the other members received the same salary. That did away with envy, the plague of all artistic collectives. His reasoning was, if you have a good voice and can sing solo, whom should I pay for that, God himself? Your voice is a gift from God, a gift, free. Zharov kept iron discipline. If anyone showed up drunk, that was the end of him.

The Bison loved to talk about Zharov. And we loved to listen, because we knew nothing about that phenomenon, which was outstanding in the history of Russian art. The Bison had several records of the choir, and he would play them and sing along.

"They rehearsed their program for a year. In 1923 they began performing and have been doing so for forty-five years now. By the end of the twenties they could earn as much as they wanted, more than German professors. The excess went for scholarships for young Russians. They helped Russian children get an education, get on their feet. Zharov knew the old modes and styles and did his own arrangements. Their program consisted of three parts: Cossack songs, military songs, and choral transcriptions. He transcribed Rachmaninoff's preludes so well that Rachmaninoff thanked him. I don't like transcriptions, but these conquered me. When the Zharovs lived in Berlin—they had an apartment there—they had a colloquium every Saturday. Musicologists lectured, all the major musicians and conductors visiting Berlin came there. Writers and scientists, too, Russians, primarily. I was there when Metalnikov talked about the immortality of amoebas . . . For your information, Metalnikov moved to France before the Revolution to head a department at the Pasteur Institute. Gabrichevsky appeared at the Zharov colloquia, so did Evreinov, Mozshukhin, and, besides Rachmaninoff, another composer you might have heard of, Glazunov. I heard Grechaninov there too . . . Those choristers were highly cultured people. Stravinsky dropped by to see them, Robert Engel gave a lecture on Russian bell ringing and bell manufacture. Boris Zaitsev read his stories, as did Remizov, and there was a very interesting writer named Osorgin. And singers like Dzerzhinskaya and Petrov. They also had Ershov . . ."

He was interrupted by a philologist, a Ph.D., who was impatiently waiting for a chance to ask his question.

"What kind of writer was this Osorgin? A pamphleteer?"

"Osorgin was a novelist, an excellent writer. Haven't you read the novel *Sivtsev Vrazhek*?"

This doctor thinks that he knows literature and art, it's his field, and every time he discovers how little he really knows, he gets mad. He's hearing about Zharov for the first time, about Grechaninov, well, he'd heard about the "mighty bunch," but sitting across from him was a man who had strolled along Unter den Linden with Alexander Tikhonovich Grechaninov. The doctor loses every time. He can't come to terms with the Bison's superiority in various arts, he can't understand that it's not a question of knowledge per se but of life; it's as if he had come to a play in the second act and couldn't understand what was going on.

Kolyusha told the Zharov group about population genetics, about how he had helped Grabar restore frescoes. In 1919 he spent three weeks cleaning the angels trumpeting in St. Dmitri's Church in Vladivostok.

Then a catastrophe befell Zharov. The choral group was traveling in two buses on a tour in a mountainous region of America and the lead bus plunged off a cliff. Everyone in it died. Zharov's wife and half the chorus were in the bus. The chorus did not perform for a year . . . Then they recruited new singers. People came from all over the world for the auditions; getting into the Zharov choir was as hard as getting into La Scala. Vacancies came about only through death or departure, as with the British Royal Society.

When the Bison talked about Zharov he showed his delight and envied him the opportunity to sing in the choir. He would straighten his broad chest, throw back his shoulders, and an unusual dreamy, happy look would soften his features.

Another friend was Oleg Tsinger, son of the marvelous Russian physicist, author of *Beginning Physics*, a textbook used for many years in Russian and Soviet schools. The Bison introduced me to Oleg Tsinger, or rather to his letters. They were unusual letters with gouache drawings. Oleg Tsinger was an artist who specialized in animals. He drew them in zoos, in aquariums, in museums. Right in the middle of a letter you would see excellent watercolors of a zoo with Indian rhinos and people sitting on nearby chairs. A paradise. The letters were in Russian on heavy paper, good for paints, and written in India ink in a clear, almost printed handwriting.

Oleg Tsinger not only portrayed animals, he also painted landscapes and illustrated the works of Gogol (in oils!); he worked in a rather broad range. I began corresponding with him after the Bison's death and he told me many things about the Timofeyevs' life in Berlin.

They met in Berlin in 1927. They were introduced by the artist Vasili

Vatagin, who made a special trip to Berlin in order to work at the Berlin Zoological Gardens. It was easy in those days. Vatagin moved in with the Timofeyevs, even though they had a small apartment. The Timofeyevs left early in the morning for the institute, and little Mitya, known as Foma, stayed with a Vladimir Ivanovich Selinov, a kindly man who tried to make a living by filling cardboard tubes with tobacco to make Russian cigarettes. That didn't pay enough and the Timofeyevs helped him out by hiring him as cook and nanny for their boy.

The Timofeyevs couldn't live without helping somebody. Selinov didn't know how to cook, and all he could make was a sort of meatball, which he served night after night for months on end. Guests came and went, but the Timofeyevs were stuck with the meatballs. They finally fell ill from the monotonous diet. But at least Selinov knew Russian poetry well.

The Timofeyevs became good friends with Oleg and he was soon calling her Lelka and him Kolyusha.

Tsinger and Vatagin spent whole days at the zoo, drawing animals, and on Saturdays Kolyusha would pick them up and they'd go to the sideshows. For a small fee you could watch wrestling, boxing, and catch-as-catch-can. Three rounds. Then you had to pay again. People were transformed at the sideshows. Decent, educated people shouted, swore, pushed, spat, cheered on the athletes, and threw garbage into the arena. The "athletes" were tattooed giants who got more applause the worse they behaved. They turned their fights into a real show, especially in catch-as-catch-can, where everything was allowed. They rubbed their opponent's face in the mud, twisted his legs, jumped on his back, bit, tore out his hair, all the while shouting, howling, and swearing. The audience loved it.

"All this was new to me, and Kolyusha was especially new! I had never met anyone like him. He had a wild charm which I fell for immediately. He shouted louder than anyone. 'Turn around, Pifik, you idiot!' He would turn to us in dismay. 'He's a fool, an idiot, no brains, crooked legs, runny nose, and God hates him!' The expressions were new to me, too. He would get furious and take it all seriously. We would get home late for dinner and Lelka knew where we had been. Guests would come for dinner. I remember Rafael Lorenzo de No, the Spanish biologist. Kolyusha liked him, and therefore everything Spanish delighted him. He didn't like Germans in that period. We always had homemade vodka with dinner and, of course, Selinov's meatballs, and his cigarettes. Kolyusha was still young and his temper boiled easily.

When Kolyusha started pacing the room and talking about something, a new guest would be astonished. It didn't even matter what the topic was. I remember how I emulated Kolyusha. When he talked about himself you had the feeling he was a man who had lived more than one life. He had been a student, a Cossack, had been wounded and his horse had saved him. He had starved and eaten sparrows, which he killed with snowballs. He had fought off an attack of wild dogs in the Ukraine. Once he had jumped down from a tree and fell barefoot on a viper. All his stories were colorful, and I loved them. There was something Gogolian about them, with an admixture of Leskov. That was what evenings at the Timofeyevs' were like."

Apparently the evenings became famous. Kolyusha's temperament, manner of speech, shouting, and ebullient talent upset the rather proper German scientific milieu at the institute. That unworthy Russian was dragging everyone into a whirlpool with his enthusiasms. He was served up as an oddity, people were invited to meet and see him, and almost everyone got trapped. Once they met him, they wanted to see him again and again. They felt wonderfully unfettered and relaxed in his company, without concern for rank and age. Naturally, skittles became popular in Germany, at least in Buch. Kolyusha was the cheering section. "Three 'almosts' make a whole only in China!" Pretty soon respectable professors found that they were shouting things, too.

The patients of the Buch hospitals stood behind the fence of the hospital yard and watched adults who otherwise seemed normal throw sticks and shout, playing the game of *gorodki*. Their leader was a barefoot, hairy Russian with his shirttails hanging out who looked like a gang chieftain. His mane of hair shook and he shouted incredibly loudly.

Every pin in *gorodki* has a name—"grandma in the window," "deceased," "steam engine"—and knocking them down was accompanied with juicy commentaries that gave the game its fire.

In winter or bad weather they played tiddlywinks with the same passion. And in this silly game Kolyusha gave his all. He would sprawl on the table by the lamp, aiming, his lower lip trembling, his eyes shining. "Serves him right, the bastard!" His passion inspired others. There are people who create calm. He had the opposite talent—he made even phlegmatic types grow agitated, his presence shook up the most inert souls.

The new, larger apartment which the institute gave them had a dining room and a large study for Kolyusha. The guests were usually jammed in there. Kolyusha walked from corner to corner, lecturing, arguing, exhorting. The rug wore out in the corners, where he turned sharply.

He paced the same way many years later in Obninsk, and before that, in the Urals. From those apartments which I knew I could picture his house in Germany, though I couldn't tell you anything precise about the furnishings in Obninsk, I only remember the shelves with files of clippings. Everything else was worn and impersonal. The Timofeyev house was memorable for the people, for what happened there, for what was said. The furniture, paintings, wallpaper–all that receded and became invisible. That was the Timofeyev style–no interest in fashion. No one was interested in carpets, vases, dishes, couches. The apartment had everything necessary to live comfortably. It never occurred to anyone to shop for stylish furniture, to change it, to fill up their lives with candelabras, armchairs, standing lamps. The many guests did not notice the absence; it did not strike them as poverty. There was no wealth, no effort to be fashionable, no pseudo-artistic taste, nothing to distract a guest or take on a life of its own. A chair was nothing more than an object on which to sit; no one noticed whether it had leather or vinyl cushions. Certainly not Kolyusha. It was that way in Germany and in Russia, it was always like that. He did not change fundamentally.

Once I asked him, "What evolution did you undergo?"

"Evolution? I'm afraid I had no evolution. Once I looked for evolution in myself and did not find it. It's kind of indecent. How can I live so boringly, how can a man have no evolution? Nevertheless, there was no evolution in me after the age of eighteen. Then I thought, what can I do if I don't have any? All right, I don't. The hell with it, I'll live without evolution."

Another son was born, Andrei, whom Kolyusha called "an incredibly insignificant person," but he said it with unusual tenderness. In the meantime he berated Foma for failure at school. "Stupid fool, ignoramus, this isn't schoolwork, this is pathetic," he would mutter, pacing from corner to corner of his study.

"I spent so many evenings in that study," Oleg Tsinger recalls, "and so many different people were there! Old friends, barely known scientists, ladies, young men, important Germans, and, toward the end, Soviet military men. Kolyusha would sometimes fall into extreme chauvinism, extreme orthodoxy, proclaiming that the lousiest Russian muzhik was better than

Leonardo da Vinci and that double-damned Go-e-the (he always pronounced it in three syllables). Then he'd insist that the Germans were the best after the Russians, that you could count on a German, while a Russian would sleep through everything or spend it all on drink. Of the Russian artists, his favorites were Nesterov and Surikov. I preferred not to argue with him on the subject."

People, both students and friends, were afraid to argue with him: he literally blew them away. Nevertheless, he thirsted for real opponents and missed the company of informed, worthy foes.

In the Soviet Union, in the biological schools, when people met around the campfire at night just to talk and listen to his stories, sooner or later the question about Russians abroad would come up—how were they doing, who were they? The enormous first wave of émigré Russians—almost three million ended up abroad—had attracted and excited our interest; we felt a secret pity for them and an unconscious sense of being related to them. Most of these people did not leave because of a conscious decision of their own, they were pushed out by tragic, complex circumstances about which we knew little. Among the émigrés were brilliant names. Once they had formed the glory of Russian thought and art, but for the most part their talents were not lost in the West. Vague, fragmented rumors of their success occasionally reached us. But their names were crossed off, and clouds of suspicion covered everything Russian abroad.

The Bison talked about this reluctantly, but kindly. "Most of them were not involved in politics and had no desire to be. They were frightened away from politics for life. The very word 'politics' nauseated them. They tried to settle down and lead a quiet, inconspicuous life. Politicians were a tiny minority among the three million. Most were refugees and workers . . ."

Once he talked about something we knew little or nothing about. "In 1922 they said, and the lie was repeated frequently, that Lenin threw many intellectuals out of Russia. Actually, and this is very interesting, Lenin told a group of people, primarily in the humanities: If you reject the Revolution, you may leave. It is understandable that a mystic philosopher, an idealist would have nothing to do in a proletarian Marxist dictatorship. Many did leave, especially since there was hunger and ruin."

The Bison mentioned Pitirim Sorokin, Berdyaev, Frank, Shestov, Lossky, Stepun, literary historians, historians, journalists . . . A group of about two hundred. Most of them lived in Europe right up to World War II in

81

a most curious situation: they had Soviet passports and were formally considered Soviet citizens but did not have the right to enter the U.S.S.R. There were three centers where they lived: Berlin, Prague, and Paris. In Prague an important role was played by the so-called Russian Free University, where the Bison once lectured. It was created around the Kondakov seminars. An academician, historian, specialist in old Russian painting, icons, and frescoes, Kondakov was an old man, he died in 1925, but he managed to set up this seminar, which brought together the best Russian scholars abroad. And they formed the university.

The Bison recalled Russian writers he had met or had heard–Shmelyov, Zaitsev, Bunin, Teffi, Aldanov, and then names that meant nothing to me; then he listed scientists and scholars–Timoshenko, Zvorykhin, Bakhmetiev, Sikorsky, Chekrygin, Kostitsyn; and artists–Chekhonin, Larionov, Tsadkin, Sudeikin. He'd mention, for instance, Lev Botas, who was chief artist of the Berlin Opera, and then some choreographers, musicians, chemists, whom we did not know because of our ignorance and lack of information.

A few years ago I visited the Russian cemetery of St. Geneviève near Paris. It was a warm, sunny autumn day. The cemetery paths were neatly raked red sand. Little old men and women strolled down the paths, speaking softly. There weren't many people, but there were many familiar names. I found the graves of Ivan Bunin and his wife, Boris Zaitsev, the actor Ivan Mozshukhin, the writer A. Remizov, and, under a wooden cross, the artist Dmitri Stelletsky. Ivan Shmelyov's wife, Olga, is buried in the same grave with him. There was a white marble cross for the art historian Sergei Makovsky, of the family of artists. Over the grave of the chemist Alexei Chichibabin was a bust of black stone and fresh flowers in a pail. My favorite artist, M. Dobuzhinsky, was buried there, too. Above Evreinov's grave was a medallion with his picture, next to him the biologist K. Davydov and the artist K. Korovin . . . This was where I found the people the Bison had talked about. A funeral service was underway in the small cemetery church decorated with icons by Albert Benois. Rusty leaves swirled silently in the warm air. The grass was still full of life. Black ravens, yellow beaks down, minced among the bushes. This cemetery held the deceived and the deceivers, the refugees and the fugitives, those who dreamed of returning to their homeland and those who recalled it as they lay dying, people of different convictions and varying fame, but they all considered themselves Russians.

Chichibabin went abroad in 1930 and stayed. A bit earlier, another wonderful chemist, Ipatiev, was sent abroad on business and did not return. The term "nonreturner" appeared. Feodosi Dobrzhansky, one of the creators of the synthetic theory of evolution, went abroad and stayed. So did the famous theoretical physicist Georgi Gamov, who, by the way, proposed the first model of the genetic code. There were many such incidents, and they were treated calmly in those years. Now these nonreturners are returning, reappearing in the encyclopedias and dictionaries, they are being given their due, they are cited, they are written about . . .

Many White émigrés and nonreturners lived in Berlin and the Timofeyevs could not isolate themselves from them. With the years the Russians began streaming to their house, attracted to Kolyusha with his charisma and inner Russianness. Soon that attraction was to play its role and took a dramatic turn.

In the meantime, life in Buch went on. Oleg Tsinger saw the domestic part of that life and had only a vague idea of how his friend's personality boiled and seethed in the laboratory.

It is pointless trying to catch the Bison in inconsistencies. Cursing everything German, he was surrounded by German friends. Cursing the German nation, he defended German punctuality, decency, German philosophy, the German postal system, German engineers, German pencils, and many other German things. Of course, he continued to maintain that an individual German was good and wonderful, while a group of Germans was horrible and a large mass of them intolerable.

16

A LOST LAYER
OF THE RUSSIAN
INTELLIGENTSIA

The year 1933 arrived, Hitler took power, and conditions in Germany quickly took a horrible turn. However, the situation changed most radically for the Germans themselves. Probably the Timofeyevs did not notice anything much at first. Buch was on the sidelines, the Bison was not interested in politics, and, most important, none of the events had any direct bearing on him personally or on his work. He was Soviet citizen and felt independent and a nonparticipant.

"In the summer we took a vacation together in the Baltic, in Pomerania," Oleg Tsinger recalled. "We rented a big peasant house with a thatched roof. The Timofeyevs took one half of the house and my wife and child and I took the other. Kolyusha rose early. Tanned until he was almost black, wearing shorts, with a walking stick in his hand and a mystery under his arm, he headed off every day to sunbathe nude in the dunes. We did not accompany him. Sometimes Kolyusha made soup for everyone, putting beans, peas, carrots, a piece of meat, tomatoes, everything in the house, into a pot. He would wrap the pot in a blanket. In the evening he would unwrap it, pour the soup, all in silence, and then everyone would say with a deep sigh, 'Fantastic!'

"Sometimes we went off together and once we came across a dead dolphin on the beach. I wanted the skull. We had a camping knife, and Kolyusha crouched and said, 'Well, let's recall our anatomy,' and he very deftly separated the head from the body. We boiled it, and I got a marvelous dolphin skull."

THE BISON

The German intelligentsia was slow to appreciate the inhumanity of Fascism. The Timofeyevs were even slower. They were much more worried by the news from the Soviet Union. Things began going bad for biologists in 1929. Sergei Sergeyevich Chetverikov's laboratory was razed and he was exiled to Sverdlovsk. They heard that he was accused, in part, of creating the Drozsoor. Attacks on N. K. Koltsov increased. Most of the attackers were philosophers, but there were biologists, too, using an ideological basis for their criticism. Semashko was replaced and sent to the department of hygiene at Moscow State University. The physicists were also getting into trouble, especially the theoretical ones, who were accused of wasting time on things that could be of no help to the economy.

Soviet newspapers and magazines announced that famous professors had fallen under bourgeois influences, teaching young people the wrong things, devoid of practical use. Students denounced them. They heard that the nephew of Rimsky-Korsakov had declared that as of a certain date he no longer considered himself a relative. First the philosopher A. M. Deborin denounced people, then he in turn was denounced. Discussions ended with firings. Letters from their friends in Moscow referred to all this guardedly, in hints. Articles appeared in newspapers. The tone got harsher with every month. Arrests began. They exposed—what words appeared!—"mechanists" and "Morganists." They recalled Slepkov from Buch and arrested him in Moscow.

Journals arrived from Moscow reporting the discussions, the rantings of I. I. Prezent, T. D. Lysenko's chief ally. They printed letters of authoritative scientists who recanted . . . God only knew what was going on, and the pattern of viciousness grew.

At about that time Kolyusha began receiving invitations to return, either to Belaya Tserkov, to head the Institute of Sugar Beet Genetics, or to Pushkin, near Leningrad. He informed his teacher Koltsov of all these invitations and asked for his advice. Through friends—the Swede Kuhn, the plant physiologist Max Hartmann—Koltsov replied: Don't you know what's going on here? Stay there and work. Your business trip was for an unlimited duration. Why can't you stay put?

Another time Koltsov gave a more precise warning: When you arrive, you will definitely get into some scandalous affair, with your temperament, and you'll end up in the north. And all your friends will get into trouble, too.

There is a legend that when Koltsov, on his last trip abroad, met with

Timofeyev and gave him the same advice–be patient until passions die down back home, stay out of trouble–Kolyusha said he wanted to go home, he was homesick, and moreover, all his winter things were there and he couldn't afford to buy new ones in Germany. Koltsov took off his fur coat and handed it to him.

I never heard anything about this from the Bison, and I think it's one of those stories people made up about him. Various people told me this story in different versions: the coat was fox, the collar was beaver of course, an *ancien régime* coat, a skunk coat . . . The legend, really incredible, says a lot to the careful reader. "A good story has to be both real and credible," the Bison said, repeating Niels Bohr's words. "Do you have to follow the facts too closely?"

Officially he had the right to remain abroad. He was still on business with his family, they had Soviet passports. The institute was German-Soviet. He could wait it out.

In 1935 news came that A. I. Muralov (someone unknown to the Bison) had been appointed president of the Academy of Agricultural Sciences in the place of N. I. Vavilov. (Muralov was Deputy Commissar of Agriculture and two years later, in 1937, he was shot as an enemy of the people.)

There had been small attacks on Vavilov before that, but after his removal from the Academy of Agriculture the campaign against him picked up momentum.

Every time Nikolai Ivanovich Vavilov came to Germany, he stayed with the Timofeyevs. The route to America, Italy, and other European countries lay through Berlin. Both Nikolais–Vavilov and Timofeyev–were as healthy as bulls and were developing the ability not to need much sleep, and so they could stay up nights talking. They would sleep three or four hours toward morning and get up at eight fresh and ready to work.

"I was useful to Nikolai Ivanovich by correcting his German lectures. He would travel to Halle, a major center of applied botany and varietal study. He would speak there, writing his lectures in German, and I had to touch them up."

The Bison would get sidetracked here, recalled Handel's house in Halle, the cathedral, its patterned vaults, and the cast-iron figure of Christ falling from the cross . . .

The friendship with Vavilov, begun in Moscow, did not end with Kolyusha's departure; separation only strengthened it. From a distance Kolyusha was able to appreciate Vavilov on a European scale rather than just on a Russian one. He was a formidable figure. Four years after his expulsion from the Academy, at the Seventh Genetic Congress in Edinburgh, which Vavilov was not allowed to attend, even though he had been elected president of the congress, Professor Crew came out onstage and before donning the presidential robe said, "You have asked me to play a part that Vavilov would have played well. This robe does not fit me. I will look awkward in it. You must not forget that it was made for Vavilov, a much bigger man."

That robe fit no one in 1939 but Vavilov.

Timofeyev had a childlike love for him, as for an older brother. They had many things in common: Moscow, genetics, friends, a love of art. Vavilov had visited all of Europe's major museums, he knew the classics, and, most important for Timofeyev, had a personal relationship with many paintings and artists: some touched his soul, some his mind, some repelled him. Kolyusha was just as passionate. They grappled over and over, never ceding to the other. Despite his awe for Vavilov, Kolyusha shouted and bellowed, but no amount of noise was enough to overcome Vavilov. They were representatives of a lost layer of the Russian intelligentsia, those who knew how to develop their own, non-tour-guided attitude toward art. They were not taken through museums; they wandered through the halls, seeking out what interested them, spending hours looking this way and that, determining an artist's power, mastery, and secrets. They read art history books, checking themselves, and suffering seriously when they discovered their blind spots. Their judgments were often naïve and crude and their taste bad. Oleg Tsinger was outraged by the Bison's feelings about certain paintings. Another colleague of the Bison's, Grebenshchikov, told me with a frown how his chief used to go on about French opera. Wrong but interesting. And they read books, the classics—for themselves. They read, pondered, memorized, quoted. Lines, phrases, verses rang through their speech.

He couldn't understand how one might not know Nekrasov, Lermontov, how one could not remember Griboedov and Gogol, not to mention Pushkin.

They also knew Latin. And Latin gave them the roots of most European languages. Therefore, without bothering too much with grammar, they spoke French and English and had a smattering of Italian.

"Vavilov had great simplicity, he did not like acting the big shot," the

Bison went on. "He treated people without regard to their rank, he spoke the same way to a minister, an academician, and a student."

Suddenly he laughed, remembering an interesting occasion. When Hermann Muller, one of the founders of radiation genetics, came to the Soviet Union, Vavilov decided to take him and some other foreigners around the republics. They flew from Baku to Tiflis. Something held them up, a storm probably, they had to make a detour, and the pilot whispered to Vavilov, "I'm running low on fuel. We are going to perish, there's nowhere to land, all mountains. We won't make it back to Baku either." Vavilov told Muller, who pulled out his notebook, to make his last testament. Vavilov made himself comfortable and stretched out his legs. "Well, there's nothing we can do, might as well rest and have a nap!" And he fell asleep. Actually, there was just enough fuel to get to an airfield outside Tiflis. That's when the two friends came up with their formula: life is hard, but at least it's short!

"Not drowning in diversity—that was his rare gift. You specialists cannot imagine the enormous material on variability that Nikolai Ivanovich had mastered. And not drowning in that material, managing to find genetic laws in that diversity, was a special gift he had. I can judge because I spent some time on systemic variability and I can imagine the talent young Vavilov needed not to go under, the way most people do. To find regulatory patterns in millions of cultured plants—millions! . . ."

That is an excerpt from one of his lectures on Vavilov. He gave it at some biology school and luckily had it tape-recorded.

Luckily, because he prepared his lectures in his mind and never wrote notes. His lectures were lectures, not manuscripts for future articles, the way people lecture today. "Why let good things go to waste?" a young Ph.D. explained to me, obviously considering each and every lecture of his a good thing.

It's a pity that his lectures on Niels Bohr, Max Planck, Georgi Dmitrievich Karpechenko (the Leningrad geneticist), Julian Huxley, and N. K. Koltsov were not recorded. A pity! He knew as no one else how to create portraits. The cassette with the Vavilov lecture reached me after passing through many hands. I am pleased and amazed that so many people appreciated the uniqueness of what they were hearing and taped his lectures. His students, co-workers, and journalists often attended his lectures with tape recorders. Thanks to the efforts of S. I. Shnol a large collection of tapes is stored in Pushchino, some twenty-five kilometers of tape, dozens of reels. A collection of stories taped by people at Moscow State University has also been unearthed. Also dozens of cassettes. I hope that there are still other tapes somewhere. If all this were set down on paper, it would make a nice collected works. I didn't have the strength to listen to all the material, I felt I was losing my mind, drowning in that abundance of thoughts, recollections, and names. I had no idea Timofeyev's memory could hold so much. I had to limit myself. Of course, there are blank spots. But the more material I used, the more blank spots there were. A biography can never be complete.

The ones who didn't make recordings memorized, sometimes word for word, turning on a recorder in their brains.

People from several countries participated in gathering material for this book, everyone felt obligated to help me. They came from Moscow, from Obninsk. Igor Borisovich Panshin, for example, flew in from Norilsk. (He had already sent me fifty pages of letters and memoirs.) People put off their work, looked for witnesses and friends of the Bison, wrote down their recollections. Some wanted to restore justice, others felt beholden to the Bison, still others understood this was History. Meeting the Bison was the most vivid moment in the lives of many people.

The Bison was easy to remember. His uniqueness worked on memory, people realized his significance and at the same time they understood their part in History, they felt like eyewitnesses.

"Of course, Vavilov learned a lot from William Bateson, who was one of the most accomplished British geneticists. In the eighties Bateson published a marvelous book, *The Variability of Animals*, a huge work, with a wealth of material on morphological and physiological variability. You can't read it, you can use it. In general, you shouldn't read scientific works, you should use them. You should read Agatha Christie . . .

"Vavilov told me a few things about his conversations with Bateson. I knew Bateson, too. I was fortunate: I knew all the idols of physics, of mathematics, those who created a new concept of the picture of the world: Einstein, Planck, Heisenberg, Schrödinger, Born, Laue, Dirac, Jordan, Wiener, Bridges, Muller, Bernal . . ."

He could have gone on and on. He wasn't exaggerating when he said he had known them all. His sociability and his fame in the eighteen years he lived abroad brought him together with many scientists. He also traveled to all kinds of seminars, universities, congresses, visited laboratories and institutes, gave lectures. I don't understand, of course, how he also managed to do so much scientific work—not theoretical work, not thinking about this and that, not calculation, but heavy experimental work: sitting at a microscope, fussing with seeds and then radiation, fussing with flies, counting, astronomical figures when you have to handle thousands upon thousands of flies. He had to spend days on end in the lab. Where did he find time to meet all these people? Innumerable conversations, not just chitchat, but serious topics. I don't understand it. But I can visualize his appearance in any group: the focus of attention shifted to him immediately. He attracted interest. He stunned. He had to rid himself of accumulated thoughts and ideas and he disgorged them without worrying about his audience. This noisy shaggy zoologist, the "wet zoologist," as he introduced himself, had a streak of madness that allowed him to see things in the heart of nature others did not see. I suspect that he was not the one to instigate meetings with the idols—they sought him out. They all perceived the world slightly askew, not the way others saw it. He was one of them, and he could describe it juicily, passionately. What he was struggling with was incredibly important and decisive for all science. The famous German physicist Robert Rompe recalled what a sensation the Bison's lectures made in Germany in the thirties.

"I wasn't particularly interested in Bateson. He was old and weak by then. Now, the man who really was a teacher of Vavilov to some extent was our geographer and biologist Lev Semyonovich Berg. He was a bit older than Vavilov. From Berg and Vernadsky, and in part from Dokuchaev, Vavilov got an exquisite sense of the earth as a planet, as an environment, as a biosphere. The practical side of his work dealt with what we would be eating in the twenty-first century . . ."

The digressions in the Bison's lectures are splendid. Sometimes he went off in all directions, and those freewheeling excursions often led to unexpected ideas, paradoxical thoughts, or memories of events from his life and the life of famous men, historical events that were never written down.

For instance, in mentioning the celebrated British naturalist J. B. S. Haldane, he told a funny story of how Haldane started as a soldier in World War I and came out a major with a Victoria Cross. Haldane liked fighting so much that he asked to be sent on the attack. He found sitting in the trenches boring and he kept pestering the commanders to start an offensive "just to get out of the trenches and fight—without any tactical reason!" After the war some British military genius came up with the idea of hurling small iron arrows from aircraft. The arrows were supposed to penetrate steel helmets, and special metal helmets were made for protection against them. Haldane volunteered to test them. He wore one while they threw arrows at him. The noise inside was incredible. He almost went deaf . . .

Not a single biography of Haldane has this story, which he himself told to Timofeyev at some dinner party.

In the same Vavilov lecture he suddenly started talking about biochemistry: "In our country people call it biochemistry when lousy chemists do dirty and bad work on materials ill suited for chemistry. That's not biochemistry. Biochemistry is the physical and chemical analysis of active macromolecules. That's biochemistry and not those instances when some girl fresh out of college has learned how to find starch in potatoes, for pity's sake!"

His natural element was the argument. A lecture devoid of lively dialogue did not interest him much. As his scientific and personal stature grew, the opportunities for argument and discussion narrowed. People were afraid to take him on.

"In every era of cultural upsurge there are great men whose range is clearly above the average. These flights of culture and the abundance of such men seem accidental to us. Russian science is part of the great European complex, but at the same time it is an autonomous phenomenon inside that complex. If you were to build a system of cultural human types, the Russian type would be subsumed under the general European type. The stormy interaction of the Russian cultural type with the European cultural type began in the late eighteenth century. It did not flow smoothly, a fact which is evident in the Russian language, which was flooded with so many foreign words that Russians could not understand each other, speaking in their own language. Perhaps that explains the tradition of the Russian intelligentsia switching to French . . . Then Russian culture went through its own renaissance, which affected science. Centers of Russian and European culture blended. Russian physicists took an active part in reshaping the physical picture of the world, from the old classic picture of absolute determinism to the modern, much freer, more interesting picture, rich with theoretical and practical possibilities . . . Russian culture created an explosion of great Russian scientists in the late nineteenth and early twentieth centuries. Among them were Nikolai Ivanovich Vavilov's teachers: the founder of modern soil study, Dokuchaev; the founder of all agrochemistry, not just Russian, Pryanishnikov; and finally, Vavilov's immediate teacher and friend, before whom he bowed and before whom I bow, one of the great scientists of our age, Vladimir Ivanovich Vernadsky . . . Unfortunately, Vavilov did not do everything that he could have done, he did not live long enough. A mathematician can achieve a great deal in a short period, but semi-descriptive, semi-experimental works need time. In that sense, Vavilov was not given enough time . . ."

There were many extraordinary people around him, marvelous biologists, physicists, chemists, mathematicians. He had a weakness for talent, for talent and for beauty. Those qualities always astonished him, they represented the triumph of nature, something divine, inexplicable. The term "divine spark" made him think. A particle of a miracle. Something of higher matter, something mysterious and beautiful that entered into an ordinary human organism. Not subject to normal reason; alien, not achievable, not creatable by any effort of education. A splash from on high, an explosion, a vision that lets us see something different . . .

A weakness for talent, but not worship of it. He worshipped only one man, whom fate brought to Berlin for two extended periods. That was Vladimir Ivanovich Vernadsky. Anything to do with Vernadsky was holy for him. I never thought him capable of such respectful, protective feelings. He didn't even talk about him at first. He began with actions, he couldn't get to the point, as if circling a cliff. He'd talk about Vernadskology—that's what he called the teaching he was developing in his late years—or about Vernadsky's son. When they were in the United States he talked Lelka into making a special trip to Yale University to meet Vernadsky's son, who was a professor of history there.

They addressed him the way his father had, as Gulya. He had told the Bison a lot about Gulya when he was in Berlin. Gulya was dean of the philosophy department, taught Russian history, and had written a three-volume history of Russia, which the Bison praised vigorously, insisting that the father had nothing to do with it, he liked the work because it examined the development of the Russian state from the ninth century as the inheritance of steppe empires, including the Scythians . . . And also because the work had been published by Eurasian specialists whom the Bison knew, Trubetskoi, Savitsky, Suvchinsky, and about whom I, of course, hadn't the foggiest idea.

"How can that be?" the Bison reproached me. "And you're a writer. The Eurasian publishing house brought out many interesting books. The lives of the Russian saints, the history of iconography . . ."

He had even published an obituary of Trubetskoi in some German magazine. He knew about Sergei Trubetskoi as well, the rector of Moscow University, who was elected in 1905 and died soon after, and about Evgeni Trubetskoi, an interesting philosopher, whom the Bison had met back in Moscow. That Trubetskoi was a follower of Vladimir Solovyov and a friend of his. His nephew, Nikolai Trubetskoi, one of the creators of Russian phonology, left Russia with Lenin's permission. And this was followed by a new story about how the intellectuals who felt that they could not be of any use to the Soviet regime left the country. They were given six months to find a country that would take them. They were given Soviet exit passports, lived with them a long time, and then received so-called Nansen passports.

These were all celebrated people and well-known stories, but we had never heard them, and no one ever interrupted the Bison when he lectured. So it was a long time before we returned to Vernadsky.

According to the Bison, Vladimir Ivanovich Vernadsky was an exceptional phenomenon, practically an ideal hero. There are good people, there are very good ones, there are a limited number of remarkable people, and, even rarer, very remarkable ones. And then, among the very remarkable ones comes the completely remarkable man. Vernadsky was the completely remarkable man. A very foggy classification, but we must make allowance for the fact that the Bison met more remarkable and very remarkable people than any of us. He had the means for comparison.

The Bison could not understand why there was no monument to Vernadsky in either Moscow or Leningrad. Vernadsky should be studied in school, there should be a Vernadsky Museum, there should be a Vernadsky Prize.

He never did define accurately what he idolized about Vernadsky:

". . . Universal scope of thought, a cosmic man . . ."

". . . Interested in everything: art, history, geochemistry, mineralogy . . ."

". . . There was never any noise or scandal around him, no one got excited, he did not get involved in politics after the Revolution. His liberal-democratic nature united many decent men. There were no scoundrels around him. Of course, there weren't as many scoundrels in science then as there are now . . ."

". . . In Berlin, Fersman, Koltsov, Lunacharsky, Kostrychev, Platonov —an extraordinary Russian historian—as well as the most important medical men gave lectures. The Germans loved Vernadsky most of all. He lifted them up, made them think about the main problems of life on earth and of man . . ."

". . . He was invited to lecture in France. He came back in several years, when he felt like it, in 1926. He came back without any scandals, any penance, a free man."

". . . Abroad he did whatever he wanted: he lectured on whatever he wanted—for instance, on geochemistry at the Sorbonne."

". . . In Berlin he lectured in good German. His French was flawless, he didn't know English, though he spoke Russian well. That wasn't unusual in those days. Now, finding someone in our great homeland who speaks Russian well is hard to do. His Russian was delicious."

What did they talk about? The Bison was planning major experimental work. He decided to utilize marked atoms to determine the coefficients for accumulation of radioisotopes in plants: where they accumulate, how they are distributed, their fate in the system of plant and soil. The Bison called this work "Vernadskology." They discussed problems of the biosphere, Vernadsky's views of the role of living organisms on our planet. They had a few taboos. For instance, they forbade serious discussion of the origin of life on earth. The Bison retained that taboo till the end of his days. I once heard him in the seventies answer a persistent lady who wanted to know how life originated. He pulled in his neck, huffed and puffed, and then, blinking stupidly, spread his hands in dismay: "I was very little then, I don't remember." Then he added consolingly, "Ask Oparin, he knows for sure."

What Vernadsky liked best was Arrhenius's theory of eternal life. He painted a picture for the Bison of a universe filled with embryos of microorganisms that find a suitable environment on some planet and colonize it, beginning evolution there. That was the concept of Svante Arrhenius, the famous Swedish physicist and chemist. Life appeared from the universe. Life in the universe is eternal in the sense that the universe is eternal. Life is a part of the good of the world. According to many philosophical and religious viewpoints, absolute good is the whole universe. There is no absolute evil, only the absolutized evil of some fallen creature, defined differently in various religious systems.

The Bison always regretted not meeting Arrhenius, whom he admired greatly.

He and Vernadsky talked about space and time, about the relativity of time. That was just when Bohr and Dirac began their arguments over the possibility of quantum space and time. Mass was quantum and energy was quantum, but space and time seemed to still be uninterrupted and subject to classic mechanics, not quantum mechanics.

The Bison liked to talk on this topic, from the general philosophical, ontological point of view, not the physics and mathematical one. He felt that there were quanta of time and of space.

Some thirty-five years later—and what years!—he could reproduce their dialogues almost verbatim. The point was that chemical and biological nothingness was known. He explained: when we die, we cease to exist as living creatures. That is biological nothingness. Chemical nothingness is the Torricelli emptiness, you can get space that doesn't have a single molecule left in it.

The effort to comprehend reflected on my face annoyed him.

"It is hard to visualize," he would console me. "It's pure fantasy for now."

They both heartily disliked scientific fantasy in literature, science fiction. Mysteries, though, were something else. Without mystery novels their mental life would have dried up. They themselves fantasized, and they considered their fantasies to be Scientific, Fruitful, and Legal, the Unknown from the point of view of the known picture of the world. Chatting about things like that was very cozy.

The noosphere in the nuclear era demands a restructuring of the human consciousness. The "I" is reduced and the "we" is enlarged. We must think about "us," not "us" and "them," but all of us. The entire noosphere is "us."

Hamlet's "to be or not to be" seemed personal. Now the phrase relates to us all. Nuclear and biological threats unite mankind in a common danger, a common dependence . . .

I would have liked to eavesdrop on their conversations, watch them stroll down the lanes of the park in Buch. There is always something exciting in the meetings of the great: Beethoven and Goethe, Tolstoy and Gorky, Einstein and Bohr. Their attraction, their repulsion. Usually it is repulsion.

Ordinary mortals cannot understand that unwillingness to communicate, even to meet. I remember how upset I was when I learned that Leo Tolstoy and Fedor Dostoyevsky were once in the audience at a lecture, saw each other, and did not become acquainted.

Sometimes I look at an old photograph apparently taken in Pasadena, California. Three people are in it–Thomas Hunt Morgan in the center, Vavilov and the Bison on either side. They are striding along, the sun is hot, they are oblivious, engrossed in conversation, they are agitated, practically shouting and laughing at the same time, friendship and love of life fill them to the brim. Morgan is much older than the other two, but you don't see that in this picture, all three are so erect and strong. If only you could hear their voices!

The deep friendship of the Bison and Vernadsky was based on the fact that the Bison, in developing Vernadsky's views for his own work, accepted them publicly as law and wrote about his gratitude in print, calling his movement "Vernadskology."

His experiments were conducted under the simplest conditions: the mutual exchange of marked atoms between plants and soil was done in slat boxes and rain barrels. The barrels were filled with boxes of earth, a mixture of radioisotopes was poured in from one end, and the components could be measured as they came out the other end, thereby determining the migration of individual isotopes. Only now can we see how farseeing the Bison was: this work is the foundation for protection against radioactivity.

There are branches of chemistry and physics that require perfected and complicated equipment. But the Bison felt that our laboratories–and labs the world over–were too concerned with getting equipment for themselves just for the sake of having it. Many young scientists are certain that the more expensive the equipment they use, the more valuable their work. Some sincerely think so, others figure that the more they spend on the lab, the more their bosses will appreciate their work.

"If you use work as a measure, then the more complex and expensive the equipment is, the stupider the science being done on it." The Bison narrowed his eyes and smiled conspiratorially. "The Stop button is the wisest technological invention of all. That's the first thing I look for in any piece of equipment. The apparatus should be of optimal, not maximal, accuracy."

Contact with Vernadsky broke off in the second half of the thirties. His work—"Vernadskology" and "Vernadskology with a Sukachev tendency"—continued and expanded, but he could not discuss it with Vernadsky anymore.

None of them had any idea where the work would lead or what purpose it would serve some ten years later. Just as the physicists from Bohr's institute did not know that their discussions, calculations, and estimates would give birth several years later to the atom bomb, they did not suspect that the work of the Bison and his colleagues would help devise measures of biological defense against radiation from a nuclear explosion. Both groups were in a happy period of ignorance, when the science they were working on seemed pure and free of political authorities and industrialists alike. The sacred love of knowledge alone motivated the physicists of that golden age.

17

KETTI TEIK
MEETS A
MAHARAJA

Humor was their safety valve, salvation from the life they entered once they left the walls of the institute. Fascism was becoming the norm. Portraits of the Führer, marching Nazi units, inhuman slogans, the swastika, warlike threats, exhortations and racist speeches—that was the fetid, toxic air of Berlin they had to breathe. Germany was changing, it was impossible not to notice it. Even though they consoled themselves with the fact that Buch was not changing much, racism reared its ugly brown head everywhere. The Jewish workers at the institute were fired one after another. In school Foma had to write compositions such as "A German Boy Does Not Cry," "A German Boy Does Not Know Fear," "What Joy Being Born German." Chauvinism was everywhere.

By 1936, when the Olympic Games opened in Berlin, the Nazis had toned down their propaganda and tried to appear more democratic. They banned anti-Jewish rallies, discrimination, racist statements. Many foreigners, colored, black, came to Berlin and they were treated with marked politeness.

Max Delbrück had a cousin, a young film actress named Ketti Teik. Not very talented, Teik decided to use the Nazis to promote her career. Anti-Semitism was the easiest way. You didn't need knowledge or courage. It was so easy to blame Jews and international Jewry for everything. Demand their expulsion, demand their destruction. Consider them a race that defiled German blood . . . You had to say it louder than the others. Shout it. She tried hard and succeeded.

Delbrück decided to teach her a lesson, and Kolyusha worked out the scenario. They told Ketti that the maharajah of Sukugunia was coming for the Olympic Games. Sukugunia was supposed to be part of the Dutch East Indies, but it was a free state with a population of twelve million. The maharajah spoke only Sukugunian and the little Dutch that he was obliged to know. Why did they invent Dutch Sukugunia? Only because Delbrück had a friend at the Netherlands embassy who had a car with diplomatic plates. Ketti, who had played bit parts in two films, was told that the maharajah was a big admirer of hers. He had seen those movies and he had liked her so much he had purchased the films. Now he would like to bestow on her the Order of Sukugunia. Kolyusha had her psychology figured out: the vanity of a minor actress made her believe anything, as long as it was flattering.

Ketti lived rather well in a good lodging house on the Kurfürstendamm. They told her to be prepared for the maharajah's visit in about a week; she would need the proper clothes and she would have to learn the court curtsy. He would speak his own language and someone from the embassy would translate. She should have good coffee, liqueurs, and cake ready. Only a few people would be present at the ceremony: the maharajah's slave, a secretary from the embassy, and another Dutchman (to be played by Oleg Tsinger). Kolyusha chose the role of a Russian specialist on Sukugunia. Max Delbrück was the slave. The ceremony would go as follows: When the maharajah appeared, Ketti had to curtsy, the maharajah would extend his hand, and she would kiss it reverently, then he would sit down, have coffee, and tell her how much he liked her. Everything would be repeated when he left.

The maharajah was to be played by a theoretical physicist, a Jew. That was the point. He was three-quarters Jewish and one-fourth German. People like that could still keep their jobs but could not work for the state. Ketti was very nervous; she ordered a beautiful gown and prepared a lavish table. She got real Bénédictine and even bought new furniture. She spent quite a bit. Oleg Tsinger made up the maharajah, who played his part beautifully. They dressed him in flashy clothes: oxblood slippers, orange tie, huge cuff links, a gold watch chain. The slave wore white robes. A friend of Lelka's helped with the costumes. They ornamented the slave's robes so that he looked better than a real Sukugunian, had there been such a thing.

They arrived in the Dutch diplomatic car and a private car. The maharajah came out majestically and offered his hand. He was a big curly-haired man, his face bronzed with makeup. Ketti curtsied and kissed his hand. The slave stood in the corner with a package. The group sat down to eat and drink. The maharajah gabbed in Sukugunian, the Dutchman translated. When they had finished, the maharajah clapped his hands and the slave crawled over from his corner, handed over the package, and crawled back. The maharajah unrolled the scroll, a certificate written in gold with a large seal. Ketti melted with delight and kissed his hand several more times. She saw him out to the car.

They drove off. Then they realized that they were still full of fun. It seemed a waste not to use the makeup and costumes some more. They drove down the Kurfürstendamm and pulled up at an expensive café. A waiter hopped over to them and they ordered all the expensive items on the menu. They ate, gabbled in Sukugunian, and asked for the bill. The owner said, "No, no, it's an honor for us to have such important foreigners visit us . . ." They went on, then stopped at the Automat. That was the latest thing then. A long corridor filled with automatic dispensers of sandwiches, beer, and wine. The maharajah was impressed by European technology, got excited, demanded tokens. The owner appeared with a fistful of tokens. The maharajah stuffed them into every slot, and the food and drink flowed. The maharajah laughed and slapped his thighs while the others bowed and congratulated him. The crowd was delighted.

A big department store was nearby. An announcement by the door said the store had translators in all languages. They asked for a Sukugunian interpreter. They didn't have one and the maharajah grew very upset. The manager explained that they would correct the error and find an interpreter through the Dutch embassy. The embassy official calmed the manager down. "Don't worry, the maharajah is just showing off. I can translate for him. He's interested in music records." They went up to the top floor. Along the way they lost the slave. He spoke nothing but Sukugunian. How would he find his master? But he did. The crowd and the salespeople helped him. The retinue picked out records and the ones the maharajah liked they set aside. They got a whole pile, which the manager then presented to the maharajah. When they counted them later, they had forty records. This was the maharajah's last stop.

Ketti adored her certificate and showed it off to her colleagues. She began demanding better roles. Two weeks later Max Delbrück and Kolyusha read her the text. It was written in incredibly stylized Gothic lettering, but once you knew that you could see it was copied from the Minimax fire extinguisher advertisements so ubiquitous then, which proclaimed: "Fire won't spread if you have a Minimax extinguisher at home." People wrote the same response on the ads all over Berlin: "A Minimax isn't worth shit if you're not home to use it." (It rhymed in German.) And that's what the Sukugunian certificate said. Soon everyone at the film studio knew about it. They learned that Ketti had kissed a Jew's hand. After that, her anti-Semitism made people laugh.

After the Olympics, after 1937, such jokes became impossible. Yellow-painted benches—for Jews—stood on the boulevards. A decree on compulsory military service was issued. With every trip to Berlin the Bison noticed changes. They were hard to miss. The Fascists took over, poking their noses into people's private affairs, interfering with the age-old life of the city. The Games were over, but the granite sculptures of discus throwers, wrestlers, and horsemen were everywhere. Gigantic figures embodying the triumph of the Nordic race. Conquerors and Victors. Harsh, militant faces. Proud and beautiful, for the Germans were superior to all other races. The sculptors observed the exact proportions of skull, neck, lips, and ears for Aryans. The women were perfect Aryan breeding machines for pure German men. Buildings were decorated with allegorical figures of steelworkers and peasants, soldiers and miners, groups titled *War and Brotherhood, Warrior's Vow, Call to Struggle*. Determined athletes brandished swords and called their brothers to battle against the enemy. Descendants of the Teutonic Knights, the future masters of the universe . . .

Explosions boomed near the Brandenburg Gate, raising clouds of brick dust, as the old houses of Berlin, so dear to the Bison, were torn down. They talked of amazing palaces that Speer would build in accordance with the Führer's wishes, squares and arches, but no one knew for certain, it was all top secret.

The Bison liked the old Berlin neighborhoods. The city had almost no face, but the stone byways with small beer halls, cafés, and bakeries were charming. The morning markets in the squares, the flower stalls, the fairs and festivals. All this was disappearing, cringing in fear. A new, Fascist Berlin was rising: heavy, concrete, rectilinear buildings like gigantic, sturdy barracks. Gloomy dark gray buildings created not to please the eye but to terrorize people and to demonstrate power.

18

AN ACKNOWLEDGED
LEADER; A ''NO''
TO STALIN

Life in Buch, as in all scientific towns of that type, moved quietly and persistently, preserving its agendas and customs. The pattern of lab experiments did not change because the Nazis were in power. At least not for the Bison. No one bothered him or his colleagues, the Vogt Institute was still considered German-Soviet, and the Tsarapkins and Timofeyevs were still Soviet citizens. The research was going very well, the Bison's works were being published, his fame was growing, especially after the publication of the *Green Notebook*, written with Zimmer and Delbrück. This was a pioneering work that laid the groundwork for radiation genetics. It made clear that genetic information was concentrated not in the whole cell but in its nucleus, in the small part that could be affected by powerful doses of radiation.

Perhaps I should say something here about his main published works, which completed the cycle of research up to 1935 (with Zimmer and Delbrück), and then the works of 1936. They laid the groundwork for modern molecular biology. Their significance can be imagined if you compare them with what Rutherford did for atomic physics at the beginning of the century. The Bison's works were fully appreciated only after the publication of Schrödinger's *What Is Life from a Physicist's Point of View?*

Genetics as a classic science matured in the thirties. All its basic laws were discovered. Biologists knew how the parents' genes combined in the offspring's chromosomes. They compiled complicated chromosomal maps of fruit flies and also of one of the most important grains, corn. These maps plotted with scrupulous accuracy the position along the chromosome of hundreds of genes that carried hereditary characters. They discovered that the rate of change in the genes—mutation—was very low in ordinary circumstances and could be increased a thousandfold by the use of X rays. But no one knew what the gene was. Some biologists thought that it was one of the great secrets of nature that would never be solved, like the question: why does the universe exist? Bohr himself thought that genes, as life's smallest elements, were so complex and "delicate" that any attempts to determine their nature could destroy the object, and we would learn nothing.

In those years the Bison had to field many questions on the nature of the gene. The physicists were particularly persistent. But what could he reply, if no one even knew the size of genes? What if the gene did not have a size but was just a complex system of biochemical reactions? And then the gene would be a process, not a body. Nonetheless, the strictly determined distribution of genes in the chromosome, their transmission from parent to offspring, their ability to mutate, all suggested that the gene was a body and therefore had to have a size. The Bison had an idea: what if they used the gene's ability to mutate under radiation to determine its size?

Koltsov had said: molecule from molecule. The Bison said: covariant reduplication. Not only does the molecule reproduce itself, but it also reproduces the random changes (variants) that occur between acts of self-reproduction. This is the beginning of molecular genetics. The Bison had come upon the source that creates the fairy-tale variety of life on earth.

The changes were created by ionized radiation. Going over their data, the authors calculated the probable size of their target. They decided that the cell had to have a separate particle which, when hit, caused mutation. Even putting the question this way is astonishing. The Bison had the highest art of the experimenter—he knew how to ask Nature questions which required a yes or no answer.

Easy to say, but hard to do. The frequency of mutation of all the genes put together is still low, and here he wanted to measure a tiny part, for just one gene. Bent over a microscope, staring at hundreds of thousands of flies! But the Bison and the physicist Zimmer reported on their results: on average a chromosome contains no fewer than ten thousand and no more than a hundred thousand genes. That meant that a gene was not a "spot" on a chromosome, but a very large formation in the molecule world, built out of tens of thousands of atoms. That was the first dependable estimate of the gene's size.

One can argue whether this work or his research on the genetic basis of evolution was his main achievement. But this is certain: it was the estimate of the size of genes that served as a bridge between classic genetics and molecular genetics, which began in 1953, when Watson and Crick discovered the double helix of DNA. Then it became clear that genes were extensive sections of DNA. The size of genes was determined first by the Bison, who figured out genes the way Rutherford had figured out the atom's nucleus.

From that time on, he was an acknowledged leader in biology. He was in the full bloom of his powers and energy. His temperament, curiosity, and strength kept him from settling down, resting on his laurels; he gave the lands he discovered to others to plow while he hurried on. He was not a colonizer, he was a discoverer. He moved on to evolution, to a completely different continent, studying the systematics of gulls, experimenting with the viability of individual mutations. What was the necessary minimal and maximal population for mutations to take place?

Engrossed in his work, he paid little attention to German political life. He was much more concerned with what was going on in his homeland. More and more scathing articles appeared on famous biologists, denouncing them as reactionaries. It was hard to tell what was under discussion, something philosophical, not concrete. Some biologists were considered "idealists," others "anti-Darwinists," and discussions were ended by "administrative means." Filipchenko was called a bourgeois scientist and he was forced out of Leningrad University. Even after his death I. I. Prezent, Lysenko's disciple, continued slandering him: "Prof. Filipchenko, brought up by bourgeois standards . . ." They exiled Levitsky, then Maximov, Popov, Kuleshov; something was happening to Karpechenko, but he couldn't find out what. Professor Rainov was arrested.

He couldn't believe it, these were major scientists, people of perfect honesty and integrity, how could they turn out to be saboteurs or scoundrels or enemies of the people? These labels did not fit them. Why was the cream of Soviet science being destroyed? Who needed that? What for? The daughter of Professor B., who was accused of idealism, renounced him. Such renunciations of parents were happening more and more frequently. Finally came the news that Koltsov himself had been forced to leave the university.

Trofim Lysenko, who was not known to the Bison or to scientists abroad, and his ideologist and scribe, Prezent, were gathering strength. The Bison remembered the latter. Back in Moscow, Prezent had asked to join their seminar, the Drozsoor; the quick-witted young man offered his services as theoretician; he had no intention of doing independent study. They told him that they knew how to theorize themselves. And now this Prezent was Lysenko's theoretician, busily exposing "mechanists," "Mendelists," and "Morganists." A scientist with no original work to his credit, only exposures. With a list of victims instead of a bibliography.

The terminology Lysenko and Prezent employed seemed fiendish to the Bison: both Mendel and Morgan were classics of biology, their works were used by biologists the way electricians used Ohm's law, why would Mendelist and Morganist be dirty names now? And even worse, why weren't these people allowed to rebut the attacks? Lysenko and Prezent had started attacking Vavilov himself. A Swedish scientist returning from the Soviet Union passed a letter from Koltsov to the Bison. After some unconsoling news, Nikolai Konstantinovich repeated his advice: don't hurry home, wait it out. In today's situation, and with Kolyusha's temper, he would be in instant trouble. And his foreign ties were inappropriate right now. He had to be patient, wait for things to become normal again. It couldn't possibly go on this way for long.

The letter was in response to Kolyusha's question. Where could he return to, Moscow University or Koltsov's institute? He was drawn home, to Moscow. While Vavilov, Vernadsky, Koltsov, and others visited from Moscow, while there was free communication between Moscow and Buch, he had not been homesick. But as these trips were cut back and ties were severed, he began suffering. He was oppressed by the lack of contact with Soviet science.

His "target theory" had been picked up by institutes in England, the United States, and Italy, he was the toast of the lecture circuit. Genetics is the same everywhere. Wherever he lectured, he was accustomed to feeling like a representative of Soviet science, of Russian science, he was promoting its fame and the work of his teachers and comrades. But now, things were different. Scientists were no longer in charge of Soviet science, it was in the hands of ignoramuses who hated genetics. They denied its existence and tried to root it out. They were persecuting the people he quoted and of whom he was proud.

In 1937, Hermann Muller, the Bison's friend and famous American geneticist, subsequently a Nobel laureate, returned from the U.S.S.R. He had made his name ten years earlier by proving that X rays could cause mutations. In 1933, Muller went to the Soviet Union to work. He wanted to help build socialism, to be part of the new world. He wanted to be close to Vavilov. The scientific climate had changed sharply, however, and Lysenkoism had denied him the opportunity to do any serious work. Month after month he tried to compromise, but nothing helped. He came to Berlin in a depressed state and vented upon the Bison all his accumulated anger. There were tears in his eyes, and the Bison didn't know how to console him.

The Bison learned that his brother, who had worked in Leningrad with S. N. Kirov,* had been shot, as had been Slepkov, who had been recalled from Buch.

A month after Muller's arrival, the Bison was called to the Soviet embassy in Berlin. A young man with chubby cheeks, a curly mop of hair, and a sweet regional accent suggested that the Bison go home. Immediately. Why immediately, he couldn't explain, just go. He was arrogant and condescending and he kept tapping his pencil and demanding to know why the Bison was in Berlin in the first place, what was he doing, why was he hanging around with émigrés? What flies, what mutation? Was that something like that science we were combating back home? Now he understood why the Bison's works were so readily printed by British and other bourgeois journals. Hearing the name Semashko, he dared to raise his voice at the Bison, who was getting too big for his britches–picking up lousy liberalism in the West!–and then used a strong swear word. The Bison wasn't used to language like that, but he hadn't forgotten it either. He responded with much stronger words and stormed out, leaving the fellow with his jaw hanging and giving the door a satisfying slam. He had never learned to bite his tongue, much less to watch what he said. He knew it caused trouble, but it didn't stop him.

Lelka sighed when he told her what had happened and then announced that perhaps it was for the best. It would be crazy to go back now, suicide, they had the children to consider. The Tsarapkins also decided not to go back. The advice of all their friends boiled down to wait, at least a year, when this campaign of repressions and excesses had to end. The Bison calmed down, he was busy with his work. He couldn't abandon it halfway, without getting his results. He couldn't pull himself away. The way a surgeon

---

* First Secretary of the Leningrad Party organization, assassinated in 1934 on Stalin's orders.

couldn't leave an operation, or a mother leave an infant. He didn't think about the consequences, he couldn't care less, he just had to finish his experiment.

The widow of Alexander Leonidovich Chizhevsky, the biophysicist famed for his study of the influence of the sun's rays on life on earth, told me how Chizhevsky asked for permission to set up a lab in the camp where he was a prisoner. One day in 1955, a truly splendid day, the decree for his release came. Chizhevsky responded with a request for permission to stay on in the camp and finish his experiments. He fought and got permission, even though it was against all the rules.

I once asked D. B. Lebedev, one of our respected geneticists, who was expelled from the university in the thirties and from the institute later because he would not denounce Mendelism-Morganism, why they had attacked genetics so furiously, why there had been such a bloody battle around a seemingly nonideological issue—do genes exist, what is the nature of heredity?

"The biologists were harder hit than the physicists and other hard scientists," he said. "On the one hand, they could be blamed for crop failures and the like. But the real issue was whether their science could develop independently, without interference from above. Many of them knew that their resistance was really resistance to the cult of personality."

"What do you mean?"

"Lysenko told everyone that he was supported by Stalin. And suddenly there were people who dared speak out against Lysenko. Called him an ignoramus. How was that to be understood? What was that supposed to mean? After all, there was a sculpture at the Tretyakov Gallery showing Stalin and Lysenko sitting on a bench, Lysenko holding a stalk of wheat. Wasn't that clear? Vavilov and the rest had to admit that he was right! The other disciplines bowed to Stalin's wisdom, but the biologists refused and struggled. The biologists knew they were fighting more than just Lysenko."

During all those years the Bison had felt pity and sympathy for the Russian émigrés. He felt the secret superiority of a man who had a homeland. Now they were threatening to turn him into an émigré, or into a "nonreturner." Horrible word!

Luckily, his refusal to return home and the scandal at the Soviet embassy were not seen as a political act. He kept his Soviet passport, especially since relations with Germany improved, leaders made mutual visits, exchanging pleasantries and vows of friendship. Perhaps the fact that he had refused German citizenship helped, too. They persistently offered it. It was tempting, because then he would have been able to travel freely around the world, without requesting visas.

But the threat remained, the chubby-cheeked fellow had not forgotten or forgiven.

Forty years later a book was published, the memoirs, daring for the times, of a man who had suffered from Lysenkoism himself and had fought it bravely.

As I read the book, I came across a reference to the Bison. The author criticized him harshly as a nonreturner. That was unexpected. I knew that they had been friends. As soon as I had an opportunity to meet with the author, I brought up the Bison, who by then was no longer with us.

"Why did you say that about him?" I asked. "Do you think he could have returned then?"

"Why not?"

"Remember the year."

He frowned, looked around, and then his face hardened.

"What difference does it make? Whatever year . . ."

"A big difference. Would you have asked him to return in '37? Would you have written him a letter—come back with your family?"

"You're putting the question on another plane."

"That's not an answer."

"You know . . . I'm not the one who condemned him."

"What would have been the use of his death? He would have been destroyed, that's certain."

"I wrote that he broke the law," he said stubbornly, and there was no sign of his amiability left.

I recalled that this same man had been among the greeters at the Kazan Station when the Bison returned to Moscow in 1956. They had embraced and wept with joy. I also recalled that his picture was among the photographs that hung over the Bison's desk in Buch. It hung there all those years, in Nazi Germany.

"You see"—he sighed—"he didn't take it into account . . ."

What? Who? Why, the author and their old friendship. In a lecture, the author had criticized Koltsov for his interest in eugenics, a harmful science with a racist tendency. Koltsov's students had counterattacked. They did not defend the principle, they defended their old teacher. The Bison had joined them.

"So that's the problem!"

I stressed the "that's," but he didn't notice. He shook his fist.

"They should have been ashamed of themselves!"

He was furious, forgetting that they were all dead. They were gone, leaving him with unspent hatred. And it was so simple: they had had a quarrel, he had written that the Bison was a nonreturner, and for those who didn't know the background, what he said seemed idealistic and profound. And no one did know the background.

Was the Bison's decision not to return a deed, an exploit, or an act of self-defense? Can you expect suicide from a man? If a man refuses to step into an abyss, is that a deed? Every age has its own concept of deed and action. In those days, the norm was obedience. So they obeyed. Without question. Everything.

The Bison did not attribute anything to his disobedience and certainly did not think about the consequences.

His whole life consisted of deeds, one after another, but for him they were not deeds, not exploits, but a way of life.

19
WAR

He did not go back, and that was the end of it. He forgot the episode and plunged back into his work at Buch.

In 1938 he delivered a speech at the annual meeting of the Genetics Society, "Genetics and Evolution from a Zoologist's Point of View." He published a book, *Experimental Research in the Evolutionary Process*, as well as two works on ornithology. His book *Population Genetics* came out in Italy. To us, a book sounds like something major, but to him, it was just the opposite. He wrote books because there was much he did not understand and he had to express himself at length. When everything became clear, he would write a brief article, and that would be more than enough.

World War II interrupted communications with scientists in Europe, Britain, and America. Then he learned that no one could leave Germany, the borders were closed. The doors slammed shut.

Buch's cloister first saw Nazism as the persecution of Jewish scientists. They were fired, they kept vanishing. Then there were attempts to find hidden Jews, questions of who was half Jewish, a quarter Jewish, an eighth. Fears, denunciations, blackmail . . .

Racism revealed itself. The Bison had never noticed such fierce nationalism in the Germans. Science trains one in the international brotherhood of scientists. Biology, mathematics, physics, all are indifferent to nationality. The laws of genetics and evolution are the same for all living things. Fish, lilies of the valley, and ravens do not know state borders. At colloquia and symposia, no one asked about a colleague's religion, much less his national background. What difference did it make whether a person was Jewish or not? The important thing was talent, diligence, the ability to solve a question, find the truth. As a true Russian intellectual, the Bison was revolted by anti-Semitism. He had grown up with hatred for anti-Semitism, for the "Black Hundreds" reactionaries of tsarist times, for clericalism—all the stinking, rotten pillars of the Russian Empire. That is why he gladly participated in a secret operation that was planned by German scientists.

No one knows exactly whose idea it was. A number of official organizations had the right to retain Jewish specialists in their jobs, but they needed expert opinions on how essential a given specialist was. That is where the plot came in. If a question came in about the qualifications of scientist X, they replied from Buch that X has done the following excellent work, but as for his work in the field that interests the questioners, scientist Y can give them an answer. So the paperwork would go to Y. He would pass it along to scientist Z. And so on. The paperwork would roll along slowly, bringing in half-Jewish scientists as consultants and experts, thereby making them essential specialists. Finally, after numerous responses and evaluations, X would become certified as a highly qualified expert, and the same procedure worked for several other non-Aryan scientists. This tricky system worked for quite a while and saved many people.

A Nazi Party secretary showed up in Buch, a man named Girnt. One day he started a conversation with the Bison, offering him German citizenship once again. This was an unusual offer, Girnt pointed out, quite a flattering one from high up. The Bison rolled his eyes in feigned surprise. Why me? I'm very happy as it is, and I don't want to be greedy . . .

Before the war with England and France, and even afterward, he had a few opportunities to travel to Scandinavia, the United States, and Italy. Fascist Italy seemed much more tolerant than Fascist Germany. But nothing that was not Russia tempted him. It was all the same to him. At least in Buch things were working smoothly, he had a system. Moving would mean losing two or three years of work. As well as his momentum, his train of thought.

As the philosopher said, "There is no second time."

Buch was not Germany, it wasn't even Berlin. Buch was a hothouse, an oasis, separate from what was going on in the country.

Hitlerism was intended for the Germans. The Bison was a foreigner, and no one paid attention to him. It was a unique position, envied by Germans and by his friends in Russia.

Nothing had changed for him. He was free of fear, free of obligations. He could do what he was doing.

The Berlin movie houses were showing a documentary film: the Kremlin, a solemn moment—the signing of the 1939 nonaggression pact, Ribbentrop warmly shaking Stalin's hand, embracing Molotov. They all chuckled happily, but Ribbentrop had a special smile intended only for Germans.

The newspapers quoted Molotov's speech at the Supreme Soviet: "We were always of the opinion that a strong Germany is a necessary condition for lasting peace in Europe . . . Germany is striving to bring an end to the war as quickly as possible, while England and France . . . are for a continuation of the war . . ."

He blamed the British and the French, who were trying to depict themselves as fighters for the democratic rights of people against Hitlerism, and insisted that you cannot destroy ideology by force: "It is criminal to have a war 'to destroy Hitlerism.' "

They began selling *Pravda* and *Izvestia* in Berlin. The Soviet newspapers attacked the British, carried nothing against Fascism, and printed material on Stalin's sixtieth birthday. Sometimes there were long articles on the state of biology in the U.S.S.R. "Many members of the so-called genetics camp are displaying such arrogance, such unwillingness to think about what the country and the people really need, are evincing such elitist isolation, that the most decisive means are needed to battle against this." Or: "There is no room in the Academy of Sciences for pseudo-scientists." This barb was directed against Lev Semyonovich Berg, Mikhail Mikhailovich Zavadovsky, and Nikolai Konstantinovich Koltsov.

Soon freight trains began arriving from Russia loaded with grain, sugar, and butter.

In Buch, they could not understand what was going on.

In 1940 horrible news reached them: Nikolai Ivanovich Vavilov had been arrested. Then they heard that Nikolai Konstantinovich Koltsov had died. The two events seemed to have an inner connection. Both Vavilov and Koltsov were incompatible with what was happening in Russia. They could not exist with the likes of Lysenko and Prezent. They could not live in an atmosphere of pseudo-science. The Bison understood that. But still—to arrest Vavilov, a great biologist of world renown, the pride of Soviet science! How could they do that?

In Buch the Russians made all sorts of guesses, and each time Lelka said that if they treated Vavilov that way, you would have had even worse treatment from them. It looks as if they are getting rid of all the geneticists who didn't agree. You would die, in dishonor, as an enemy of the people, and for what? The Bison said nothing. He would snort, sometimes in irritation. He had survived. He had made the right choice. He had protected his family. But what was the point of being right? He couldn't even attend his teacher's funeral. He felt ashamed and vile.

He had not missed Moscow before. He hadn't had the time. Now he dreamed of Ostozhenka, the Arbat, Moscow byways. He dreamed about Kaluga and the birch trees on their estate. It wasn't nostalgia. He didn't suffer from nostalgia. It was the injustice and baseness of history, which had caught up with him at the worst time.

Held up by the war, the news that reached them was no longer fresh, but it was still incredible: the arrest and death of N. Belyaev, the problems of other friends, A. Serebrovsky, D. Romashov. The former participants of the Drozsoor were called members of an "organization."

They seemed to have forgotten the Bison, no one called him to the Soviet embassy, he was not anathematized. In Europe he was still a major figure of Soviet science. Pro-Soviet circles still used him as an example of the achievements of Soviet science. A man who embodied the Soviet genius, with an advanced mind and a colorful personality.

There were many well-known scientists among the émigrés, but everyone always stressed that the Bison had no relation to the émigrés . . .

World War II was gathering force. German troops moved along the roads of Poland, airplanes bombed Warsaw. In April 1940 the Nazis marched into Denmark. In the north their units took over Norwegian ports. A month later Hitler occupied Holland, Belgium, and Luxembourg. After brief fighting German troops bypassed the Maginot Line. Tank battalions, with crosses on their turrets, moved across France to Paris. The French capital was proclaimed an open city and Hitler walked up the Champs-Elysées toward the Arc de Triomphe wearing a long, shiny brown leather coat and carrying white gloves in his left hand.

Germany began grabbing, annexing, taking over, enslaving openly, without justifications or excuses. The Germany the Bison had learned to love, the Germans, the most honest, hardworking, talented people, so many of them his friends.

Germany no longer existed for him, Russia was taken away from him, now all he had left was science. The blue walls of his lab, the view of the grounds from his window—his world had become very small.

Nations collapsed and fell, cities burned, bomb shelters turned into homes, suitcases into houses. The acrid smoke of defeat, helplessness, and shame hung over Europe.

How could he sit over his microscope, fuss with flies at a time like this? What kind of a brain, what kind of nerves could disassociate themselves from the rumble of war? Tune out, and not in America or Africa, but here, in the middle of events, in Berlin?

I never did fully understand his behavior. There was something challenging and unpleasant in his actions as far as I was concerned.

But some of his remarks made me think that it had not been that easy for him. Something nagged, gnawed at his conscience in those years. It must have been hard for him. And even though he knew how to respond to all reproaches and put himself in the right, that righteousness made him sick. His friends and like-minded colleagues were being blasted, and there he was, cozy right in the middle of Germany.

I realize I am entering the shaky ground of guesswork and psychological reconstruction, which I vowed to eschew in this book. The Bison did not like psychologizing. Once I persisted, trying to squeeze out something more definite from him. But he waved me away and then burst out, "How did you bear everything? Why did you put up with it?" And jabbing his finger at me, he brought up things in our society we had long ago agreed not to touch upon, things we tucked away into dark corners.

He had never been an anchorite, a man obsessed, or a science fanatic. He had lived a full life, in all directions, stormily and greedily. But now science had become his refuge. He immersed himself in it like a diver, like a speleologist going deep into a cave, retreating from the sounds of war, from the tears and cries, from the bombs, the bitter taste of Nazism.

He was thinking about a synthetic theory of evolution. Microevolution was being formulated. It began with populations and developed from elementary evolutionary material–mutation and simple, known factors–into population waves, isolation, selection. A divine picture of millions of years of effort by nature was developing, he could see how the best combinations from an infinity of choices were selected. The selection mechanism at work, speeding up, slowing down . . . There were patterns, signals, changes . . .

He recalled a conversation he had had with Einstein about the secret of touching. That is the most beautiful and profound of all feelings accessible to man. It is the source of true science. Those who are unable to marvel, to feel the wonder of nature might as well be dead.

The act of touching was merely a signal of the world, blindingly beautiful and wise, that existed in the actions of nature and that was inaccessible to him.

What did war mean beside the magical processes of life? Not so much . . .

The battles of Dunkirk and the Vistula became just a few more in a series of battles that had once been considered historic and glorious. Had they held back or speeded up the course of history? Every nation's history was made up of the history of its wars. Endless wars had decided nothing, added nothing to human reason. The very existence of the Thousand-Year Reich seemed like nothing more than a crazy instant when set before the eternal laws of nature. He was proud of science's majesty and his part in it. It let him be part of the great processes of life. His ear picked up things that he understood before others. It was not much, but it was more than most. He knew the letters, the words, he just didn't know the connection between them. He watched the intertwining of fine threads, carefully stepping on the glittering high wire with a new, fresh sense of wonder. It was easier to understand the tangle of the movements of the planets, the starry sky, than the actions of a simple bug. He considered a caterpillar wiser than his own mind. Every leg, every hair was organized with such genius in the caterpillar! Seemingly unrelated phenomena suddenly joined into something stunningly simple. A cathedral made of single bricks.

Later people asked whether the Bison was a discoverer or an understander. Was he someone who found out things or someone who was the first to understand and explain them? Most people would tend to call him an understander; he measured results by their proximity to the truth, and things were true if they were fruitful. His efforts were only a step on the stairway to heaven. And can life be measured by results? Life is lost in the list of results. Life is greater than any results. Life is first of all love. You can learn only what you love and you can understand only what you love.

But this seemingly obvious truth was incomprehensible to most people. The Bison sometimes was infuriated by the indifferent methodical approach, the detached calmness of his colleagues.

News from the noisy outside world grew fainter. He was breaking through to the secrets of the mastery of nature, how it started life, which then went on to develop on its own. He had to understand nature's successes, the stability of its creations, why the gull remained a gull for millennia, why variety in birds and bugs was so important. The hardest part was to see what was before your eyes. To see in a fly what no one else has seen, even though it is visible to everyone.

20

"A RUSSIAN PROFESSOR WHO HELPS FOREIGNERS"

Hitler's attack on Russia in June 1941 exploded the Bison's world and forced him to surface. The war with the Russians was unexpected, shocked him with its shamelessness and baseness. All the vows of German-Soviet friendship were still in the air. Ribbentrop had gone to Moscow . . .

Lelka, the children, the Tsarapkins, they were all in a trap. There was no Soviet embassy, they were turned into prisoners. By law, like all citizens of an enemy country, they were required to show up for registration at the police precinct. A check mark was put next to their names to show that these people were not in hiding. They had to report weekly. All correspondence was broken off, with Russia, France, and England. The only radio broadcasts they could listen to were German.

Shipments of booty from the Ukraine, Belorussia, and the Baltic states came to Germany by the trainload, stolen clothing, food, paintings, furniture. Military maps hung in beer halls, and every day the flags were moved eastward. But strangely enough, after a few months something began rattling in the brass thunder of victory marches, the first whiff of decay touched their nostrils. The German troops were still forcing their way toward Moscow, blockaded Leningrad was starving, but the Berlin man in the street saw the early signs of trouble: cars of wounded arriving from the front, the beer halls filled with invalids. The war, which had been moving so briskly to the east, had bogged down by winter, it was barely crawling along, the tank treads

117

were creaking, the engine of war was overheating as it pushed against the defenses of the Soviet troops. Yet the German radio had reported that those troops had been destroyed long before. The careful ear caught the morbid strain in Goebbels's screaming propagandists.

Through the Bison I began to learn about the German side of our war, the face unknown to us.

The inevitability of Germany's defeat was an idea that occurred early in Buch, first among the Russians, but by the winter of 1941, after the German defeat before Moscow, the German scientists were thinking it, too. With scientific thoroughness they analyzed the strength of both sides and became convinced of the madness of the war with the Soviet Union.

In late 1942 the head of the Buch police precinct told the Bison, "Herr Doktor, you have known us over fifteen years and we have known you just as long. All those years we lived in friendship. Why should you bother coming to see us? I will make the check marks for you myself."

The high reputation of the famous Russian scientist, immersed in research on flies and birds, helped both the Bison and some of those around him. After the war, documents showed that whenever someone denounced the Bison, the local *Gruppenführer* threw out the case, saying that it was impossible.

Thus, he was under no personal threat. Here, in Buch, he was safe, he could "tend his garden." No one prevented him from continuing his work during the war. But something broke in him. His feelings awakened, and his interest in his work vanished.

That lump inside him which had seemed to respond to nothing suddenly became alive. What had happened? No one knows. He knew that in Hitler's Germany a scientist had to try to survive, to save culture, to pass it along. Now everything had changed. He still felt that it was not his job to throw grenades or cut barbed wire; destructive work was not for him. Saving one man was more effective than killing ten bastards. Had he been in the army, he would have fired his gun, but in his position, he preferred to save people. At any rate, he could no longer remain inactive. His country was at war with Germany, and he had to participate.

He demanded that from himself, but he would not let Foma do it. This was their first argument. Foma, his older son, was eighteen then. His behavior worried the father. He guessed a few things and didn't want to know about others. He merely repeated to Foma: every honest man must do what he can and no more than that. "Your work is science," he insisted. "That's where you can do the most good. In science!" He dreamed of Foma's becoming a biologist.

It gradually became clear to me that there was a group of German anti-Fascists associated with the Buch institute who helped Russian and other foreign military prisoners to escape. It was futile to try to escape from Germany without help. This underground group set about transforming the fugitives into civilian workers documented as *Ostarbeiters* brought to Germany to work. The group learned to forge church registry affidavits, *Ostarbeiter* identification papers, and other documents. I never obtained the details.

This network operated around the Bison, near him. He was not in on it. Foma told a bit more to his mother, with whom he was more frank.

Then the resistance leaders had to find work for the fugitives. Distant farms were best for this. They sent them off to be hired hands. Sometimes they asked the Bison to hire them in his lab. There were quite a few of them in the course of the war. Some say that the Bison and his friends helped as many as one hundred people. Some of them have been identified, particularly those of the scientists who were given jobs at the lab. I spent a great deal of time searching for them. One eyewitness account could disclose much information. Forty years had passed. Where were these people? Where had fate taken them, who was still alive, how was I to start looking for them?

If the Bison had told me about how they had saved people back then, I could have found more eyewitnesses and facts. But he had never mentioned it. Why? Much later I guessed—rather, I was given a hint.

How we searched for this material is another story. The Bison's friends and students helped, we had a whole group working. Once again I saw how devoted they were to his memory: Masha Reformatskaya, Kolya Vorontsov, Valeri Ivanov, Anna Benediktovna Getseva, Volodya Ivanov . . .

Grebenshchikov was the first one we found. He lived and worked in the German Democratic Republic. By chance I was sent on a business trip to Berlin, and from there to Weimar.

That month of June was unbearably hot. The car wound its way through

German villages. We kept checking the map. None of my friends in Berlin had ever heard of the town of Gatersleben. It was shown in tiny type on the map. We tried calling Gatersleben from Berlin, looking for Herr Grebenshchikov. After a few tries, we connected. They asked Grebenshchikov to see me, but he refused. He was sick, he was busy, our meeting was impossible. My friend Ewa D. spoke with him. She felt badly for me, she had not expected that kind of cold refusal, and she tried to soften his words. I had no idea what kind of a man he was. According to what Vorontsov in Moscow had told me, Grebenshchikov had lived in Gatersleben ever since the war, working as a scientific associate in a genetics institute, and was a very sweet and decent man.

"Did you tell him I wanted to talk to him about Timofeyev?" I asked Ewa.

"Of course, I repeated everything you asked me to say."

I didn't doubt that. Ewa was impeccable in these matters.

"Please call him one more time. Tell him I'm coming anyway," I said. "On this date."

Ewa shrugged. She did not understand how one could start this conversation up again after such a refusal. Nevertheless, she spent a lot of time getting through by phone. I had no other choice. Grebenshchikov was one of the men he had saved, a living eyewitness. The thread would start with him.

The institute had well-tended grounds and low brick lab buildings. Igor Sergeyevich Grebenshchikov was a gaunt, tall man, resembling Don Quixote without the mustache. He spoke flawless Russian, with a pleasant old-fashioned air that can still be found in Russian provinces. I found him in the lab. He had been head of the applied genetics section for many years, working on corn and gourds, but now he was merely an associate, since he was over seventy. He had studied in Belgrade. His parents had taken him out of Russia during the Revolution when he was a child.

He answered after a moment of hesitation, as if probing for the reasons for my questions. His shoulders were hunched and he was alert and wary. Luckily, he could not maintain his formal attitude for long. His natural amiability took over.

As a child he had loved the theater and beetles. Dung beetles. War found Grebenshchikov in Belgrade, a stateless person with a Nansen passport. According to the German law of 1941, he had to go to work in Germany. Arriving in Berlin, he tried to find a job, but could not, since in his position he could work only in government enterprises. He was told he would be sent to the eastern provinces. Grebenshchikov did not want that. That would mean helping the Fascists directly in their occupation. And then he heard about a Professor Timofeyev who helped foreigners. Timofeyev was a biologist, and that fact made up Grebenshchikov's mind for him. He called Buch. Here he imitated the Bison's voice, whose manner of speaking was the same in German, Russian, and English. Grebenshchikov explained that he had been working with beetles since childhood. Come to see me, said the Bison. That was early 1942. Thus, even then people in Berlin knew that there was a Timofeyev who helped people find work. He went to Buch. The meeting, according to Grebenshchikov, was marvelous. After all his questions, the Bison said, "I'll make you a free-lance assistant."

"And he did it! It was hard. Afterward I still was anxious when I went to the Eastern Ministry to tell them I couldn't go since I had found work in Berlin. A certain Wrangel spoke to me. One of *them*, I guess. But just imagine, he was happy for me! Congratulated me. Think what kind of zigzags happen in life."

Grebenshchikov met others who were being sheltered at the lab in Buch: a Frenchman, a Greek (now at Saloniki University, he said in passing), and then S. N. Varshavsky, a Soviet POW, appeared (he heard that he was alive and well, working somewhere on the Volga). There was also Birulya, who had been brought out by convoy from Rostov to work in Germany. Of course, he might have been a POW, too, but he had been documented as someone brought out. There was also a Dutchman, a half-Jewish secretary, he had forgotten the names. He didn't understand how the Bison had managed to shelter all of them. It helped matters that Buch was in the outskirts, out of the mainstream, because Hitler's people did not care about science, especially genetics and biophysics, which could have no bearing on the war effort.

Grebenshchikov warned me that he knew only a small number of those whom the Bison had saved, only those with whom he had come into contact directly; there were others, but he didn't know who or how many; he felt that it wasn't his business to inquire.

In a short while Grebenshchikov was able to send for his wife in Belgrade and plunge into the work his chief was piling on him. They were hungry and they all did whatever they could to manage. The fruit flies were given molasses and cornmeal, and the workers took the food away from the flies, putting the test subjects on a starvation diet. Rabbits were sent to the labs for radiation experiments. Exposed rabbits could not be eaten. The hunger was getting worse. Therefore they cut back on the dosage of radiation. The experiment results were still valid, and they could eat the rabbits. Later, he decided not to expose the rabbits to any radiation at all: science could wait, it was better to eat healthy rabbits. So they did. The feasts were held at the Timofeyevs'. Elena Alexandrovna would cook a rabbit and invite everyone. When they didn't have rabbits, they made pudding from molasses and cornmeal. The Bison would dump it on a cutting board for "general devouring."

"Even here he remained a collector. There are collectors like me, I collect beetles (I'll show you my collection later), there are collectors of knowledge, but he collected people. He didn't collect them by appeals to do something, he collected them with his ideas. A volcano of ideas! Some talents need paper, others labs, but Nikolai Vladimirovich, we called him N.V., he needed listeners. He had to share, discuss, argue, dissect. That would spark a new thought. In discussion."

Listening to Grebenshchikov, I looked at a portrait done in black pencil. In a simple frame, behind glass, it hung over Igor Sergeyevich's desk. I like portraits in labs. They are never there by accident. This one depicted a young man, with a big nose, a shock of hair, and big lips, and I suddenly realized that it was the Bison of those years, aged forty. Oleg Tsinger did the drawing, and Grebenshchikov got it from him.

"As for art, we argued all the time. What he blathered about opera was just nonsense! It was impossible to win an argument with him. And what he said about Vrubel!"

The old outrage was still alive and made Grebenshchikov jump up. His long wrinkled face was tinged with pink, he was embarrassed by his ardor but couldn't stop himself.

The Bison's most loyal students still spoke of him with a touch of irony. That was the tradition—no blind idolatry. Nothing like the devotees of Pushkin, Chekhov, or Blok, who don't want to hear a word about the weaknesses or flaws of their idols, who are perfect as far as they are concerned.

"In Germany N.V. began attending church after his son's arrest. He considered saints the connecting bridge between God and man. He prayed for his son's salvation."

"How did you live in Buch? What was daily life like?"

"The Timofeyevs' life seemed to be a continuation of their prewar manner—as simple as possible. A few sticks of furniture. A few paintings, gifts from Oleg Tsinger. A big table in the dining room, where guests gathered every evening to drink tea. They got Germans used to the Russian practice. After tea we sat in his study. There was a couch, a desk, and books, not too many scientific tomes, mostly poetry. He had worn a path in the rug, pacing back and forth."

Many people recalled that worn path. No one recalled anything remarkable in the furnishings. But all the German friends and students remembered the way the lab was run. No one could say what the rules were, but there was a definite order. It was maintained by two female assistants, devoted to the Bison. And there was the research assistants' independence. The Bison's style of management was to have a "fermenting" effect on his colleagues (Grebenshchikov's term). The Bison handled administrative duties simply. An accountant came around twice a month to hand out money. The genetics department was in a separate shed; it was autonomous, without any bureaucracy.

"If I needed a scientific book or special tweezers, I went into town, bought it, and the Bison passed the signed receipt along to the accountant."

The Bison was aristocratically polite with the technical help. In extreme cases, when he was asked to reprimand an insubordinate young lady, he agreed reluctantly and took a long time to work himself up to it. But in scientific arguments he was harsh, crude, and unrestrained.

In Hitler's Germany, so bureaucratic and conformist, his freedom stood out sharply. Trying to fit his behavior into some framework, the Germans found nothing better than to call it *Narrenfreiheit,* the right of the fool to say what others dare not. Or perhaps they were protecting him with that jangling belled cap.

Before I left, Grebenshchikov made me look at his beetle collection. He opened box after box: tiny beetles, like jewelry, and huge beauties, the size of my hand, seemingly cast in metal, with horns, velvety brown, raven black, ruby-colored. The colors were purer and warmer than those of precious stones, and the surfaces varied as much as the colors. I was convinced that nature gave living creatures the best colors and imagination. So much creativity in that species alone. No wonder scarabs were considered sacred in Egypt and put inside mummies in place of the hearts.

On the street, saying goodbye; I asked Grebenshchikov why he had refused to meet with me. With great tact and circumlocution, he explained that he could not imagine why I wanted information about the Bison; he knew I was a writer and was gathering material, but what for? He had concerns, understandably, since there were all kinds of rumors about the Bison, and perhaps I intended to write something bad about him . . .

So that was the reason. I laughed. We were so pleased that we embraced in farewell. The car started up. The smile was still on my face, but I realized that things were pretty bad if these concerns had reached this far, to this distant German institute, and if such concerns could have been a reason for avoiding a meeting with me.

Sergei Nikolayevich Varshavsky's name came up several times in our search, but it was hard to find him and even harder to get an answer from him.

He lived in Saratov, worked there as a zoologist in an institute. Despite Kolya Vorontsov's energetic help, Sergei Nikolayevich kept silent a long time, apparently out of the same considerations that Grebenshchikov had. Finally I persuaded him to write to me, briefly, how he had ended up in Buch. Here are his reminiscences.

"I met Nikolai Vladimirovich in late 1944, after my wife, Klavdiya Tikhonovna, Ivan Ivanovich Lukyanchenko, and I fled from the factory following a bombing raid. We had worked there as *Ostarbeiter*, brought there from Rostov-on-Don to Germany.

These lines were very important for me. Grebenshchikov had been told in 1942 to apply to a Russian professor who helped foreigners. Thus, in 1942 and in 1944 there was a persistent rumor in Berlin about the Russian professor. In a letter, Grebenshchikov later explained how it had happened. He had heard about Timofeyev in the crowd that hung around Alexanderplatz. It was a market of news and information, and it included the word on the professor.

"Once we escaped from the factory," continued Varshavsky, "we decided to try to find that professor and ask him to help us, we had no other way out. Berlin was being subjected to daily, systematic Anglo-American air raids, not only at night (as was the case in 1943) but also in the daytime. We walked several kilometers from the ruined and burning city and reached

Buch. This suburban town amazed us by its untouched state; for some reason the Allies had not bombed.

"The institute where we were told the professor's laboratory was located was in a building several stories high surrounded by spacious grounds. Ivan Ivanovich and I waited outside while Klavdiya Tikhonovna went off to find the professor, to see about the possibility of finding work for us. She came back in a short while and joyously informed us that Timofeyev was waiting for all of us.

"After getting to know us, Timofeyev said that he knew our scientific work and would try to find jobs for us. He paced a bit in his office, a small workroom, I think a corner room, and then proposed that I think about working for him feeding experimental animals, adding that to his great regret he had no other positions open at the moment. I accepted instantly, of course. Then N.V. asked Klavdiya Tikhonovna to forgive him for being unable to hire her but promised to get her food ration cards as a family member. He immediately wrote a note to a friend of his, the old Russian doctor A. I. Sokolov, with a request to give Lukyanchenko a job in the neighboring hospital right there in Buch. N.V. handed me a form that would allow me to work at the lab, dictated the text to the girl at the typewriter in the next room. The form was taken care of in just a few moments.

"Our fate had been decided. We did not know how to thank N.V. We couldn't believe that right in the heart of Germany, in the capital of our mortal enemy, a man could live and function actively, risking his life, a man who not only was a Russian patriot but was openly proud of it. The walls of his office were covered with pictures of Russian scientists—natural scientists and biologists from Lomonosov to Severtsov, Mensbir, Koltsov, Chetverikov, and Ognyev."

The Bison used to call it "my iconostasis."

How could all this be? It was happening under everyone's eyes. Naturally denunciations reached the local Gestapo. So how could it happen and continue happening?

When I was in Berlin, I asked this question of Robert Rompe, the famous German physicist who in those years was doing research work at the Kaiser Wilhelm Institute, with which the Bison's lab was affiliated. Rompe had lived for a while in Buch. He and Timofeyev had worked on several research projects together.

It was hard to get to question Rompe, for it took over a week to get an appointment with him. It was the same problem I had with Grebenshchikov. They were all afraid that their recollections would be used against the Bison, that they could somehow damage his memory.

I met Rompe at his Institute of Electronic Physics. He told me, "Tim was not touched because his fame by then was so great that it was impossible. Just as they did not touch Max Planck and Max von Lauer, the great German physicists known for their anti-Fascist views. Tim already had the Kistyakovsky Medal and was considered the world's most famous geneticist. Add to that the authority of the Kaiser Wilhelm Institute."

Then Rompe recalled how Tim gave the right people vodka when he needed documents for a Jew that would show only half-Jewish ancestry, because half-Jews could work at certain jobs.

Rompe spoke Russian well. He came from a family of St. Petersburg Germans. He was around eighty when we met. He was head of the institute and apparently worked hard. We talked in his office. Rompe was thin, frail, tanned, and resembled a dried flower.

Judging by certain facts I learned and a few remarks the Bison made in his time, Robert Rompe was involved in the anti-Fascist underground. During the war he headed the lab for OSRAM, famous for its heat lamps. He worked on plasma physics, hard-body physics. Apparently he had lived through a lot in those years. It is a pity I did not manage to get him to talk about his own underground activities. I do know that he accomplished much and that after the war he headed the administration of upper schools and scientific institutions of the GDR.

"It was difficult, of course, to organize aid to Soviet POWs. They were starving to death . . ." Suddenly remembering something, Rompe switched subjects. "Tim was incredibly courageous. I lived in his house for two months. It was in '45 . . ." He stopped again. I could tell he was remembering much more than he was telling, not like the other people I interviewed. He was one of those old people who do not like to say too much, especially about themselves. It was my misfortune to come across such a rarity.

What did he mean about courage?

"Ah, that . . . Well, for example, a man came to Tim in the winter of '45 from a prison near Dresden that had burned down. He was clearly not Aryan. Tim hid him. He wasn't afraid."

It looked as if the Bison really feared no one, not our people, not theirs.

Not before the victory, not after. But first I must complete the list of people he saved.

After all the questions, gathering of documents and testimony, we established that among the rescued were the French brothers Pierre and Charles Peroux. Charles was an officer in the French army and a brilliant physicist. Also saved were: Kanelis, a Greek; Ma Sun-yun, Chinese; Bauman, Dutch; a Russian couple, the Panshins; and Alexander Sergeyevich Kach, half German, half Russian, whose wife was Jewish and particularly difficult to save. Kach later became director of an institute in Karlsruhe. There was a Frenchman named Machin, a mechanic, and another Frenchman, a laborer, whose name we could not learn. There were Peter Welt and a lab worker named Nergner, both half German and half Jewish. We discovered the name of the man who had fled from the Dresden prison: Lutz Rosenketter. This list does not include the people I mentioned earlier. Meanwhile, the normal contingent of German employees continued working, including the irreplaceable physicist Karl Günther Zimmer and the physiochemist Born.

Since all the positions in the lab were filled, and he couldn't hire any more people, the Bison made arrangements to form affiliated labs at other institutes. Thus, he sent Igor Borisovich Panshin to the Auergesellschaft.

"N.V. sent me to Rill with a formal application for hiring. Rill saw me in his large and gloomy office in one of the Auer research buildings. He was cool and official, the conversation was brief: N.V. and I should set up a lab at Auer. This must have had a *nonscientific significance* [italics mine–D.G.] for Rill and N.V., since it was soon rescinded and Sasha, my wife, and I worked in the big room next to N.V.'s office, the same room where he and his wife worked."

This is from Panshin's letter. He sent me several long and detailed letters from Norilsk, full of love for the Bison. He reconstructed the events of those years with details and with guesses.

"The first month I was in Berlin, N.V. decided to do a test run . . ."

It is possible that the Bison had doubts about Panshin, he had reason for that, but it is also possible that he wanted to prove to others that the ex-POW he took on was really a specialist and not a pretender.

". . . He suggested I give a lecture on my already published works for the institute staff. There weren't many people in attendance, but I saw a few unfamiliar faces (the head of the local Nazi Party organization and others). I spoke in German, and my reading of the Bison's work in German had helped.

I described the work I would like to set up at the lab. The lecture was successful. My plans were approved. N.V. and Zimmer nodded significantly, 'Yes, this is very important,' even though both knew that at that time it was important only for scientists.

". . . Rompe and I began collaborating on employing my method of microphotography in long-wave ultraviolet. Mercury quartz lamps, needed for this method, were being developed at the OSRAM plant. Rompe invited me to his lecture on these lamps and showed me around the plant; incidentally, Rompe helped save the plant."

Nikolaus Rill, mentioned above, was a Russian German, a marvelous German physicist, who was working on the technology of uranium in those years. He was close to Tim. Rill will reappear in our story later.

Igor Panshin was the son of a famous Soviet selectionist and biologist who was arrested in 1940. As a child he had assisted his father; when he was fifteen, he caught a new species of fish in the Dnepr River, wrote a serious article on it, and attracted the attention of zoologists. After completing Leningrad University he worked in Koltsov's institute. Everyone there followed the Bison's achievements closely and through Koltsov knew about his latest work; after all, the Bison was their representative in Europe. Of course, Igor Panshin had heard of the Bison earlier, when he had worked as a student in Vavilov's genetics lab. He was doing experiments in radiation genetics and naturally studied the Bison's work as the leader in the field. That was in 1933-34, when Hermann Muller came to Leningrad at Vavilov's invitation.

"He was a celebrity for us. And Muller was interested in my work and suggested publishing it. I wrote an article, and naturally there were references to N.V. But what amazed us then was the awe and delight with which Muller spoke about Timofeyev. He had worked with him in Buch."

And Panshin recalled yet another meeting with the Bison, a very important one for me.

This was in the summer of 1938 at the genetics institute.

"I was in the greenhouse and ran into Vavilov. He said, 'We'll be going to the Genetics Congress soon and we'll decide the question of Timofeyev-Resovsky's move.' It was said without the usual Vavilov optimism. Muller was no longer in Moscow, Vavilov's institute no longer had a chief of the theoretical directions staff, and we were all in a depressed state."

What did Vavilov mean? Apparently, learning about the Bison's conflict at the Soviet embassy, he hoped to smooth things out at the international congress. This was on the eve of the Seventh International Genetics Congress. The Soviet organizing committee had been approved two years earlier and they had worked out the agenda and the composition of the delegations. Seventeen hundred geneticists from around the world would be attending. Vavilov and his people had great hopes for the congress. The greatest scientists of the world would confirm that they were right in their struggle with pseudo-science, with medieval views.

Vavilov expected to see Timofeyev at the congress or, at the very least, in Moscow once the congress had reestablished true science and Timofeyev could come home without risk.

In the fall of 1937 it was decided to postpone the congress for one year, and then the new president of the Academy of Agricultural Sciences, Lysenko, began doing everything he could to keep the congress from meeting in the U.S.S.R. The international organizing committee had to switch the congress to Edinburgh in September 1939.

The Bison, along with Muller, Harland, Dobrzhansky, and others, proposed electing Vavilov president of the congress. Scientists from other countries supported them. The Bison waited for Vavilov to come, to help him find a way to return to Moscow. He thought Vavilov could do everything. The Bison held fast to his hopes until the last moment, until the congress was opened and it was announced that Vavilov would not be attending. He had not been allowed to go.

And so they waited for each other and never met, remaining on either side of the door that had been shut on them.

Illusions were shattered. From that moment on, the Bison could count only on himself.

Panshin now lives in Norilsk. He left biology a long time ago. When I located him and wrote to him, I began getting letter after letter from him, detailed recollections of the Timofeyevs, dozens of pages of tiny script. Then he flew in from Norilsk and I listened to his stories for several evenings. Despite his age, he was sturdy, an avid skier, and a professional photographer. His own life was not simple. He had gone through the war and prison camp, where he had worked as a translator in the tank division. His adventures were complicated, with unexpected twists of fate, he had an interesting love-and-marriage story. But I had to limit him and myself. I firmly stopped Panshin, would not let him get sidetracked, kept returning him to Berlin, to Buch, to the lab. I behaved like a businessman sorely lacking in normal human compassion—that's who I was. Every time. Merciless, indifferent—how strangely compatible with literary work.

". . . The next news I had about N.V.," Panshin continued, "was in the spring of '42, in prison camp. I was talking with Rakel, a Munich architect and ski instructor. He told me that he was designing a villa for the famous German geneticist Wettstein. Then I asked him if he had ever heard of Timofeyev-Resovsky. He had and was certain that Timofeyev was living and working in Berlin."

Panshin began looking for a way to get to Timofeyev. That required time. But by then horrible events had taken place, turning the Bison's life upside down.

21

THE BERLIN
UNDERGROUND:
FOMA

The fate of their older son was never discussed in the Timofeyev household, it was too painful. Everyone knew that Foma had died at the hands of the Gestapo.

Foma was born in 1923 and brought to Germany as a two-year-old. Only those who had been to Buch ever knew him, and there weren't many people like that left. For them Foma was an almost legendary figure.

To her dying day, Elena Alexandrovna retained the wild hope that Foma was alive. She and the Bison avoided talking about it. I think that deep in their hearts each blamed himself for Foma's death. At least, I sensed the guilt gnawing at the Bison.

In those days I wasn't planning to write about Foma. I simply put the microphone in front of the Bison to save his words. One time he was talking about Germans and war:

"The feeling was growing that Hitler was losing. Everyone said that the Germans were bound to repeat the mistakes of World War I. They did not follow the English precept. The British allow themselves to lose every battle except the last one—you must win the last one. The Germans win all the battles except the last one, and therefore lose the war."

We laughed and then, forgetting the taboo, I asked what had happened to Foma.

The Bison looked grim and said angrily, "What for? . . . Foma isn't an indulgence. Do you want to add to my image? A writer needs a plot device, is that it? How can you do without it! The crown of thorns . . . Justification . . . All your plots are lies. Life has no plot . . ."

I had forgotten to turn off the tape recorder and I have his curses, his angry trampling of me and my books and everything that I planned to write and was capable of writing. In his wrath he was unjust and unstoppable. To this day I can't listen to that tape to the end, that roaring, rattling recording, full of below-the-belt blows and painful comparisons.

The next day he called, asked me to come over, and without explanation or apology, leaned toward the microphone and recounted Foma's story drily and briefly.

"My son was arrested. He ended up in Mauthausen and died there. Yes, he died! . . . He lived with us but spent time with Russian groups in Berlin. They were doing important work: saving Eastern laborers, trying to get food to POWs, helping those who could still move to escape from the camps, giving them *Ostarbeiter* documents so that they could allow themselves to be recaptured and sent to the camps for Eastern laborers, which were more bearable then the other prison camps. Since my son spoke several languages well, he typed and photographed identification cards for all the camps that also had Western and Southern workers: Yugoslavs, Frenchmen, Belgians, Dutchmen, Danes, Czechs. There were several underground groups like that, basically composed of Russian émigrés. The rest were Germans, sons of big bureaucrats. Foma was arrested because there was an informer in their group. Close to fifty young men were arrested. That was in '43. Foma was a biology student. His surname was Timofeyev-Resovsky. The double name ended with him, because our younger son, Andrei, is simply Timofeyev."

That was all he said in his only story about Foma.

When I started writing about the Bison, I began collecting everything known about Foma as well. The Lyapunov family kept photocopies of Foma's letters from camp and letters about him. Then I talked with Robert Rompe, with Oleg Tsinger, learned a lot from his younger brother, Andrei. I talked to everyone who might have known something. And this is what gradually emerged:

Foma really did belong to a clandestine organization. Along with children of Russian émigrés it included children of important German physicians, including some from Hamburg, children of famous people and government figures. Rompe mentioned the son of Karl Kautsky. What did they do? Besides what the Bison had described, they got medicines, treated POWs who were afflicted with gingivitis and dystrophy, and helped hide fugitives. Foma, we know, hid two French pilots.

Foma did not tell his parents about his activities. He was protecting them. He particularly wanted to keep his father out of these things—he was too open and uncontrolled. Everyone who knew the Bison even slightly understood that. Under interrogation, Foma apparently convinced the Gestapo that his parents knew nothing. The Bison was not called in for questioning. Nevertheless, he had guessed that Foma was involved in something in the underground: he would disappear for days at a time, people would come to spend the night and then vanish.

Everything Foma did came about from the example set by his father, his views and convictions. Nevertheless, the Bison told Foma that he should stay out of illegal secret organizations—that was not for a scientist. The old story of Koltsov and Mensbir had soaked into the fabric of his heart. He felt that Foma had to become a good scientist, he had the ability for it.

Foma was arrested on June 30, 1943, and taken to a Berlin prison.

The anxiety began. Heisenberg, Weizsäcker, and other German scientists appealed to influential people, begging, pleading. They got the Timofeyevs an appointment on a high level. The Bison didn't want to go. Elena Alexandrovna forced him. She knew how to free him from hard decisions, taking them upon herself. She understood that it didn't fool him, but it made it easier. She was the only person who ever saw him dispirited, depressed, pathetic, or weak. After their son's arrest, no one expected the frail woman to show such energy and persistence. Nothing stopped her. No warnings or threats had any effect. During their appointment, they managed to extract a promise to save Foma's life.

But soon the person who had granted them the visit refused to help: too many damaging facts had emerged. Foma had played a significant role in the group. They did get some vague promises. They were allowed to see him, they could get food parcels to him. They celebrated Foma's birthday on November 11 in Buch. He was twenty.

A copy of a letter to Foma from a Frenchman survives. Apparently it is from the man Foma had hidden and who was arrested with Foma. Perhaps he was a pilot. He was exchanged for someone else later. Elena Alexandrovna once said it was he. It was important for me that Grebenshchikov confirmed this:

"Foma was arrested by the Gestapo for hiding French pilots and helping

Russian POWs in the camps. We don't know if he was tortured or not. N.V. was depressed. Elena Alexandrovna did all the visiting, she was terrific and supported her husband."

The Frenchman's letter is marvelous, not only in conveying the personality of the writer and his feelings for Foma but also for the image of Foma it depicts.

Berlin, October 17, 1943

My dear friend Dmitri!

I do not want to leave Berlin without saying goodbye to you. That is understandable, since we spent long weeks together, the saddest time of our lives, the saddest because we did not have freedom, and only freedom can make man happy. It is fate that I am leaving here first, but I assure you, my dear friend, that I would rather see you leave first.

Bidding you farewell, dear Dmitri, I want to say that you are a rare person in my life, one who never loses the feeling of friendship. You showed me and other comrades a feeling of incredible value, a great and perfect feeling, the feeling of comradeship. Chance let me know you not as simply a young man, but as a mature man, with an exceptional character and extremely sensitive feelings.

Dear Dimitri, save those qualities throughout your life and thank providence that you were given parents whose perfection brought forth the qualities in you of which I speak. There is no need to ask you to remain true to yourself, because a man whose mind and soul has already formed like yours will never betray himself. Live for the future, my friend. You will get out one day, the war will end, and a new era will begin. And then we will be able to renew our contacts and perhaps see each other. I will receive the first news of you with great joy, I will wait with great impatience for an opportunity to see you in other circumstances.

All my life I will recall those sad evenings we spent sitting together on the edge of the window in our cell, watching the stars, making plans, thinking of the future, dreaming of freedom. We had moments of despair, but hope never left us.

There is no need to add that our friend Petrov is also a person I will never forget. He is a man of great spirit and he has the right character.

Tomorrow I return to Saloniki to take up the work. I am incredibly happy to be going there. Nora is waiting for me, of course. Without special permission from the secret police I cannot return to Switzerland. That does not upset me so much, even though my wife would like to see me. You know that Greece has become my second homeland and not being able to go there would have been torture for me.

Farewell, my dear friend! I thank you a thousand times again for everything. The future will show the full measure of my gratitude. My best wishes to you in case you get home soon. If not, I wish you courage, much courage, to bear your prison suffering. I embrace you in friendship.

There is no one to ask who Petrov or Nora is. An excerpt without a beginning or a continuation.

The consolation and hope conveyed in the letter are imbued with a sadness the author may not have been aware of. Did he understand the danger Foma faced? Or is it something we are able to see, knowing what will happen? Either way, the image of the twenty-year-old young man was revealed to me.

In July 1944 an attempt was made on Hitler's life and the situation worsened for all political prisoners. The Nazis were killing now without any care about people's names. The son of Nobel laureate Max Planck, mixed up in the Stauffenberg conspiracy, was shot. Planck could do nothing. In August 1944, Foma was transferred to Mauthausen. There is a letter from a Nikolai, Foma's comrade from the Berlin prison, about this.

29.7.44

Good day, dear Elena Alexandrovna, your husband, and son Andrei!

Please forgive me for starting this way, but I couldn't begin any other way, because Foma and I spent over seven months in prison together and I consider him a brother. He must have written to you about me. My name is Nikolai. I will write you a few lines about how we were separated. It was yesterday morning, at 4:30. He was told on July 27 that he would be transported at 7:47 to Mauthausen. And he told our mutual friend (you know who, of course) to pass you a note about getting him something for the road. He planned to bring it here at six in the morning. But things were changed that night. Instead of 7:47, Foma had to leave at 4:50, almost three hours earlier. The mutual friend brought the parcel to me, but when I went to give it to Foma, I was told that he had left early in the morning. I was very sorry, of course. Before this I had managed to get all the parcels through the old man you left in the bureau. It's inevitable, something had to happen, you know the Russian saying: it can't be dairy week for the cat all the time, there's Lent, too. This man left the parcel with me, because Foma told him to do that in case of a problem. I think there will be good people there, too, through whom good contact can be arranged. We said goodbye like brothers, shaking hands, kissing, and wishing each other freedom as quickly as possible from the bars and convoys and a return to a free life.

I understood his inner striving to be with you, but I always told him, you're still young, and you must learn to bear all misfortunes. I dare to write a few words about myself. I was an officer in the Russian army, was imprisoned by accident, escaped and made my way to Germany, where I worked for a year and a half and through a mistake ended up in prison with Foma. I am also from Moscow, the Taganka Square. I have heard only good things about your husband in Moscow and in Berlin. I want to tell you one more thing. Alexander Romanov, the officer who visited you and told you about Foma, has been arrested again and is here. I saw him today. The dark Georgian who also visited you was arrested and is in solitary confinement here. Well, I don't want to bother you any more. I can't tell you anything about the concentration camp, because I don't know myself. I am ending this letter, which Foma asked me to write. Forgive me if it is hard to read, but I lack light and a table. I wanted to ask you one thing. If you get any word from Foma, please let me know, if I am here, through that man. Give him my best wishes.

I am alive and healthy and wish you the same.

Respectfully yours and Foma's,
Nikolai

We don't know who this Nikolai is.

Only one letter (actually a note) of Foma's from Mauthausen exists, on a camp form, written in German. It may be the only one he wrote.

Mauthausen. 8.12.1944

Dear parents and brother!

I am healthy and everything is going fine. I received your letter of 6/9 and also of 13/9, thank you. I haven't received the parcel yet, but was informed about it on 25/9, for which I thank you. I think often of each of you and send you heartfelt greetings from a faithful son.

Dmitri Timofeyev

Two other notes—crumpled scraps passed secretly—were from Russian prisoners.

7.12.44. Good day. Hello. Thank you for the parcel, I got tobacco, bread, butter. Many thanks. No changes in our life yet, don't know what the masters will decide. Still have not removed my handcuffs. Warm greetings to Foma . . .

[illegible] to Sergei. I'm still able and well, wish you the best, good luck at school, Andrei, nothing comes without work. Thank you again for the parcel, wish you success in everything. Goodbye for now. Writing at night in moonlight after lights out, please send a needle.

Fomenkov

It is possible that this man had visited the Timofeyevs, since he knew about Andrei and his schoolwork? Or was he one of Foma's prison friends?

The second note is written in a hurried, slanting hand. Apparently, there was an opportunity to send notes that day.

7.12.44. Good day. Many thanks for your kindness, got everything, butter, bread, tobacco. Send regards to Foma. Still alive and well. Still shackled, no changes.

Alexander

On the reverse:

No time to write a lot, time [illegible] sincere thanks to all my friends. So long.

Alexander

I did not determine who Foma's prison friends were. These notes were in the Timofeyev family archives, kept by the Lyapunovs. From them it follows that the Timofeyevs continued to help prisoners even after Foma was transferred to Mauthausen, passing food parcels through their channel.

Foma was betrayed by a man who had lived in the Timofeyevs' house, and Foma was told about it almost immediately. Foma had a few hours before his arrest; he could have gone into hiding, he could have gone to Hamburg and tried to escape to Denmark from there. There were several possibilities. But he knew that if he had done so, according to Nazi law his father and mother would have been thrown into the camps in his place. So he did not try to escape then or later.

Mauthausen concentration camp left little hope.

The Bison forced himself to go to work in the morning, to listen to his colleagues, respond, advise. Once Vogt left, there was more work for him. He spoke, signed, moved according to schedule from office to lab, to the animal room, up, down, but his soul was frozen, his mind absent.

If he had only taken his family to America, or Italy, or anywhere . . . If he had only agreed to return to Russia back in 1937 . . . If only he had not set an example for Foma, had not helped to rescue people . . . If he had only not thought in his pride that there was nothing higher than science . . .

Retribution had come. Inexorably.

There had been ways to prevent Foma's arrest, but now it was a question of the boy's life. He felt that Foma would not get out, would not survive. Germany was going from one defeat to another, the Nazis were getting more vicious, and the chances to save Foma's life were getting slimmer.

He began going to church. He couldn't pray at home. The Russian Orthodox church was unheated and the stingily thin candles barely illuminated cold faces. He knelt on the icy tile floor. He prayed fiercely. He did everything fiercely. Prayer kept him from feeling helpless. Nothing but a miracle could help. Who else could he turn to? What could he hope for? If there were anything he could do . . . He suddenly discovered how dearly he loved his son. Science, success, truth, discoveries—everything that seemed to be the center and meaning of his life—dissolved, shattered into a meaningless shell. There are no values left when it's a question of your child's life. Foma was a child again and his father was ready to give away everything he had—his knowledge, his work, his fame—to save him. How had he not realized that before, thinking children were just a concomitant of marriage? He recalled how Foma had gone to the French *lycée* as a boy and had loved learning French. He recalled how he had picked on Foma in recent years: too dull, no original thoughts, and yet a student. His son had to be exceptional. Ability was not enough, he had to have talent. The war? What about it? The war would pass. He had shouted at him, called him stupid, dumb, ignorant. He had called handsome, sweet, dear Foma those names . . .

He was stupid and dumb spiritually himself . . . He didn't notice his son. Found him when he lost him. He was too late, just a little bit too late. Lord, save Foma, forgive me, have mercy on us all! Spare him, Lord, don't let him die!

He slept apart from Lelka, so as not to disturb her with his despair.

If Foma died, it would be his fault, he hadn't managed to protect him. When had he missed it, when? The Bison avoided politics as best he could, never making statements, never joining organizations. But damned politics found him anyway.

Oleg Tsinger wrote to me about Foma:

"Once Foma and I went into town to buy him a good penknife. We bought the knife we wanted and then had tea in a café. And suddenly Foma told me that he wanted to kill Hitler and that he was in a conspiracy with his friends, and he was sure they would manage it! He spoke cheerfully. He said he would never tell his father, it was too hard talking to him anyway, he only scolded him . . . Then Foma spoke about Russia, which, in his opinion, had the fastest trains, the best roads, the biggest rivers and eagles, and the best people in the world. I was touched that Foma was so frank with me, but I also felt sadness and great fear . . . I could see that Foma had absorbed everything that Kolyusha had told him about Russia, how childishly he had perceived it, and how dangerous his plan was. I had to promise not to tell anyone about it."

Many residents in Buch could not understand why the young man with such a famous name, with a good future, would get involved in these frightful things. He was destined for another life.

The Russian professors' laboratory had more and more fugitives, *Ostarbeiters*, Russian and non-Russian. They all needed shelter and documents. Two months after Foma's arrest, the Bison sent a letter to the Tushenwald camp asking for permission to use "the famous scientist Panshin and his wife, Alexandra Nikolayevna, in my laboratory." And he hired them.

You would think this was the best time to lie low. Be quiet. Not make any careless moves. The thin thread connecting them to Foma could tear at any second. They could be deprived of the right to correspond or to send parcels. The slightest mistake could affect his fate. He should have refused everyone: go away, my son is in danger, you will destroy him, we don't have the right to do anything . . . That's what he should have done. No one can reproach him. He tried—but he couldn't. His character wouldn't let him. He couldn't behave like a hostage.

Robert Rompe was astonished by his behavior: "That man had no fear nerve!"

He had a fear nerve, like any human being, but something suppressed his fear—the desire to be himself. He couldn't change that any more than he could make himself shorter. His obligation to Foma might have been in fearing nothing.

Once the great physicist and former president of the Kaiser Wilhelm Institute, Max Planck, came to visit Buch. He and the Bison took a long walk through the grounds. They were united in sorrow. After the attempt on Hitler's life in July 1944, Eric Planck was arrested and shot. Planck was bowed down by sorrow, his darkened face retained only his shy smile.

With that smile he recalled a visit from Hitler long ago. He had hoped to persuade the Führer to change his attitude toward scientists. To make an exception, for instance, for the chemist Fritz Gaber, to whom Germany was indebted. The Führer began shouting at Planck and shaking his fists. That rid him of the illusion that the Führer knew nothing and that the people around him were guilty of everything. They were all one gang of bandits who had taken over Germany.

Recently Planck had been thinking about the power of faith. Did religion have a tie with science? Did the very development of science increase one's sense of not understanding the fundamental things? Science was accepting more and more on faith. There could be a unity there. The two men did not argue, they considered the position that the individual consciousness is beyond the limits of science. What about the soul? Did it exist? With age, man becomes convinced that it does and believes that he has one. How does it appear, what is the evolution of the soul? Is there a mechanism that directs the evolutionary process in general?

"Of course, this thing—life—was begun by God," the Bison said with a laugh, "but then He took up other things and let it flow on its own."

Planck was tormented by thoughts of Germany's future. There was no doubt it would lose the war. What would happen then? The only thing he wanted was to save German science from total destruction. Without it the

Germans would not be able to purify themselves spiritually and be reborn in the near future. He did not want to talk about it with Germans.

The war separated people, breaking off connections, heightening disagreements. The Bison fell into long silences; no one wanted to interrupt them. It looked as if he had lost his goal, did not know what to say to people or how to unite them. He did stupid things. Once coming home from a visit at night, drunk, he began singing at the top of his lungs on the Friedrichstrasse. At the height of the war in the middle of sleeping Berlin he bellowed Russian songs. He got away with it, as he did with so much that was headlong and daring.

Now people would reminisce around the big Timofeyev table. The past was what they had in common, and it had receded far away. The past, which elicited sweet sorrow. The Bison sometimes joined in, recalling how he and Lelka had visited America. On the return trip, the Royal Society in London gave a dinner in his honor—a rarity—and at that dinner he wolfed down an entire plate of caviar, which he had missed.

Oleg Tsinger recalled how the Bison had rushed to their side when he heard of the death of Oleg's father. The father's last request was to have his body donated to Moscow University. Oleg's mother was horrified, and Oleg didn't know what to do. "Kolyusha convinced me tenderly and tactfully to give my father a Christian burial, that his last wish was his last gift to science but now we had to think about the living—that is, my mother."

The food rations in Buch were cut to starvation minimum. Varshavsky told me that their ration cards were not enough. Lukyanchenko was having the same problem, as was the tolerant Chinese geneticist Ma Sun-yun.

But some parts of the German machine continued to function with irrational punctuality. The experimental animals were brought paper bags of feed on the old rations. The bags held carefully wrapped hard tack biscuits. With the chief's blessings, the workers took some of the biscuits for themselves. They shared it equally. Varshavsky recalled that he got two portions—one for his wife, who was not on staff. Sometimes Elena Alexandrovna added to their portion.

Elena Alexandrovna was saving a lab worker then, managing to make her only one-eighth Jewish. They also found a job for a French woman,

Chouchou (only her nickname was remembered). Somehow Elena Alexandrovna still managed to get false identity documents.

Sometimes habit brought the Bison back to his normal active state.

"He told me to familiarize myself with the literature on genetics," Varshavsky said. "After liberation from the Fascists he planned to develop population genetics. He must have found me satisfactory as a biologist working in the ecology of populations. I was astonished by his optimism: Buch could be turned to ruins at any second, but he was planning our scientific work."

By spring ration cards were done away with completely. The authorities recommended that people gather herbs, mushrooms, and snails, make coffee from acorns, and bake bread from rapeseed.

22

THE RUMBLE
OF SOVIET TANKS

The Bison climbed up to the seventh floor, and from there up to the icy roof of the institute. He could look out over Berlin. The city's familiar profile had been changed by the bombs. Fires blazed across the horizon. Black columns of smoke rose to the clouds. The Bison looked eastward, toward an unfamiliar, one-note sound, not like the roar of planes or the crackle of gunfire. Something was buzzing deep in space. A heavy, low rumble spread below it. There was also a barely perceptible vibration, not yet familiar. A new sound of war was being born somewhere on the Oder River. The Bison twisted his binoculars, vainly trying to see. A few of his colleagues came up on the roof. They listened and wondered, but were afraid to voice their guesses. They waited for him to speak.

The Buch institutes were hurriedly evacuated to the west. The physicists left. Heisenberg and Weizsäcker left. The medics left. Workers at the other institutes vanished somewhere.

Three months earlier, in November 1944, the Bison had been sent to Göttingen to make plans with the university there to move the lab. Soon afterward came word from Göttingen that everything was ready for them. They should have started packing, but the Bison announced that first they would have to dismantle their most valuable possession, the neutron generator. People would have plenty of time to leave. They had no specialists for dismantling it. Rill could have helped, since his factory was nearby in Oranienburg, but Rill had more pressing work. When he came to Buch, he and the Bison sequestered themselves and talked about something. People were concerned about the delay. Buch was emptying. Just recently their neighbors from the Brain Institute had strolled around in their summer uniforms (they were doing work for the air force), but now the corridors were deserted and the doors sealed. The Bison listened to the arguments, but shook his head. How could people panic like that? We had to set an example of calmness. The newspapers and the radio carried reports about the impregnable fortifications on the Oder. Posters all over Berlin proclaimed: "Bolshevism is facing the decisive defeat of its life!" "If you believe the Führer, you believe in victory!"

One day an American bomb landed on the grounds near the lab. Windows shattered. The Bison had them replaced.

He was praying on the roof. The hollow new sound could mean only one thing—tanks were coming! Soviet forces had broken through the German fortifications on the Oder, tanks were headed for Berlin. It had come to pass! He had lived to see it. Could it be true? His heart was thumping, he felt hot. The Russians were coming, it was an end to Fascism, the damned Reich was crumbling, the death throes were starting. Hurry! Nothing could help Hitler now, no secret weapon, there would be no atom bomb. He knew that from Rill and from Rompe. The rest was nonsense, like the impregnability of the Oder.

The decisive battle was coming. People were waiting for the Bison's orders to leave. His German workers demanded that they go west, to Göttingen, anywhere but here.

He understood that fate was bringing him to the crossroads, the turn that would determine the rest of his life. Not only his, but the lives of his family and everyone who followed him.

The terror increased daily. The field courts-martial were swift and ruthless. People were shot for defeatism, for dissatisfaction; deserters were hanged. Specially created units of Waffen-SS, police battalions, frenzied bands of former Hitler Youth, drunk on blood, were marauding.

East or West? Leave or stay? America or Russia? The question tormented people, and every evening they gathered at the Bison's house, discussing, guessing, picking up rumors. It would be horrible to be caught in the middle, ground to dust in the final battle. They had hopes for the unity of the Allies. Perhaps their friendship would last? The Nazis were trying to cause a rift between the Americans and British and the Russians. It wouldn't work, the Allies would remain friends, there would be free communication with Russia, there would be joint laboratories, scientific centers . . .

Dreams, illusions, they are also documents of history.

How did the Bison view this problem for himself and for others? I don't know. My past got in my way, my own war with Fascism. I couldn't imagine myself in Germany, in Buch, among Germans, I couldn't imagine what they were feeling. I could see myself only shooting. It was a war complex. I couldn't do anything with myself. I couldn't imagine myself on the other side, that meant being a traitor, I couldn't cross the front line without a weapon or a mission . . .

Aircraft were crushing Berlin into ruins, streets had turned into burning tunnels, whole neighborhoods were in flames. Flames raised blazing whirlwinds to the skies. Steel girders were contorted, melted, fire raged, purging everything that had been there—parades, torture, fear, hope . . .

Into the inferno of war, Fascism tossed quickly mustered units of sixteen-year-olds and pensioners. Women, lugging children and suitcases, scrambled in the search for safety.

The incredible occurred: the ruins were declared sites for the construction of a new capital. Signs were hung over smoking holes: "We hail the first builder of Germany, Adolf Hitler!" No one saw the absurdity in this.

Goebbels made all propaganda workers screen the film obtained abroad about the defense of Leningrad, so that they could teach Berliners stoicism and sacrifice from the enemy's example. However, for some reason, Fascism did not give rise to resistance heroes or heroes of the underground struggle. We did not hear of German partisans in East Prussia or Silesia. As our troops moved toward Königsberg, no one bothered us from the rear. The Fascist units fought fiercely, they had fanatics loyal to the Führer, but there were no fanatics for an idea worth fighting for after they lost the battle.

Friends and acquaintances of the Timofeyevs were fleeing Buch. At their house you could see those they had helped: Soviet POW pianist Topilin, Oleg Tsinger, a French mechanic. Robert Rompe came and went.

The institute was quiet and almost deserted. No one dealt with the laboratory anymore. The snows melted. The grounds were empty, blackened, ready for spring. The birds began to return.

The Führer appealed on the radio: "I expect even the wounded and sick to fight to the last!"

A sign appeared on the hospital wall: "Better to die than to surrender!"

The next day someone wrote "No!" in black paint over the sign. That "No!" was being painted fearlessly on the walls of ministries, on shop windows, at subway entrances.

The multilingual, multinational Noah's ark of the laboratory separated and reunited over the issues. The Germans, brought up to obey orders, wanted to do as they were told–move to Göttingen. They were afraid to stay. They heard that the Russians would wreak revenge, send people to Siberia. They wouldn't care if you were a scientist or not. Especially with geneticists–they didn't like geneticists in Russia.

"Why would we be needed in a country in which Lysenko has won?" they asked the Bison, including him in the question. "They imprison all geneticists, and they'll do it to us."

Everyone agreed that the Bison and his family should move to the West. The British and the Americans would be glad to have him, his fame was great there, he had many friends, any university would be honored to have him. They would supply him with anything he wanted. Hungry and worn out, they thought about where one could be warm and well fed. Their conclusions were logical. Logic demanded that he leave. And that they move westward, too.

Refugees moved past Buch. Wagons pulled by horses, carts, wheelbarrows, bicycles. They carried children wrapped in newspaper or curtains. A half-mad old woman walked past, bent under the weight of a portrait of Hitler. The suburbs of Berlin were fleeing. The flow increased daily. The panicky desire to flee infected the most rational lab workers. Only the Bison's will could keep them. He was silent, not disclosing his decision, and they huddled around him. Formally, they did not need to obey him. He gave no orders, but he was the leader.

Actually, he could not know how the Russians would treat him, and he felt no certainty. He must have realized that it was safer to go to Göttingen, at least for a time, to avoid both Germans and Russians in the heat of the moment. He could go back later . . . But he did not budge.

Sometimes he did give orders. His actions of that time were marked by caution, I would say by farsightedness, so you could say he was on top of the situation. Panshin found guns abandoned by the *Volkssturmer* in an empty house near the institute. He and the older Peroux, a French officer, suggested that people arm themselves, so that they could fight back if SS bands attacked. The Bison did not allow it. They argued, he attacked and categorically forbade them to bear arms. And as it turned out, he was right.

It is hard to explain why they believed him, harder still why they obeyed. He was politically naïve and formally without power. Perhaps because he was a Russian, a Soviet? He was a Soviet citizen. On the other hand, all the others—the Soviet POWs and the Germans—agreed that he could expect nothing good when the Soviets came.

Hope turned to despair.

The front moved slowly, too slowly for the Bison. It was moving too fast for the Germans. Everything looked different for the Bison, like a negative. Rumors of General Wenck's army coming to rescue besieged Berlin brought him to despair. Victory for him was coming with Soviet tanks, and it would be the salvation of Foma.

Not everyone is capable of thinking differently from the rest, it is always difficult, and it must have been especially difficult amid the shouts of Goebbels's propaganda and the fleeing Germans. Two decades of life in Germany had left their mark on the Bison, he had some German in him. That's not surprising, what is surprising is how little German there was about him. Now the German part of him sympathized and was horrified, responded to the wailing and the deaths, while the Russian in him triumphed and rejoiced.

The Soviet tanks were not rolling down the highways, they were breaking through barriers and ambushes, fording rivers, struggling every inch of the way . . . The anticipation was unbearable. Would they arrive in time to liberate Mauthausen?

Time broke down. There is nothing worse than stuck time, when everything stops, the hour and minute hands don't turn, and the same meaningless thoughts spin in your brain. The Bison knew only one way to try to escape from that paralysis—drink alcohol and tune out.

His powerful constitution made it hard to drink to unconsciousness. Red eyes bulging, he would sway through the institute, the grounds, and once he dragged in somebody's cow by the horns, shouting, "I've caught a devil! A devil!"

He found a fellow drinker, a small hunchbacked German from the neighboring institute. He was either a glassblower or a mechanic. With drunken casualness, he insisted that when the Russians came, they would hang the Bison.

"What about you?" the Bison asked.

"See my hands?" He would show his singed, work-roughened hands. "I'm working-class. And if Hitler holds on, they'll hang you anyway."

"What for?"

"For sheltering enemies of the Reich."

The hunchback's eighteen-year-old son had been killed near Tilsit. "And where's your Foma?"

They would embrace and weep, and then the hunchback would push away the Bison. "The Russians killed my son, the Nazis took away yours. You're my enemy, but it turns out there's no difference. We've both lost our sons."

"Foma's alive!" the Bison would shout.

"If he's executed, the Russians will go easier on you. They'll take that into consideration. But why would you want to live after that, Professor?"

The hunchback stung him. The Bison could have flattened him with one blow, but he would get on his knees. "It's what I deserve."

The hunchback shook him by the shoulders. "What happened to my idea? I had a life's idea—a great Germany. I shared it with my son Ralf. What happened to it? Germany is just big shit. Ralf died for shit."

In April on the day the storming of Berlin began, the hunchback hanged himself. The day before, he had brought news for the Bison: Foma's group, Melk, had been returned to Mauthausen from Vienna, probably to be executed.

Later this was confirmed. In response to my question, the Central Party Archives of the Institute of Marxism-Leninism of the GDR checked all sources and informed me: "Dmitri Timofeyev, born 11 September 1923, student, confined to Mauthausen 10/8/1944; sent into Melk group 14/11/1944. They returned 11-19/4/1945." The Central Party Archives could not establish what had happened to Foma after that. All that was known was the construction sites in Austria where the prisoners in that team had worked. The archive people suggested consulting the Viennese archives for resistance documents. Vienna responded that they had no further information and sent me to the French archives that had the Mauthausen documents. I knew that Elena Alexandrovna had asked there herself and had received no satisfaction. Someone had said that Foma had died during an uprising of the prisoners in Mauthausen just before the Americans came. Those rumors reached his parents later, in the fall of 1945. That spring they believed that he was alive and expected to hear from him any day. Foma had to come back and they had to wait for him.

Everyone knew that the Bison was not staying in Buch merely because it was the first place Foma would go. He would have found them elsewhere. The Bison wasn't someone you could easily lose.

All scientists are interconnected. If they do not know one another personally, they nevertheless know a lot about one another—personality, family, prejudices. They have an international community, a fraternity, a system of information and mutual aid. Thus, both Peroux brothers ended up in the Bison's lab thanks to the concern of the Paul Rosabud scientific publishing house, which published scientists from many countries. The older brother, Charles Peroux, a French officer and physicist, had been released from a concentration camp on the excuse that he would translate material for the atomic scientists. German physicists helped him. Once Charles Peroux was set up with the Bison, his young brother came to Buch. He came with a promise from Frédéric Joliot-Curie to defend Charles from any accusations of collaboration with the Nazis that might be hurled at him after the war.

Through these secret channels the Bison received word that they were waiting for him in the United States and would be glad to set up a lab for him in any of the universities where his friends, such as Delbrück, Gamov, or Morgan, were working. He did not respond to the invitation. He was constantly drunk. Rompe was the only one who could get him interested in work; they wrote a joint article, "On the Principle of Intensifiers in Biology."

"Only the force of his talent could drag him out of the morass of alcohol," Rompe told me.

23

WAITING FOR
THE RUSSIANS
TO COME

They were both named Nicholas and were born in the same year. The Bison called him Mikola. Rill called him Kolyusha. In public they spoke German; in private, Russian. Nikolaus Rill was of Baltic German extraction and had begun his work in physics with such fine scientists as Otto Hahn and Lise Meitner. Their high moral principles undoubtedly had an effect on Rill. The day would come when this would be called upon. But his path was a twisted one. In the early years of Fascism, Rill was inspired by the possibilities opening before him, applying his abilities as a physicist in industry. It must be remembered that from inside, for the ordinary German, Fascism looked quite different from what it did from the outside. Everything in Hitler's Germany was done under the slogan "For the good of the people, in the name of the future of great Germany." This created illusions. Yes, of course, anti-Semitism and nationalism were bad, but at least the homeland would improve.

Before the war Rill was already in charge of the central radiological laboratory at the Auergesellschaft. He showed enterprise, business sense, and extraordinary ideas for experimentation. The scientist coexisted with the businessman in him. He began helping the Bison in 1939 in his radiological research, supplying him with radioactive materials. His love for the Bison was his secret dues payment for his childhood memories of Russia and his loyalty to the pure science that was quickly disappearing in Germany.

War with England was starting. Rill was called to the War Ministry and asked to work on the production of uranium for a uranium project. It became clear that actually they wanted uranium for atomic bombs. The Germans began working on the atomic bomb even before the Americans. The problem interested Rill. For a scientist any interesting problem is a great temptation that often overrides moral considerations. Rill worked enthusiastically. His energy and inventiveness made it possible to get a quick start on the industrial production of metal uranium. They had to create the technology for this new production. By then Rill was chief chemist at the Auergesellschaft.

The history of work on the atomic bomb in Nazi Germany is complicated and mysterious. Despite the efforts of historians, much is still unclear. One serious work states: "The failures of Germany in the creating an atomic bomb and an atomic reactor are often explained by the weakness of its industry compared with that of America. But as we can now see, it was not a question of a weak industrial development, for it was industry that supplied the physicists with the needed amount of metal uranium."

And in fact seven and a half tons of uranium was manufactured by 1942.

Opinions are divided among historians. Some contend that German physicists were pursued by failure, the bomb didn't work because of miscalculations and misfortunes. Others argue that Heisenberg, Weizsäcker, and Diebner were secretly sabotaging the project. Their failures were not accidental but intentional. They clearly understood that such a horrible weapon could not be put in Hitler's hands. They pretended to work, used pull to get talented scientists out of the army, saved German physics. They did not put science in the service of war. "War should serve German science!" That was their slogan.

The atomic scientists in Buch worked not far from the Bison. It was a different institute, but the Bison knew them, at least Heisenberg's group. As for Lise Meitner, he helped her find work in England, where she fled from the Nazis. We know that he helped other physicists, too. The Bison told me, in response to my questions, that he doubted that Heisenberg and his people were trying to create a bomb, it didn't seem that way. At least, they were in no hurry at the start. He avoided more specific statements. The work was secret and he might simply have been guessing, judging from Heisenberg's moods or comments. But the Bison's opinion is substantial. When it came to someone's reputation, he was careful.

In 1942 Rill began gathering all the reserves of thorium in occupied

Europe. It formed real capital, the value of which was understood only by a few. Gradually he had his hands on enormous wealth, supplies of uranium and thorium.

Besides Heisenberg's group, another independent group under Diebner was working on the bomb. They worked successfully, spurred on by rivalry. All good intentions paled before the heat of the race: who would win? The excuse was scientific curiosity. A pure, selfless feeling that gave rise to science. A dangerous feeling when you forget about taboos just so that you can get to the secret, find out what's behind the curtain.

But Rill, Heisenberg, Diebner, and Weizsäcker, no matter how clever they tried to be, ended up in a trap. Even if you take their anti-Fascist feelings at face value, they still would have failed. Everyone who set foot on that path ended up in a trap.

The groups alternated in obtaining encouraging data. A little more, just a bit more, and they would have a good reactor. The bombs had nothing to do with it, they told themselves, the reactor would be for atomic energy. It would provide the capability of sustaining a chain reaction with the materials they had. Clearly, Germany was losing the war, but the reactor would help it win the peace, it would be ahead of the rest of the world in atomic energy. Germany would sell energy to rebuild the country.

Later Werner Heisenberg formulated his attitude toward the creation of the bomb this way: "Research in Germany never went so far that a final decision about the atomic bomb needed to be made."

It never got that far because the advance of the Soviet army did not let it.

And who would have made that final decision? I doubt it would have depended on the physicists.

And if it had gone that far? Would the German physicists have resisted the temptation to create the bomb? Test it?

I will have to go into what happened to the German bomb later, because it is connected to the fate of Nikolaus Rill, which in turn is connected to that of the Bison.

Thus, as the rout of Germany approached, as the armored tread of Soviet tanks rumbled closer, both groups of physicists hurried to create a working atomic reactor. Evacuations, air raids, and alarms interfered. They began building a big reactor in a Berlin bunker in late January 1945. Everyone who could do so had fled Berlin. Panic was growing. People were worried.

When the experiment was basically prepared to start, the orders came to evacuate. Another two or three days would have been enough for the experiment. But they didn't have those days.

It was a question of hours. Weeping, cursing Hitler and the Soviet army, the physicists demonstrated the reactor without testing it first. Loaded trucks moved toward Thuringia on January 31. Then they moved farther, to Haigerloch. In late February, Heisenberg's group settled down and began assembling their equipment in a cave. They set the reactor working on February 28. There was no reaction. Heisenberg realized they needed more heavy water and uranium. The materials were available, but it was impossible to get them from Berlin. It was too late. Telephones were down, electric power was uneven, roads were bombed out. Germany was in its death throes.

Back in September 1944 the uranium-purifying plants were destroyed when Frankfurt was bombed. They tried to repair the factory in Rheinsberg, but Soviet troops intervened. That left the plants in Oranienburg. Both Oranienburg and Buch were going to be included in the Soviet zone of occupation. By then the Americans had learned about the Germans' atomic work. They didn't know the details, but they knew that the Germans were working full blast. They set up the ALSOS Mission, a group ordered to seize materials, documents, and the physicists themselves. The Americans were afraid they would fall into Soviet hands. General Groves, head of the American atomic project, set Oranienburg as a prime objective for ALSOS. They decided to send an engineering team to disassemble the uranium factory and take the specialists, including Rill. They had already captured Professor Fleischmann, a specialist in dividing uranium isotopes, and seven other physicists. They also bagged Otto Hahn, Bagge, Weizsäcker, and then Diebner, Laue, and finally Heisenberg himself. The war was being aimed at the atomic physicists directly. The Germans realized it, but too late. History took revenge on the Germans for slighting science, for disdaining highbrows, for hating the intellect and their own culture.

The Americans, however, could not penetrate into Oranienburg. General Groves asked headquarters to send an American unit there, but the military feared repercussions from the Soviets for an illegal action. Then Groves demanded that General Marshall bomb the plant before it was too late. Marshall delayed, seeing no military necessity. Groves insisted, threatened, and finally got what he wanted: on March 15 six hundred Flying Fortresses bombed the city, turning it into ruins. Everything was destroyed.

Rill miraculously escaped from the burning city and went to the Bison in Buch. To him, the reason for the terrible bombing seemed clear. The Americans had to have known, at least from the German scientists they had already captured, that there was no possibility of a German atomic bomb; they hadn't even had time to build a reactor. Therefore, Rill concluded, the uranium plants were destroyed in order to keep them out of Russian hands. That was why Oranienburg had been leveled. If we Americans can't have it, no one can! Rill was furious. While the Russians were fighting the Nazis, the Americans were fighting the Russians. Was that any way for allies to behave? No high-flown words about political expediency could serve as justification. To destroy the manufacturing plant Rill had set up with such effort, his brainchild! A shameful act! He repeated Rathenau's words that if the means are immoral, then the ends are immoral. The ends are the favorite justification of the immoral.

The bombing of Oranienburg moved Rill. The decision he made then was not so much for Russia as it was against America.

"Until the thunder and lightning," the Bison said in a huff. "Well, all right, and amen to that."

Bucked up by the Bison, Rill stayed with him to wait for the Russians to come.

In the meantime, SS officers were searching for Rill in the ruins of Oranienburg. Their mission was to find any remaining important secret research groups left near the front. Everyone they located was sent south to the Alpine Redoubt on the border of Germany, Austria, and Switzerland. People were shot if they didn't obey. The SS were gathering atomic physicists, as well as engineers working on the new ballistic rocket, the V-2, when they learned that the Americans were hunting for them.

The SS were not interested in the Buch institute. A genetics laboratory was not an important site. Those people fussed with flies, had no special assignments. Rill could hide out there calmly until the Soviet army came. Calmly only in a manner of speaking. There was no calm. "How will the Russians receive me?" Rill thought aloud. "They'll receive you wonderfully," the Bison assured him. Rill need not worry about the Americans from ALSOS. "They won't come here, they're afraid of us." By us, he meant the Russians.

There was a hunt on for brains, the first of its kind in history.

Rill knew that the Bison could have no precise information, that his confidence was unfounded. Nevertheless, it helped. More than anything, the fact that the Bison was staying there convinced him.

He would have had to leave behind not only Rill but his German colleagues, the nucleus of the laboratory. Separately, they did not have the value they did together. The war was forcing them to make a decision in the final days and final hours. Flee or stay? East or West? Zimmer was accustomed to trusting his boss, he had been right too many times. Born mocked his trust: what can the boss promise, where's the guarantee? Hard labor in Siberia was what awaited them.

There was an organization of Russians in Germany that helped people get to the West. Fears grew and people were confused.

Zero hour was approaching.

"Do you remember, Nikolaus, how afraid you were when we went to see Niels Bohr?" The Bison shuddered visibly in imitation of Rill.

Everyone laughed, but it was forced, and Zimmer said, "What do you care? Bohr received you, and the Bolsheviks will receive you, too, but what will they do to us?"

All conversation and all thought came down to the zero hour.

Reason and logic didn't help, something else was needed to keep people there.

At that time they received a visit from a young Englishman, actually an Irishman, more precisely an Irish Austrian who could pass for a German, a Swiss, a Dutchman, a Dane, or a Tyrolean. They knew that he was a biochemist and had letters of recommendation from Cambridge. After their first conversation it was clear to the Bison that this sweet fellow in army boots and feathered hat had been sent by the ALSOS Mission, this time on a delicate mission. The Bison was sober and listened without interrupting, lower lip pouting.

"What are you counting on?"

"On my people, the Russians," the Bison barked.

The fellow looked at him carefully and then went on about conditions in American universities, salaries, housing, and then as if in passing mentioned the rumors about Vavilov; their information was that he was dead, had been killed.

"Nikolai Vavilov? Nikolai Ivanovich Vavilov?"

The Bison's voice cracked. It couldn't be, impossible! But instinct told him that it was the truth. Vavilov was gone. The support had cracked, part of his own life had broken off. He was not as alive as he had been, and he felt the dead part, the chilling part of his soul. The future, the hopes connected with victory, were buried there.

He returned to the present on the grounds of the institute. Firmly holding his guest's arm, he was leading him out to the road. He thought that the guest had not mentioned Vavilov randomly, he had intended to use that: anything to get the job done.

He did not have the strength to be angry. Steadily and softly he explained how disgusted he was by the manner in which the Americans were hurrying to grab brainy Germans, stealing the intellect of this already mutilated country. Like picking up the spoils of war. You would think that the Americans were the ones who had won the war in Germany.

The biochemist was not offended.

"All politics is dirty," he said. "We're not politicians, you and I. We scientists flourish in conditions conducive to doing science. After all, it wasn't bad for you here, was it?"

He landed this second blow without pity and right on the mark. The Bison grimaced in pain and imagined how many more such blows he would have to take in the future. It would be useless to try to explain that he had been a Soviet citizen here and that he would be an immigrant in the United States. That here he was standing fast, while if he went to America, he would be running away.

He walked the biochemist out to the road, not letting him talk to any of the lab workers. He protected his flock from predators.

"Why do you think you won't be hanged?" they asked him at the lab. "And us along with you?"

"Because they're Russians, not Fascists. They saved Europe," he replied, knowing these answers satisfied no one. He had nothing except his fierce faith.

He suddenly realized how strong his roots were, how they had not dried out over all these years. Now nothing could budge him.

It wasn't even a choice. The powerful press of propaganda squashed a man, the "divine clay" was flattened and remolded. There was no free choice. I don't understand how he withstood it.

They found bodies of people who had committed suicide or who had been executed on the grounds. No one left Buch. Everyone huddled around the Bison, lying low, ready for anything. Panshin's wife counted flies in test tubes and sang Soviet school songs and Pioneer songs.

24

"DID YOU THINK THAT GOING BACK WOULD BE CHEAP?"

In one of his letters, Oleg Tsinger described those days of 1945 rather colorfully.

I was living in Berlin, there was nothing to do, there was no food either, and usually I lay on my cot and strolled around the ruined city. I spent the nights in some bomb shelter. I made plans with friends to end up in a more dependable bunker. I ate poorly, I wore three shirts and three pairs of socks at a time and always carried a small case with the things I needed most. Our apartment had burned down, I was divorced, and I lived in the studio of a friend who had moved to Austria. My wife and son lived in a room in Buch, not far from Timofeyev's institute. Once in the spring I decided to visit my wife, which I did regularly. At the subway station I learned that the trains were going only as far as Buch and not to the terminal of Kero. I saw incredible bustling, a multitude of armed soldiers in helmets, with rolls of camouflage netting. On the train everyone said that the Russians were in Kero and were firing at the trains. At the station in Buch I saw craters from aircraft fire. My wife was at home. Our friend Selinov was there. Over the radio they asked people to go to the bunkers. The three of us headed for the big bunker in the park. We spent two nights there, and there I opened the doors for the first Russian soldier. They were boys of nineteen or so. I won't describe the touching scenes.

My wife's room in Buch was confiscated by the military and so as not to sleep on the street we took our little suitcases to the

157

Timofeyevs', of course. Kolyusha and Lelka greeted us joyfully. They had been through a lot in those anxious hours.

Here I insert an excerpt from Igor Panshin's letter.

At night we all gathered in the cellar of the house where the Timofeyevs lived. Rill, Rompe, both Peroux brothers, Kanelis, all of us, the Germans—the Zimmers, the Erlenbachs—and people I didn't know. It was quiet at night. We slept on the floor. In the morning and during the day the sounds of battle came ever closer. Of the retreating German unit, only two batteries pulled by horses were left. Then machine-gun fire nearby. Bursts. I came out of the house. Several of our soldiers were walking across the field. I took a white rag and went toward them, shouting, "It's Russians here, no Germans!" One of the soldiers took aim and advanced toward me, saying, "I know these Russians . . ." We approached the Timofeyev house, entered the vestibule, lots of people speaking Russian. Another Soviet unit entered from the institute side, with senior officers. I was seeing the shoulder-board insignias for the first time, I couldn't distinguish among them, but Nikolai Vladimirovich knew it all. The explanations began, who we were and why we were here. No time to go into details, the units were on their way to storm Berlin. I wanted to go with them. A lieutenant asked, "Do you know Berlin well? If you do, we'll take you." I didn't know Berlin well . . .

Here is more of Oleg Tsinger's letter:

And we were left in a deserted Buch. Many people had left the institute. Some doctors had committed suicide, there were only a few Germans left on the grounds, and Kolyusha with his wife, the Tsarapkin family, a Soviet pianist, and Kolyusha's scientific colleagues and lab assistants. How it happened, I don't know, but we immediately became a "separate state," and Kolyusha became commander in chief. Kolyusha gave himself the title Director of the Institute. That was naïve and had consequences, for Kolyusha did not know the whole institute, didn't know what was happening in the hospitals, and couldn't have known, since he was in charge only of the genetics department. The first task was to protect the institute from looting and damage to the equipment. We sent Selinov out with some signs I made up to post them around the grounds. In Russian they said that this was a scientific institute and it was forbidden to damage or take anything. At first the posters didn't help.

The institute had reserves of methyl alcohol. The Bison had it destroyed, to avoid accidents. At night it was flushed down the toilets.

He talked to the medics in some unit and the institute was assigned a Soviet guard with a rifle. No more unwanted visitors.

The spring of 1945 was warm and sunny in Buch. No one had left the lab yet. Everyone was waiting for something. No one could work, they all sat at their desks, fed the animals, moved pieces of equipment around. Oleg Tsinger continues:

> One morning a truck came and we were arrested. The selection was rather strange: Kolyusha, me, the pianist Topilin, a Soviet biologist, and two Soviet zoologists. We were terribly frightened, of course. First we spent the night in a barracks, then we had to walk. We were led by a soldier who kept offering us Russian cigarettes. Kolyusha kept trying to get the soldier interested in genetics. The soldier kept saying, "Take it easy, Professor!" He used a map and wasn't allowed to tell us where he was taking us. We walked until late that evening and arrived at a place we could have reached in half an hour's walk. Kolyusha was interrogated daily. The weather was excellent. Every morning we heard the Katyushas firing in Berlin. Bees buzzed in the apple trees. The sailor guarding us gave us smokes. There was also a German prisoner, the owner of the house, who kept complaining about the bucket they took away from him and which he wanted back. We pointed out that cities were burning, people were being shot, and he was complaining about a bucket. But the German insisted he wanted it back. We laughed at him, offered him money, which, we figured, meant nothing anymore. The German took all the pieces of paper. It turned out money still had great value. Eleven days later we were released. We walked back to the institute. And a fantastic life at the Buch institute began. Kolyusha turned into a dictator and policed us, so that we were afraid of him. Everyone had his title. I was artist in residence. My wife, son, and I were given a marvelous apartment with a kitchen, which had been abandoned by some fugitive German. Grebenshchikov also got a good apartment. The French prisoners got good rooms and titles: two were scientific workers, one a gardener, one a carpenter, and one a mechanic.

Kolyusha continued his work, but he seemed lonely and nervous. He berated me, telling me that I was pretending to be a rich Englishman and had no sense of what was important! It wasn't pleasant; it was incomprehensible. The "Buch evenings" in their former form ended, but we still got together sometimes, as usual, at Kolyusha's . . .

What Oleg Tsinger and others could not understand had an explanation. During those eleven days of arrest the military found out about the Russians in Buch. The situation was simple with Tsinger and the others. It was more complicated with the Bison. Many questions came up about him and it was not easy to find answers. Luckily, word of his arrest reached Zavenyagin. Avrami Pavlovich Zavenyagin, the legendary director of Magnitka, builder of the Norilsk combine, was by then Deputy Commissar of Internal Affairs. He was in charge of some objectives of Soviet science development. He had come to the front for a reason: our physicists were interested in the German projects. One of them was linked to the problem of biological defense; they were also working on the atomic bomb.

When Zavenyagin visited Buch and met the Bison, he zeroed in on the significance of the man, the value of his work and the importance of the research center itself, which was turned over to him fully staffed and in perfect shape. The Bison articulated his ideas about restoring Soviet genetics, but Zavenyagin tactfully brought the conversation around to a more pressing problem, the atomic one. Apparently Zavenyagin was pleased and impressed by this man. Zavenyagin could understand better than most his reasons for not returning to the homeland in 1937. And he was impressed that Timofeyev had waited for our army, keeping Rill and his co-workers there. Without hesitation, Zavenyagin entrusted the institute to Timofeyev until the question of his move to the Soviet Union could be resolved. Timofeyev's reputation apparently did not worry Zavenyagin.

The Bison was delighted by their conversation. He liked the man very much. This reaction corresponds to the opinion of many physicists who worked with Zavenyagin in those difficult years.

The Bison was appointed director. Zavenyagin returned to Moscow.

And now our Bison went all out. He set up a billboard on the highway announcing that the institute was Soviet-German (no one had ever officially abolished the title of the twenties) and that it was under the control of the main Soviet command. All our military units passed by the institute without a fuss. Then the booty hunters came and began taking equipment to send back to Russia. The Bison interfered so energetically that they first took him for someone sent from Moscow. The Bison shouted, "You fools, what do you need these for! You're garbagemen! Why are you taking these microscopes and other antiques! We'll make new ones. Why don't you take the patents, reports, most of all, take *people*, the specialists!" He pushed them around and gave orders, until someone asked, who is that man? And they found out. They grew angry. How dare you yell at us! You served the Fascists! That's why you're trying to save their equipment! They were so angry they wrote a denunciation to the right place. So we could say that the Bison threw a monkey wrench in the works of his own good fortune.

Oleg Tsinger writes:

> We celebrated the taking of Berlin, Germany's capitulation, we watched the grand fireworks from our grounds. I loved going to the theater put on by the soldiers and professionals for the wounded. They set up the stage among the chestnut trees, hung lanterns, and played all kinds of silly stuff, but with great humor and talent. Skits like "Front-Line Katyusha," dances to the accordion, and even poetry readings. I was very attracted to this, it reminded me of commedia dell'arte, *Petrushka*, Vakhtangov's *Turandot;* at least these performances were very spontaneous. Kolyusha did not attend them, he didn't go to the new Soviet films. He kept looking for something all the time. Something important that he lacked. It must have been peaceful scientific work.

Tsinger was right, the impossibility of working tormented him, but there was more to it than that. Other things had happened by then.

Lev Andreyevich Artsimovich, a physicist already famous by then, flew in from Moscow. He was introduced to the Buch scientists, including Rill and the Bison. Artsimovich greeted them all pleasantly. He was very pleased to meet Rill, but when he reached the Bison, he said, "Yes, yes, I've heard of you, but forgive me . . ." and refused to take his hand.

And the Bison stood there with his proffered hand. It was one of the most shameful moments of his life. He had been publicly insulted, dishonored, and he had no way to defend himself.

He froze like a bull in a *corrida* when the matador's sword enters his neck, the steel reaches the heart, the moment of truth comes, the second between life and death . . .

Artsimovich later recalled his gesture without regret. But they eventually developed great respect for each other.

That year I would not have shaken hands with a Russian who had worked for the Germans. That year we were implacable. The fire of war had purged our souls and we wanted no compromises. We approached everything from a front-line point of view: where were you, on which side of the line? If you fought Hitler, you were one of us; if you didn't, you were the enemy. We soared over the complexities of life, free and happy conquerors who understood all. We were full of condescension for the Germans, but it was hard to separate the Nazis from simple Germans. And Russians in Germany were also suspicious.

Not shaking hands was normal. Ah, I was a happy holier-than-thou lout for such a short time. And then I shook so many different hands. About some I didn't know, about others I didn't believe, and about still others I knew but was embarrassed or didn't want to make a fuss. What was it to me? Judge not so that ye will not be judged . . .

The Germans understood what had happened. They stood watching their idol, waiting for his response. He was suddenly alone, separated from everyone, marked by dishonor. He did not have the right to respond with a slap, he did not respond, he just stared into his life.

He had come face to face with what, from now on, he would have in his homeland.

"Well, what now?" Zimmer asked.

He could change his mind, go away. Why put up with the humiliations? That was Zimmer's question. They were walking through the institute grounds. The Bison was staring at his feet. "What did you think?" he said, not looking up. "That going back would be cheap?"

Oleg Tsinger writes:

That summer I became close to Grebenshchikov. Igor's wife, Nina, was a marvelous poet. Igor himself declaimed well. Selinov, who loved literature and poetry, always spent evenings with us. The evenings were long, summery, warm. Elena Alexandrovna often joined us. In general we were very happy in that "enchanted garden," as Nina Grebenshchikova called the Buch grounds. Kolyusha did not visit our literary evenings. He kept away from all amusements and diversions and listened to his inner thoughts.

The people closest to the Bison did not understand what was happening to him.

He regarded their amusements from the outside, pretending to be busy, pretending so well that he fooled even Lelka. He was moving further away from them. Something had changed. They, his colleagues, were finding peace and hope, while he was losing those very things. A gap had opened and dark indifference was flooding in.

That first postwar summer was generous with warmth, day and night. Flowers bloomed and filled the air with scent. A multitude of butterflies appeared. Birds sang, warbled, and chirped without cease. Small sounds, long unheard, filled the air, redolent with the scent of grass. The flowering earth rustled, buzzed, and hummed. The juicy verdant foliage hurried to cover the signs of war. People plunged into the sweet, healing peace that helped them forget.

The Bison meanwhile directed, demanded, scolded. He made Selinov the concierge. Seated behind a glass wall, he had to check all visitors, but there were none. He had a phone that didn't work. Everyone sat at his desk and pretended.

Before, everyone knew what to do, didn't need to be nagged, and the Bison did not interfere.

All attempts to learn about Foma were futile. From Mauthausen came rumors of an uprising in which many prisoners had died. The revolt had taken place before the American troops arrived. There were no details, no lists of the dead, but someone allegedly saw Foma killed in the cross fire. They could get no precise information.

Nikolaus Rill soon left to work in the Soviet Union. He was followed by several German workers and their families. Everything took place just as the Bison had predicted.

Finally they came for him. They came late at night. A few days later it was learned that he had been arrested and taken to prison.

Subsequently it was learned that he had been arrested by another Soviet organization which knew nothing about Zavenyagin's orders and plans. They took him in a convoy to Moscow, where he was investigated and tried. He was found guilty of refusing to return to the homeland. End of conversation. The regulations were harsh, the times were heated, no one bothered with scientific achievements and other nuances, everything was clear to the investigator, no need to complicate things. He was sent to a camp with both dirty and clean inmates—former collaborators, deserters, bandits, Vlasovites,* Banderovtsy,† all kinds of men were there.

When Zavenyagin became aware of the situation, his organization could not find the Bison; they may truly have lost his papers, as they later explained. At any rate, it took a year to find him. In early 1947 he was brought back to Moscow and then sent to the Urals. And there he began doing what he had agreed to do with Zavenyagin back in Buch.

---

* In the first two years of the war, at least two million Soviet soldiers, perhaps three million, were taken prisoner. Many of those who joined General A. A. Vlasov's "Russian Liberation Army" were only trying to save themselves from starvation, hoping at a suitable moment to cross over to the Soviet army or to the partisans. After the war, despite official promises that they would not be prosecuted in their native land, prisoners who returned were treated like traitors—ed.
† Ukrainian nationalist leader Stepan Bandera led armed resistance to Soviet authority in the western Ukraine (1947-49); his followers were called Banderovtsy—ed.

25

EXILE IN THE URALS: A NEW MISSION

The lake was blue, the mountains a light shade of blue. Dark green stands of fir descended the rounded slopes. Their peaks glistened in the sun. Deserted sandy beaches stretched along the lake, beyond the village lands. The cottages, lab buildings, warehouses, and garages made up the village, lost in the Urals.

The first few weeks the Bison sat on the balcony, getting used to the peace and quiet. He used a cane when he walked. He could not climb the stairs alone. Lieutenant Shvanyov and Lieutenant Colonel Vereshchagin, who had been assigned there to aid him, half carried him up to the second floor.

"I could put my foot on the step by myself, but it had no lifting power," he recalled.

Doctors told him he needed months to recuperate, but either the southern Urals suited his constitution better than anything else or his own impatience and longing for work urged him, for his strength returned quickly. His head functioned.

"You know this about the mind: the more it works, the better it thinks."

The director came over in the evenings. His name was Alexander Konstantinovich Uralets. The Bison was lucky in his director in the sense that he was a sweetheart. That's probably the most important quality in a director. What the Bison liked best was that Alexander Konstantinovich did not get involved in the work, making corrections and suggestions. Instead, he made a point of figuring out who the Bison was, and once he knew, he trusted him as a specialist.

Elizaveta Nikolayevna Sokurova told me, "Other administrators pretend to understand, use fancy words, but Alexander Konstantinovich was not embarrassed to admit he knew nothing about our work and that he depended on Nikolai Vladimirovich. We had the greatest respect for him because of his admission."

Decades later people still recalled his decency and tact.

With disarming directness he asked the Bison to teach him as much biology as possible. The Bison was overjoyed—he loved inculcating his ideas, enlightening people.

"Well, sugar is sweet all over, and every day I gave a lecture in biology, special genetics, and radiobiology at the blackboard in his fancy director's office. I gave him the essentials. He was a graduate of some economics institute in Kharkov, the kind you attend just for the diploma. He was taught a lot of nonsense, naturally. He listened to my lectures two hours a day for the whole summer. He started a notebook. On Saturdays he showed me his notes and asked for corrections, told me to cross out the garbage."

The Bison did not begrudge him the time. You would think that it was too late to make a scientist out of him. Nevertheless, the Bison stubbornly did his work, never suspecting what it would give him in return.

In the meantime he had to organize his laboratory. There were several labs in his section—radiochemistry, physics, radiobiology of plants, radiobiology of animals, radiology, and some workshops, too. He had to write requisitions for equipment and supplies, build stands, take care of ventilation and electrical wiring, manage, settle, direct. The sweet and healing flow of work and concerns engrossed him more and more. He needed people, both specialists and lab assistants. He suggested hiring his former colleagues from Buch, people with whom he had worked well, who had stayed in the Soviet zone, had trusted him. But where were they? What had happened to them? He had been taken out of Germany a year and a half ago. He had been unable to send a single word back. He did not know what had happened to Lelka, Andrei, whether they were free, whether they had headed to West Germany or over the ocean . . .

Actually Elena Alexandrovna and their son were still in Buch. The foreigners had scattered, some of the assistants had applied for resettlement in the West. Out of a stubborn certainty, Elena did not leave. She regularly sent queries about her husband to Moscow and about her son to Vienna, to the American zone. Friends advised her to take Andrei to Göttingen, to Munich, to Austria, before she was arrested herself. She could also be accused of not returning. The Germans thought there was no hope of a speedy liberation for the Bison, at least not for ten years, if he survived. What was she getting into? Why should she stay here as the wife of a criminal? No one was inviting her to the U.S.S.R., they wouldn't give her permission—what was she waiting for? She could answer none of those questions, nor did she ask them of herself. She sat there implacably, as if he had left her at the train station while he went for tickets. The place emptied around her. Zimmer left. Then Born. They went to the Soviet Union. They were hired as specialists for scientific work.

When they arrived at the Bison's lab in the Urals, he learned that Lelka and Andrei were still in Buch, waiting for him. He calmed down. He had known that Lelka wouldn't leave, but now he knew that they were safe and sound.

He had a staff of specialists, radiologists, chemists, botanists. Naturally, the Bison knew many Germans, with whom he had worked during those years, but there were Russian specialists, too, whom he managed to find, not an easy task in the postwar period. When young Moscow State University graduate Liza Sokurova came to the Urals site, she was unpleasantly surprised by the German she heard spoken in the labs and hallways.

No wonder she was drawn to Nikolai Vladimirovich. Even when he spoke German, it was still Russian. He invited everyone to his lectures. Made them study radiobiology, the biological activity of various rays. Neither the Russians nor the Americans had any significant experience in this. They were seeking knowledge, protection against radioactivity, they were feeling their way; no wonder they overdosed themselves and, despite their precautions, grew sick. They had to learn how to protect themselves.

The work they had been doing in Buch—the biological effects of ionizing rays on living organisms—suddenly, after the explosion of the atomic bomb, took on an ominous urgency.

The Germans from Buch received good apartments and high salaries. The Bison was also moved to a luxurious three-room apartment with a balcony. The ceilings were high, it was sunny, the polished parquet floors shone. He refused the place: what would he do alone in all that space? Then A. K. Uralets asked: wouldn't he like to call for his wife? They had a job for her, too—scientific assistant at the lab. They had permission from the Council of Ministers (in those days, relatives could not work at the same lab). Their son, Andrei, could study at Sverdlovsk University, finish his education. Andrei was then studying at Berlin University.

So Uralets sent Elena Alexandrovna an official invitation.

They arrived in August, Lelka and Andrei. All three were together again. The war was over for them. They were together, and not just anywhere, but in their homeland. It had all happened in one fell swoop: the end of their separation, they had found each other, they were alive and well, they were doing work that was interesting and necessary, it was their work, which they had started back in the twenties, and the conditions were excellent for the times: good food, they got clothes and shoes—what else could they want? They considered themselves lucky.

Despite the difficulties of the new project and their separation from the "outside world," the work went well. It was Work, the significance of which was appreciated by the lowliest bottle washer: they were looking for ways to clean rivers and lakes after a nuclear fallout, studying the effects of radiation. They had to find methods to protect the living. Their humane mission inspired all the various people gathered at the site.

Sometimes, of course, there were disagreements and arguments. Liza Sokurova was working with fern spores. A young specialist, she wanted to better understand the meaning of her work. She asked her supervisor, Dr. Menke. He raised his eyebrows and replied with surprise, "It doesn't matter for you. You are a senior lab assistant and must obey my orders. Don't worry about what we're doing."

Surely Menke was not a bad scientist and perhaps she should have tried to find a way to talk to him, but for her, a Komsomol member, then, in 1949, he was offensive. What right did those Germans have to behave that way! You'd think that they weren't working for Russians, but the other way around. She did not want to work for a German supervisor anymore. She rushed to the Bison, who coolly replied, "Establish your own working relationships."

Nevertheless, she began attending his seminars. He gave her permission.

The Bison talked about miracles in his seminars: weak radiation stimulated growth. This contradicted the "hit principle" that they had discovered. At first he had mocked his colleagues and berated them for messy work.

Made them redo it. They did, and once more they got stimulation instead of damage. Strange, wondered the Bison, this shouldn't be. They thought, discussed, couldn't come to agreement. They got stimulation every time they tried, especially with legumes. And suddenly, the way it happens, that lucky suddenly, he understood what it meant and everyone else gasped at its simplicity. From that moment on they began a fascinating cycle of work on the stimulation of plants through weak doses of radiation.

Liza Sokurova had never encountered seminars like this at Moscow State University.

The Bison was understanding the solution of the problem along with everyone else, he had no special benefits. Neither prestige nor authority could help here. Yesterday's victories meant nothing. You had to win today. Every time it was only today that mattered.

In August 1948 the infamous session took place at the Academy of Agricultural Sciences (VASKhNIL), at which all of Lysenko's opponents were smashed and denounced; many had to give up their work. Biologists who did not share Lysenko's views were shunted aside from teaching, some were fired. The wave reached Timofeyev's lab in the Urals only a year later. A resolution was passed: destroy the fruit flies and not a whisper of Morganism-Mendelism. But here the Bison's educational efforts paid off. Uralets called him in and said, "You are not used to our ways, Nikolai Vladimirovich, and that's why I want to talk to you separately. Go on with your work, your genetics, but make sure that none of the reports and plans you've been accustomed to signing have even a hint of genetics or fruit flies in them."

"You mean cheat?"

"No, don't put it that way. Remember, you drink the water of the river you're sailing on."

Even the little the Bison had taught him was enough for Uralets to see the flaws in Lysenko's theories. He managed to separate genetics from Lysenkoism, to evaluate real science, and to make a rather risky decision, especially for one in his position.

"We set up tons of fruit fly experiments," the Bison told me. "We couldn't publish anything. The Americans published data from their atomic sites, but we didn't publish a thing. We were first, before the Americans, to study the complex generators for separating radioisotopes from the human organism. We worked on the biological cleansing of radioisotopes from water. We had dozens of reports prepared, but unpublished, on the water problem alone!"

During all this time the Bison did not officially exist. No biologist abroad or at home knew where he was, whether he had survived the war, or what had happened to him. Those were the conditions of his work at the laboratory. But one day he needed some Drosophila cultures. He sent Senior Lieutenant Shvanyov to Moscow, to the genetics lab of the Academy of Sciences. This was before the August 1948 session of the Academy of Agricultural Sciences; after that there were no fruit flies to be had anywhere. The Bison gave the lieutenant a list, telling him which strain of Drosophila to get from which lab. Naturally, he didn't sign the list, didn't even initial it. But the list was enough for Moscow's geneticists to understand who was working in the Urals. Several people with whom he had corresponded from Germany had recognized his handwriting.

The word spread quickly—Kolyusha was alive!

They solved a number of problems in biological protection. They eliminated radioactive isotopes left in the body by introducing complexons, elements that bound with the isotopes.

Zimmer, whom the Bison considered to be the best dosage specialist in the world, had organized a marvelous physics lab with a powerful cobalt gamma ray accelerator housed in a huge well. With Zimmer's aid, they developed comparative dosages for various ionizing rays, thanks to which they could work on experiments with fruit flies, bacteria, yeasts, and plants and could study the effects of various doses. Koch, Born, and Likhtin, all the Germans the Bison had persuaded to come to work in the Urals, worked the way they had at home, with all their hearts.

They were happy in that preserve. They almost didn't miss the "outside world." The Urals lab was perhaps the only place in the U.S.S.R. that was protected from Lysenko's terror, a place where scientific genetics remained alive. The Bison was lucky. Who knows what stupid things he might have done had it not been for the restraining hand of Alexander Konstantinovich Uralets?

"And also Zavenyagin," the Bison added, always returning to this man. "He really helped. There were many good men around him and relatively few bastards. That's what was so special about him. Zavenyagin was not only a sweetheart, but a wonderful, direct man."

Mother Nature had endowed the Bison not only with talent but also with good luck. No one knows exactly what this is, but it definitely exists in science. I knew a lab worker whose equipment kept breaking; it worked for other people, but burned or cracked for him. And you couldn't say that he was clumsy or ignorant; nothing of the sort. He could tiptoe up to a piece of equipment, plug it in carefully, and nevertheless it would short-circuit or crack. Others with bad luck will get into an accident whenever they take a taxi; they buy a book with missing pages or get a burnt matchstick in their mashed potatoes in a cafeteria. It's hard to scare off bad luck, it's pointless to fight it, that would be like fighting the absence of an ear for music. If bad luck is combined with talent, it ruthlessly cheats the poor wretch. Two or three years of work, interesting results, a pattern is discovered, and wham! there's an article in the latest journal about your discovery written by some New Zealander, Ashkhabadian, or Moroccan. They'll steal it out from under your nose and you'll never get the credit.

But when talent and good luck are combined, that's glorious. I suspect that luck is one of the qualities of great talent; it can raise such people almost to the level of genius.

Often people with good luck have a superstitious belief that those who work have luck, that success likes the patient, and so on. Yes, but not completely. A lucky man can make do with anything; as the folk saying goes, even his roosters lay eggs.

The Bison always had luck and nothing could separate him from it.

You would think that being sent into exile in the Urals after the camps, being isolated from academic and institutional scientific life, would be bad, but what happened? After the session at the Academy of Agricultural Sciences, Lysenko and his proponents destroyed genetics, and major biologists who would not give up genetic work were deprived of their labs and university chairs, while the Bison blithely went on working with his fruit flies in an out-of-the-way spot. In those years the very word "Drosophila" began to have a criminal sound. People who worked with Drosophila were saboteurs, Fascists, a threat to Soviet life. The weekly magazine *Ogonyok* published an article entitled "Fly Lovers–Man Haters." Fruit flies were made illegal. Anti-Lysenkoists were depicted in the white robes of the Ku Klux Klan. If the Bison had returned to Moscow in those years, with his hot temper he would have definitely engaged in battle and it would have ended up irreparably badly for him, as it had for several other scientists. But fate hid him away in a spot where he could remain himself—probably the most important condition for his existence. In that sense, he had always been lucky. Conditions made way for his nature.

Science was in luck, too. The Bison managed to move ahead in a new direction. His team studied the paths of radioisotopes in plants and animals, both in water and on land. Here is a polluted river, to which they add isotopes. How do they distribute themselves among the plants and soils, how do they migrate? The team studied the mortality rates of organisms under various doses of ionizing rays.

They had to work with radioisotopes having a decay period of several hours. "By the time you got them, going through all the secret offices, you had only an instant left before they fell apart!"

Elena Alexandrovna worked on determining the coefficient of the accumulation of various isotopes in seventy-five species of freshwater animals and plants.

The luck lay in the fact that his work dealt with a most pressing problem. Nuclear weapons, reactors, power stations had been built, and the whole world was working with radioactivity. Protection of the environment, of life, of man himself, was an issue that appeared for the first time in science. Even senior physicists could not fully picture the safety measures that would be needed when using radioactive elements; junior personnel even less so. An elderly woman worked as an assistant to Sokurova. Before letting her wash the cups that had held radioactive materials, Elizaveta instructed her thoroughly: wear double gloves, then wash them, check them with the Geiger counter. Once she saw her washing the cups with her bare hands.

"What are you doing?"

"I've already washed them like that, without gloves, and nothing has happened to me, so you can stop shouting at me."

All the assistants and all the workers got exposed. Sokurova's husband, a specialist in doses, and Nikolai Vladimirovich and his son Andrei were also exposed. It was hard to stay clean working with that little-known stuff.

But in getting exposed, they developed measures of protection, measures of cleaning up, limits, standards, for future generations. It was the leading edge of biology in those years, reconnaissance in battle.

If I were making up the Bison's story, I would have him an embittered man after his release from the camps. The reasoning would go something like this. Zavenyagin had promised him a rosy future, and instead he was seized, sent off, he almost died. For what? For not going to the West, for talking his colleagues into staying? That's why they put him away? I would have him working in the Urals, of course, just the way he did work, at full speed, he couldn't work any other way, just like his Germans. None of them could work badly or even in mediocre fashion. But within he would be burning with outrage. That is the first thing that would come to my mind.

Usually, though, it's better to discard the first thing that comes to your pen. My starting point was that the Bison had been insulted. He had to respond in some way. For instance, with haughtiness: aha, you can't manage without me! Or with aloofness: avoid all and sundry. If that's the way they welcomed him in the homeland, if they made him a criminal and wouldn't shake hands with him, then he didn't need any of them. Different versions begged to be used, especially since the Germans mocked him: you persuaded us, and look how they treated you! You get sent to the camps for your efforts! They sympathized and laughed.

And then, everything that happened in the camps had to have left a trace. He had to have changed!

As soon as the Bison's character came out onto the plains of my imagination, he began pulling all sorts of tricks. He could take up drink, escape, get religion, become a cynic, become a careerist (he could offer his services to Lysenko for that).

What actually happened is what I could not guess, the only step I could not imagine: the Bison did not change at all. The most incredible variant for me and the most natural one for him. In his relations with the Germans, his co-workers, and his family, his trumpet voice still blared, his lower lip still trembled in anger and in laughter. He was just as fierce, just as relaxed, just as engrossed and enticing. He didn't grow bitter, he didn't give up, he didn't grow angry. His nature was unshakable. He recalled his camp life with a chuckle, as if it were one of the amusing episodes of his biography.

Real life differs from fiction in that you really can never guess which way it will turn. There was no turn in his life at all. It continued moving in the same direction. Straight and unswervable. Not responding to outrages. Was it inertia? The stability of fine metal? I couldn't figure it out. On the one hand, it seemed simple: he stayed the same. What was mysterious about that? The mystery is that he stayed the same, didn't give in either to the demons or to the angels that were cleaving his soul in two. A person in comfortable circumstances has the luxury of being moral. But try to hold on to your morality when you're in trouble, try to be just as responsive and life-loving as you were when you were happy. The Bison returned more than once to a conversation that took place in his cell, a conversation about not dying a shameful death. Whether we're afraid of death or despise it, whether we think about it or not, we are still going to die. We have to be prepared for it always, which means that we have to try to keep our conscience clean. Death is horrible when you die in shame for the years you spent on vain pursuits, chasing after fame and riches. There is no satisfaction, there is nothing left at the moment of death, nothing to hold on to, everything is dust . . .

His thoughts boiled down to the need to think about death. To check your conscience against the thought of the hour of death.

The difficulty lay in the fact that he did not know how things worked in the Soviet Union and he couldn't adjust to them. He didn't see the point in meetings, in public work, in "socialist competition," in everything that set our methods apart from the German. Speaking frankly, he didn't want to adjust. He remained a white crow and was therefore always under some suspicion. But he attracted attention, especially from young people. Don't think that the laboratory could isolate him totally from what was happening in the country. Liza Sokurova, for instance, was assigned to teach Lysenko's progressive line, as a political assignment. She was very worried how the Bison would take it, that he might think she said the opposite of what he said behind his back. She decided to invite him to these lessons. He came, listened a bit, and dashed out, angrily. He thought she was trying to reeducate him. It was useless trying to explain about assignments and duties. He was that way in everything. Often he demanded: "Why are articles in scientific journals criticized anonymously? Why do I have to make promises when I'll do all I can anyway, without them? Why can't I buy reactor agents in the store with my own money and then be reimbursed?"

His naïveté amused some and worried others.

D., who worked at the Urals lab with him, recalled that the Bison alluded to Malthus in his lectures on Darwin: Malthus had calculated this and said that. "Malthusianism" was a dirty word for them then, and they listened to the Bison in horror.

One day one of the physicists had to check something in microbiology. The Bison referred him to Sokurova.

"Ask Elizaveta, she's our microbiologist, she should know."

Sukorova didn't know. She admitted it. The Bison said with furious seriousness, "Look, Elizaveta Nikolayevna, why don't you go back to Moscow, to the university, and demand your money back since they haven't taught you a thing!"

What money? Education is free in the Soviet Union. That didn't interest him. Everyone, including poor Liza, understood that that wasn't his point.

Things like that happened much later, at the Miassovo biostation and in Obninsk. He was capable of roaring, shaking a document sent down from above:

"What does it mean to turn in a scientific work by December thirtieth? And what if I turn it in on January second, does that mean the plan hasn't been met? What does that have to do with science? What the hell does it have to do with scientific work? Oh no, that isn't scientific work, it's paper-excreting!"

He made it sound crude and vulgar.

26

A FAITHFUL
ENEMY

I had heard a lot about D. from many people. They always said bad things about him, his conspiring and his nasty tricks, all directed against the Bison. For decades, year in and year out, he acted vilely toward the Bison, his teacher, mentor, and boss. He wouldn't let up, he persecuted him. The stories depicted a lifelong ill-wisher—more than that, an enemy, a persistent, fierce enemy locked in a blood feud. His hostility was expressed in constant bites, big and small; apparently this man's petty soul found solace only in attacking the Bison.

For what purpose? Opinions diverged here. No one knew with certainty why this D. persecuted the Bison so long and so stubbornly.

Their hostility was not mutual. I never heard anything bad about D. from the Bison. It looked as if the Bison simply avoided talking about him, as if he didn't affect him. But he created enough trouble as it was.

How did it begin? Some considered the starting point to be an incident that took place in the early fifties, at the lab in the Urals.

D. was a junior assistant there, a chemist. He had appeared under dramatic, one might even say romantic, circumstances. During the war, as a teenager he ended up in Bessarabia, met a beauty, and lived on her estate until Soviet troops arrived and tried him for draft dodging. Later he was rehabilitated. But before that, the incarcerated dropout from Kharkov University decided to put his mind to getting out of the camps, drawing attention to himself, demonstrating his usefulness. He was assisted by the same thing that had helped the Bison, work relating to biological defense against nuclear radiation. He was sent to work in the Bison's lab, where he had to live up to his promises. Surprisingly, he did so faster than anyone had imagined he would. He picked things up quickly. He had an excellent memory and a facility for languages. He was soon speaking German with the Germans, and he could read English and French. He got his candidate of sciences degree in a year and then proceeded to more advanced work. The Bison entrusted him to do an independent study.

D. blossomed in the atmosphere of trust and sympathy. He became sociable and witty. He knew poetry, even wrote his own. He read aloud readily from Tsvetayeva, Mandelstam, Khodasevich, then little known. He wrote satirical skits. He sang. Women nurtured the talented youth and predicted a brilliant future for him. He began to believe in himself. It wasn't that easy to stand out among that handpicked team of major scientists, where your reputation was not determined by the boss's attitude toward you, by your speeches, or by your curriculum vitae. Here the decisive factor was your work, how quick-witted you were and how well you worked. That was the situation at all atomic sites in those days. Deadlines and necessities dictated everything. Daily demands selected the best and cut out the mediocre. D. held his own in that race, which meant he was extraordinary, and this coincided with his own opinion of himself.

Once—no one remembers the circumstances now—the Bison blew up and publicly berated him: "Just think, so many gifts and not a single talent! Flash!" D. was stunned. His pride was injured and by the man whom he idolized and imitated, the highest authority, the Supreme Judge, the only one whose opinion was worth anything. If the Bison had called him an ignoramus, a show-off, anything at all, he would have forgiven him. But instead the Bison hit his sore spot, something deep down, personal and unconscious, and he made it public. He formulated the problem. There are unconscious things that need only be verbalized to take over your life. From that moment on, D. applied the formula to his every failure and mistake. The Bison had made him feel inferior. The pain of a blow eventually passes. But this pain did not go away, it became morbid. What if he really had no talent, the talent needed to do serious work in science? He could not escape that fear. The Bison was behind every failure, mistake, and problem in his life.

That is the general picture of his hostility.

The only way D. could get away from it was to dethrone the Bison. Tear off his halo, prove there was nothing to his fame. He was just a blowhard, no genius at all.

These were the explanations given to me.

But is one sentence enough to start a Thirty Years' War? It had lasted almost three decades. And if one sentence was enough, then how inflamed an ego must you have? Something wasn't right here. The sentence was just an excuse, for such stubborn hostility can develop only on inner antagonism, the hostility has to feed on something.

Then I learned facts that did not fit this version.

When the laboratory was shut down, the Germans were generously paid and allowed to go home, which astonished them, since they thought they would have to work much longer for the conquerors. The Soviet scientists were relocated. The Bison was sent to the Urals branch of the Academy of Sciences and he was allowed to choose his group. Among others, he selected D.

A. K. Uralets tried to dissuade him. He made it clear that D. was not simply hostile but had actively slandered him, shamelessly. That seems clear enough. But the Bison refused to understand. He's a dangerous man, they told him, dangerous. Proximity can lead to unpleasant consequences. The Bison laughed it off good-naturedly. One of the people in personnel broke the rules and showed him a report written in D.'s hand. It was a collection of the Bison's careless statements, ambiguous words and phrases. They were annotated. The personnel man put it in the Bison's hands disdainfully. Read that!

The Bison read it, moving his loupe over the lines.

"You don't make an enemy without nurturing and feeding him. You didn't pay any attention to this scribbling. Others won't either, I would hope. And he's a good worker."

The personnel man shrugged, what could he do with that simpleton? Now his hope was that D. would refuse: why would he want to be under the whip of a hated boss when there were other places and other opportunities?

However, and I felt this was important, D. did not refuse, he followed the Bison to a new job in Miassovo.

He knew that the Bison knew about his denunciations, everyone knew about them, yet he wasn't afraid to take him; therefore, the Bison did not consider him a threat. That hurt even more.

Knowing the facts, I could not put these two people together; nothing worked, they were incompatible by all parameters. At least, D. should not have wanted to follow the Bison. After the Urals lab, after Miassovo, they went to Obninsk, in Siberia. D. accompanied the Bison almost until the latter's death. Was he persecuting him? But why? You would think: get away from him, if he bothers you so much. Why did D. hate the Bison so much and, hating him, nonetheless follow?

The phenomenon of D. meant that you could not love the Bison, though you could hate him. That was a revelation for me.

I decided to meet with D. Especially since he was one of the few who had known the Bison long and well in his work and in life after the war.

People tried to talk me out of it. They warned me that he would sling mud and lies and try to mix me up.

The more I was warned, the more I wanted to meet D.

I remember Konstantin Leontiev's book on the novels of Leo Tolstoy.* Sarcastically, with killing detail, Leontiev takes apart the language and style of *Anna Karenina* and *War and Peace*. He gives Tolstoy his due and then mocks him mercilessly, without any respect. I had never read anything like it about Tolstoy in my life. I felt a thrill of fear and curiosity. Leontiev's hostile eye was sharp. I was stunned that Tolstoy could have flaws, weaknesses, that one didn't have to bow before him. Much of what I had read about Tolstoy before had been saccharine in its praise. I suddenly felt that my love had needed this nasty appraisal from someone else. It had come in handy, it had taken nothing away from my feelings for Tolstoy; on the contrary, it had added depth to them.

It wasn't easy to talk D. into a meeting. Naturally, he knew that I wanted to write about him, that I would write no matter whether he met with me or not, since he couldn't be left out of the Bison's story. He knew that he was the negative hero, but to what extent? He was not sure just what I knew. He kept putting me off, citing poor health.

"I need to hear from you what no one else can say," I cajoled. "Bad, critical, ironic, whatever you feel necessary."

"Let's call it the truth," he said. "The objective truth. The crude bread of truth. You've been getting nothing but pastries from adorers. Well, if it's in the name of truth, all right. That's what we do, you and I—serve the truth. Our profession even more than yours."

* *On the novels of L. N. Tolstoy: Analysis, Style, and Drift* (1890, published in 1911)—ed.

Had it not been for the high heels on his shoes, he would have been quite short. A narrow, nervous face, thinning hair coquettishly combed forward like bangs. Gray, darting eyes. In the stories I had heard, he was young, brilliant, powerful, and smart. Here I saw an elderly gentleman, fragile and dried up—nothing evil or dangerous about him. I had wanted him to resemble Grushnitsky, whom I had hated since childhood. Or Salieri. Or Mephistopheles. I had prepared myself for a character like Smerdyakov or Uriah Heep—treacherous, satanic, in keeping with his role.

Can you recognize a villain? That would be nice. But Satan and the devil come to us with worn faces, horns hidden beneath their hats, shaggy tail tucked into velvet tousers. Friendly. No sulphurous fumes. A series of smiles and you don't notice the smell of singed fur.

D. radiated friendliness and began with light, meaningless banter. When I moved on to the point, he settled down in his chair more comfortably, clasped his fingers, and stared at me with a vague smile. Then in brief phrases he set out the terms of a possible deal. He was prepared to help on condition that another person was depicted instead of him. A certain Mr. X. And that the circumstances be unrecognizable. Only that way. The more it's "not him," the easier it would be for him to open up. The more "not him," the more it would be "him." Otherwise it would be hard to be honest. The writer wanted to know private, secret things. Who would be willing to strip, to show his ulcers? It's easier when it's someone else.

I didn't understand how it could be done: everyone else would be real and suddenly one person would be fictional?

Not fictional, D. insisted, on the contrary, he would be more real than the rest, just given another name. Did it matter to the reader? And since the hero would be fictionalized, why not change the work to pure fiction anyway? The author would feel freer and no one could complain about anything.

Apparently D. had planned this conversation, I didn't know how far ahead. I defended myself uncertainly. I had been yearning to yield to the temptation to break out of the fetters of facts, dates, addresses. What was stopping me? Just that I wanted to talk about the man I had known and loved. About him, and no one else.

"Then make me up," he said with a smile. "You'll have to make things up about me anyway if I don't cooperate."

He was right, I had no way out. But I said, "I won't make things up. I have enough with what people told me about you."

His mouse-gray eyes scurried over me and hid in a squint. "Have they told you a lot?"

"A lot."

He depended on me, and I on him. Who would win?

"Maybe it would be better for us to make up? Like Faust and Mephistopheles?" he said gently. "Remember, you'll gain more in this hour than you could get in a year's work."

Perhaps he was right. I agreed to call him N. No, he insisted, not N. Let's give him a name, say Demochkin, Makar Yevgenyevich Demochkin, so that people would stop to think, to guess who he was. Let's create a Demochkin, who can carry all the opposition and hostility.

He began by telling me that Demochkin was in a bad position: all the facts were against him, the author was prejudiced; however, let's not make him a blatant villain. Let's imagine a man for whom everything went wrong, unjustly. A bad record, no pardons or mentors. The starting position was terrible. The only thing to do was struggle like the mouse that fell in the pitcher of cream and struggled so hard it churned up butter and got out. The best years of his life were spent doing that.

I tried to return him to the Bison, but he couldn't leave Demochkin. Apparently, Demochkin was close to his heart. He wouldn't have talked about himself, author of this and that, vice president, editor in chief, chief consultant, in a word, a Chief, like that, but poor Demochkin, green and untried, came out too soon with his own ideas. Naturally, the Bison didn't like it.

"Before that, life was one sweet *bonjour* for him."

As he said it, I chuckled, hearing the familiar expression. I shouldn't have done it. He grew wary and gave me an unforgiving look. But he went on as if nothing had happened. He talked, making ironic jokes about himself, and told me a parable about an old scientist jealous of his talented student, not letting him move ahead, mocking his ideas. He cut him down when he was going full speed.

"Power is disgusting, like the hands of a barber," he cited, and glanced at me, checking.

I knew Mandelstam's line and nodded, confirming his erudition and mine.

"But he had so many grateful students."

"Oh, he was a good teacher. Lots of boys in short pants frolicked around him, it's a harmless age, but I had cut my teeth. I wouldn't let him hurt me."

They soon blended, the person I knew from stories and the one I got from Makar Demochkin.

He felt sorry for the young talented fellow making his way in the world. It's an ancient, banal situation, it can be regarded without anger, with forgiveness.

"Live another quarter century, nothing will change, there is no way out," he recited. "A quarter century was an eternity for Blok, but we've hopped through three decades and talk about it as if it were yesterday."

"Why is it past? Your relationship continued. And developed, probably."

"Over thirty years? 'Probably'? And how." He laughed at me. "We traveled a long path, from resistance to confrontation. And beyond."

"I don't understand."

He nodded in satisfaction.

"You see, a great man must have a great opponent. For his adversary he chose the modest person of Demochkin. So in one sense he valued Demochkin highly. A genius can't fight with the shadow of an ass. He needed a worthy opponent."

"Then, do you see Demochkin as a genius?"

"A failed genius," he said calmly and seriously. "Because of him."

"Well, then, let's accept that for now. What did he do to him later? Why? Did he give him cause?"

"He did."

"There."

"You keep wanting to simplify things. You're taking only part of a phenomenon, but it began because he made him do it, he made Demochkin bad."

"He made him?"

"A bad man, say a villain, you have to become one. It's an achievement. Instead of bad men we just have small-time crumbs."

"You say he's a villain?"

"From his point of view. Actually it's more complicated than that. Is it worth explaining?"

"Yes."

He shrugged and obeyed. "Let's take the words about bad man and crumbs. People think those are his words. He got the phrase from me. He turned it into an effective flowery phrase. And then I was told that I was repeating him. That happened often. Others imitated him with delight. As for me, I had dealt with him up close. His closest associate. His speech, intonations, phrases oppressed me. Everyone repeated his favorites: 'That's not just beetle shit,' 'soul-saving,' 'up-to-now experiments' . . ."

"All sweet *bonjour!*" I added.

"You noticed? That, too. And his gestures and manner of speech. His voice was a trumpet, ever at extreme pitch. Full of temperament. You could never be calm around him. The most upright, reasonable citizens grew agitated. They'd shout and wave their arms about. Once a girl I was dating said to me, 'Could you talk to me normally, in your own voice?' I suddenly realized that I was imitating him. I didn't exist. He was with her instead of me. I thought the same way, I had the same prejudices. I insisted that Raphael was interested only in beauty, that correlation wasn't a cause and effect, that a coincidence was an incidence of cows, and other nonsense, stepping in each of his footsteps. Whatever independent thoughts I had, I voluntarily turned into a continuation of his views. I was losing myself. My uniqueness. He subjugated me more and more. It was becoming unbearable. You might say that's only external. No, it affected my thoughts, he got his feelers into my brain. I tried to rebel. I'd try to argue, he'd shout, grab my unripe, green thought, yank it out, stomp on it, prove that it was absolutely wrong, laugh at it, and leave a burned spot behind. No way back, just smoke and stink. I was a shadow, I was a copy. What is valuable in a copy? Its closeness to the original. The less it differs, the better. That means: no originality."

He wasn't upset, he didn't raise his voice. Sweetly and modestly he offered me a few corrections for my portrait of the Bison, adding individual strokes. Not about others, just about himself.

"I saw that I had to fight to retain my precious personality. Otherwise I wouldn't find these skeletons. A scientist's personality is first and foremost free thought. Independent spirit. I had to get free. But how? Leave? There was no possibility of that then. And you can't leave yourself, anyway. Push away, that was liberation. Overcome the power of attraction. In that struggle

183

for freedom I understood that I couldn't win if I loved and obeyed him. Anger helped me push away. Like a jet rocket. It took me a while to get there, growing fiercer in my struggle. I pushed away, once, twice, he fought back, my face was bloodied, it was fine. There's your answer on how to make a villain. I began looking for flaws in him. I saw that he had only approximate knowledge of physics and was weak in mathematics, worse than me. But he didn't admit it. I would trip him up. Do you know what tormented me the most? That he managed, nevertheless. For instance, he didn't know math well, but he said things and they worked. I saw that they shouldn't, but they did. Despite everything! He made me look like a jerk every time. I knew that my mind was no worse than his, but I couldn't pull it off, at the last moment I would blow it while he succeeded. How I hated him!"

"But he wasn't the one who kept you from succeeding."

"Yes, he was," D. said, controlling his voice. "People were always juxtaposing us, both in his circle and in mine. I understand why you laughed, how dare I compare myself, but my opinion of myself helped."

"It sounds like envy to me."

"Envy? That explains some of it. But not everything. Besides envy there was injustice. It gnawed at me. Why did he get everything, the full bag: background, physique, voice, strength, height? Everything worked in his favor. If I had been mediocre, I wouldn't have struggled. I would have accepted it and been happy. Others followed him blindly and were rewarded. I struggled. We don't know how to respect a man if we don't fully share his opinions."

"Depends on the opinions."

He thought about my answer. It made him wary, I must have spoken too soon. I had to be more patient.

"Take Lysenkoism, for instance," I said.

"You mean in terms of pseudo-science?" Demochkin asked. "But there's a paradox there. Lysenko was a fanatic. He believed in his idea. He couldn't force real scientists to give up their faith, they would have burned at the stake first. And I think that Lysenko would have gone to the stake for his false idea. He was convinced, that's why he promised quick successes. That was his strength. He was convinced that you could change heredity by upbringing. That's why they followed him. They sensed his faith. Wait, let's be calm, unemotional, scientific. Can false ideas have their adepts? Lysenko could have believed in his prophecies the way Savonarola believed in his and gone to the stake without repenting."

He jumped up, paced the hotel room, stepping with a soft, catlike tread. From the far corner he looked at me through his fingers forming a tube like a telescope. He was much more casual and relaxed than I, mincing no words, at ease, as if he had thrown off a heavy coat.

"But there is a difference," I said.

"What?"

"An essential one. Can't you see? You're putting real scientists together with . . ."

"Let's drop the opportunists. But the ones who were mistaken were subjectively no different. Both sides were convinced."

"Yet for all that, Vavilov would never allow himself to use illegal blows in a fight, whereas Lysenko did."

From the start there had been something else lying between us, rolled up into a ball, hiding its claws. Now it opened its tiger-yellow eyes.

"Vavilov fought honestly," I repeated, "and so did the Bison."

"He had no power."

"You can do it without power, too . . ."

I didn't finish. I waited. Demochkin came back to his armchair, sat down, and crossed his legs. He waited, too.

"Would you like some coffee?" I asked, breaking the silence.

In boxing it's called taking the punch. He took it.

"I wouldn't refuse."

While I made coffee, he continued about the struggle for his ego through hostility, which spoiled Demochkin at the same time. It made him worse than he was, developed the baseness that can be elicited in every person.

"And you didn't care about the means," I said, handing him a cup.

"Remember, we were taught: if the enemy doesn't give up, destroy him. They attributed the words to Gorky. Though it doesn't seem like him . . . But then I believed that any means were good against the enemy."

"Any?"

He said reluctantly, "We saw things differently then. What was allowed and what wasn't—it was all different. Now people kiss in public, on escalators . . ."

He sipped the coffee and smiled disarmingly. "I know what you're talking about."

And so we reached the barrier. The thing that had been between us all along unsheathed its claws and got ready.

"Try to be objective. You want to accuse me, but if you were going to justify me, you would put it differently, you'd say, Demochkin was right, he was defending the greatest value in the world–his personality. Others lost it, turned into ants, but he used whatever he could to protect himself . . ."

"Good Lord! What are you talking about!" I shouted. "How can you justify yourself! You wanted to destroy him, you wrote denunciations . . ."

He raised a hand to stop me.

"Wait. I thought we could talk calmly, without insults. What do you want–to understand Demochkin or to condemn him? Obviously, learn about him. And I'm not as interesting to you as your hero. You want to justify him and glorify him. I'm a curious exception to you because I was against him. I've told you why."

"Your version doesn't work. If you were protecting your unique soul, why did you have to destroy him? You wanted him destroyed actually. Not figuratively. Gorky has nothing to do with it. And anyway, Gorky was talking about class enemies, not personal ones."

He laughed in a friendly way. "A point in your favor."

Then he finished the coffee, wiped his lips with his handkerchief, and his face darkened, wrinkled.

"Let's look at the situation another way. Forty years have passed, and a certain Archivist comes to the old, respected scientist Demochkin and asks: Aren't you the one, dear fellow, who rose up against your Teacher? Do you understand that you did wrong? I understand, says the Student, I really lost, I see how great the one I attacked was . . . Oh, if I had known at that bloody moment what I had raised my hand against! . . . Pangs of guilt rose to the surface from the bottom of his soul, where they had lain buried forever . . . Admit it, says the Archivist, you wanted to kill the Teacher, we have the facts. What is it to you? the Student asks. We would like it better if you had done it out of envy, the Archivist responds. I know it's ugly, the Student replies, but what can I do? He weeps. I did envy him, I did. I confess!

"And do you know what happened after the Student wept? He wiped his tears and said, I'm not going to repent! Why should I? I'm ostracized by the other students–in other words, I am distinguished. They all try to figure out why I fought with the Teacher, how did I dare? If I repent, I'll be part of the herd, no one will wonder about me. This way, people will always be interested in me, the enemy of Himself! His main enemy! Say what you will, but great villains are famous. Herostratus, Malyuta Skuratov,* and so on. Judas is remembered more than the other apostles."

"Did Demochkin convince the Archivist?"

"The Archivist had a large dossier. There was everything about the Student in there—letters, applications, reports, old conversations, meetings. Things he had long forgotten. I'd give a lot to read that file. I'd read it and weep, but not repent. The Archivist wanted repentance, of course, the way all the literary villains repent. Maybe that's the way things were in the past. I've never seen anything like it myself. No one ever repented that way to me. Though they should have. They condemned me unfairly. I've never seen someone come out, if not in a public square then at least on a stage, and say, 'Comrades, judge me ruthlessly, I calumniated an innocent man . . .' I've never seen that, have you?"

He came over, hands in pockets, and leaned over me. "Have you?"

"No."

"Then what do you want from me? We're surrounded by the unrepentant. They drive their wives into the grave, steal, lie . . . And they live well, sleep soundly. Then why pick on the Student? Repentance is convenient for keepers of the law, for lazy investigators. Oh yes, the conscience . . ." Demochkin looked at me. "But why do we always appeal to the conscience? What does it have to do with it, anyway? The Student wasn't a killer."

"He wanted to kill."

"Wanted. That's not punishable. Have you never wanted to kill anyone? Since the Student won't repent, let's imagine that he is a villain through and through. Since we want to close the case. That's the goal here. Otherwise you won't be able to erect a monument to the Teacher. It won't be steady."

His half smile was triumphant. I gave into it, smiled, and said, "There is no philosophy that a smart man could not justify. Your Student would deserve sympathy if he were a real personality, and not an ant. Conscience

* One of Ivan the Terrible's chief *oprichniki,* the tsar's personal military contingent, dreaded for its cruelty in enforcing Ivan's rule over the *oprichnina,* lands set apart under his personal dominion. Skuratov was himself executed by Ivan in 1570—ed.

has to do the work of repentance. Conscience is the privilege of a real person. The fact that many don't repent doesn't mean anything. That's the behavior of ants. An ant isn't a person, it's an organ, not an organism. He fulfills a function, and no more."

"Then you think the Student was an ant?" A mean glint came into his eye. "But he was the best Student. Understand? The best! Even though he didn't get the credit. They kept him in the shadows."

"It's hard being an unrecognized genius."

"The woman he fell in love with"–Demochkin spoke louder, not listening– "also respected the Teacher. At a party when the Student asked her to dance, she waved him away, engrossed in the Teacher's story. She was pleased by his praise. If the Teacher said what I always said, she was delighted. She didn't hear me."

"But perhaps the Student never was a genius. He just had a complex."

Demochkin shook his finger negatively.

"It won't work! Only the select feel they are geniuses. Mayakovsky called himself a genius before he was recognized as one. A small poet won't declare himself a genius. He won't have the nerve . . . The Student could have been great, everyone thought so."

"The Bison didn't consider himself a genius."

"He didn't need to. He was recognized."

"No, he wasn't. You know perfectly well that he wasn't recognized. They wouldn't make him an academician. But he didn't suffer over it. Chekhov sincerely believed that he would be read for eight years, no more. But Salieri, he considered himself a genius."

He shrugged.

"Perhaps the Teacher even laughed at the Student in front of the woman. Mocked his pretensions."

It was as if he had blown ashes from coals, the heat flared, and reddish reflection crossed his pale yellow face.

"If not for him . . . I would have . . . I achieved much anyway. Despite everything, I did," he repeated, pounding the thought into me. "So I forgave him!"

"Oh, you forgave him? That's a switch!"

"It was harder for me to forgive him. I hated and loved him simultaneously. He was what I could have become. Understand?" He bent toward me and added softly, "If he had disappeared. I loved him as an enemy. Because I had no enemy more worthy or significant. Love thine enemies, for if you love those who love you, what does that require? . . . Still, I did not become like him. Isn't that right?" He looked into my eyes. "And I'm not like all his fans. You see, I defended myself."

"The question is at what price," I said. "You say you defended yourself. And what did you get as a result? Are you really yourself? Just not being like someone else is not enough."

"What do you mean?"

"What you became . . ." I stopped, unwilling to finish, before me was a sickly, elderly man, well read, wise, hardworking all his life.

He waited, watching me, suddenly leaned back against his chair, relaxed, and laughed gently.

"Lord, what are you afraid of? You're right! Why won't people ever say it to your face? Only behind your back in a whisper. You too . . . Come on, do it."

I felt myself blushing. I realized he was mocking me.

"You forgave the Bison. For what? The denunciations you wrote against him?"

"At last," he said calmly and seriously.

And I recalled one of my teachers. A handsome, gray-haired man, methodical, sweet, witty at his lectures. Joking and caressing, he ruined several of his colleagues during the struggle against "cosmopolitans," he cleared a path for himself, became a leading expert, was elected corresponding member of the Academy, was a prize laureate. He went to Moscow. He was made rector of the new institute, a member of the editorial board. Now he was invulnerable. Much depended on him, and when he came to see us, no one dared reproach him for his misdeeds of the past. He grew old amid great respect, presided at meetings, and no one ever told him to his dying day what they said about him, what his reputation was. We were sent to his funeral, we stood in an honor guard, listened to orations, carried wreaths . . .

Two days later, D. called me, asked me to come back because he had remembered something important. I tried to get out of it, but he insisted. Categorically, almost with an official threat. Our meeting was brief. He told me about the Bison's connection with Werner Heisenberg during his work on the atomic bomb. Without a doubt, he said, the Bison had aided and abetted. He was tied to Nazi science. D. had no direct proof, but all I had to do was dig around to find it. As a writer I was bound to seek it, otherwise my conscience would be compromised. At any rate, he had warned me. In fact, he would write a letter to me, and keep a copy, as proof of his official warning. After my work was published, there were bound to be people who had the goods on the Bison. Wouldn't it be better for me to create a hero, a made-up one, a physicist, or in some field I knew? Then all objections would disappear. No one would complain about an invented hero, and I could solve all the mysteries, too. For instance, he takes along his enemy to his new job because of the enemy's bride, whom he loves. The enemy goes along with it out of pride, accepts it as a challenge, and a long duel ensues. The facts remain, just change a few names.

He was full of confidence. He was energized by every concession.

"Listen, why don't you write about lost talent," he suddenly said, as if proposing something new. "About a man who was not allowed to develop fully. That's the tragedy. Typical for our times. What you're planning to write is trite, forgive me for saying so. Yet another great scientist. We've been shown so many of them! What have these models taught people? Nothing. Because a model of a fortune's darling can't teach anything. But you'll show a talent that served as a target. Everyone who felt like it practiced on it. How that wounded the talent. They would not allow him to become great. When did the Bison become great? Where? That's my point! Instead, write about a man who was forced to cut back to be like everyone else. Can't handle it? Too hot?"

It's a good theme, I thought, an important one—how bastards are created, how hatred grows. He hated the Bison to the death. There is eternal love, to the grave. This was eternal hatred. It's not that easy to acquire such a faithful enemy.

27

MIASSOVO—A REFUGE FOR PERSECUTED SCIENCES

The first time Valeri Ivanov heard of the Bison was in Moscow at a lecture in 1956. The lecturer was speaking of the position of genetics after the VASKhNIL session. Among the famous names came an unfamiliar one–Timofeyev-Resovsky. Valeri was in his third year at the university. He was interested in his friend's story about Miassovo, where that Timofeyev lived. A few bits of information from Gorky had reached them via S. S. Chetverikov, who was considered a living classic; this made even more astonishing the esteem with which Chetverikov spoke of Timofeyev. They decided to do their practical work that summer in the Urals, in Miassovo. They took a train and once they got there learned that it was another twenty-five kilometers to the biostation. They started out on foot.

There were four of them. One knew Chetverikov's brother, a mathematician, who, incidentally, liked to make masks. He made them artistically, with subtle details, very expressive. He gave each of them a mask. As they reached the station, they put them on and burst in with wild cries. They created a tumult. The Bison himself came running. They recognized him right away. People always recognized him right away, even those who had never seen him before. He was delighted by their daring. They became friends. The Bison dragged them into his study. Showed them the pictures of his favorites–Schrödinger, Bohr, Vavilov, Vernadsky–and gave the students nicknames: Chromosome, Tractor, Diplodocus, Joe.

191

Miassovo was a free range for the Bison. He could wander wherever he wanted, with his students, with bearded Lyapunov, lover of minerals and of the wonders of the Urals, he could clamber on boulders, listening to the roar of the river.

He returned to his homeland in stages. He gathered strength, will, and people. A few houses, a meadow, a lake, a campsite, with fires, songs, young romances . . .

He grew healthier there, becoming more expansive to match the scope of the wooded slopes, the enormous flowers, the wild sunsets.

His strength burgeoned. Valeri Ivanov persuaded me that the Bison could run behind horses for hours without tiring. He could play with the young as an equal. He was back home, for his homeland was Russian science, which he had left in the twenties, with its stormy style of those years—a robber brotherhood outside the lab and a mighty and assiduous working brotherhood in the lab. He had left that, and now that he was back, he was re-creating it here. He was still a student nihilist, a troublemaker, a storm. He worked up a storm, thought up a storm, spoke his mind without looking over his shoulder. His peers had long grown quiet and careful, looked like serious and responsible men impressed with their own titles and ranks. He had no titles, no rank, he was free, and when he heard the young men whooping in their masks, he went to them, found soul mates, despite the age difference. He was home in his youth.

The students responded to Miassovo as a completely new world order: work and study went on as if there were no difference between study and play. After lecturing, the Bison went to the tents and the campfire and talked about whatever came to mind—art, or Andrei Bely, or Bely's father, or the mathematician Bugaev, a professor at Moscow University, or the Sioux Indians, who taught three hundred years ago that the world's spirit is indivisible, that family ties connect us with all animals, in short, that there is a biosphere and that biocenosis, an ecological community, exists.

He didn't worry about boring people, he didn't have any complexes. If he was interested, he was sure others would be, too. He wasn't afraid of young people, he wasn't afraid of seeming out of date. They were the ones who were backward, ignorant, dumb, he teased them as much as he wanted, accusing them of being gray and boring, and they followed him around.

The Bison was the same with everyone, from Nobel laureates to lab assistants. It made no difference to him who you were—Tatar, Estonian,

Chinese—and so he didn't think about it, and with a bad accent told Armenian jokes, Jewish jokes, and was the first to make fun of Americans, Italians, and Russians, who were the butt of most of his jokes. No one could accuse him of prejudice.

They danced in the evenings. The Bison could dance till morning. It was hard to keep up with him. He was as powerful physically as he had ever been.

What the students learned over that summer at the station determined, for most of them, their philosophy of life and their approach to science.

He taught them to have priorities. Naturally, scrupulous detail work was necessary, but he managed to keep a balance. He laughed at the narrow specialist, "researcher of the left nostril of the crawfish." That wasn't for him. He valued the work, but his reasoning was: if you have to spend time, spend it on the main thing. And he knew how to find the main things in graduate students as well as in big shots.

"Mendel's fate is like Darwin's," he proclaimed. "After all, Darwin did not create evolutionary theory, as popularizers often claim, for that idea was known long before Darwin. His genius lay in being the first to see the principle of natural selection in nature, the natural mechanism of evolution in living creatures. Mendel's genius is not in discovering the laws of heredity; those laws were well known before Mendel's work. His genius lay in being the first in biology to do exact and well-thought-out experiments."

After that first summer, Valeri Ivanov and others came every year. No other places tempted them.

They didn't realize at first that they were dealing with an extraordinary and unique man. That came much later. Talking about Miassovo, each of them regretted how late he had understood. The only consolation was that it had happened that way for all of them and that it must have been necessary. Apparently, there is a reason for youthful blindness. They just felt good, very good, in Miassovo, and they were drawn there. People began coming from Moscow, Leningrad, Novosibirsk, Kiev. The rumor spread that you could learn about banned genetics in Miassovo, that there was talk there of cybernetics. Miassovo became a refuge for persecuted sciences, a bulwark of biophysics. The Bison didn't agitate for anyone in particular, he simply flung open his doors. He said what he thought, without self-censorship. It turned out that this was possible. No one really knew what was possible. People just knew what was "not allowed."

The students decided to have an art show. Of abstract art, naturally, because in those years there was a campaign against it–it was attacked in the press, over the radio, on the stage. In Miassovo they also argued whether or not it was art. The majority maintained that anybody could paint an abstract canvas. The Bison, Lyapunov, and another master were put on the jury. All comers could test themselves in that genre. Everyone did what he could. There were several dozen canvases. The question came up of where to hang them, they didn't have the wall space. Someone came up with a brilliant idea. There was a wooden canopy over the dining room. They hung the show on the plank ceiling and it had to be viewed lying down on the benches. The sign at the entrance said: "The First Exhibition of Abstract Art in the Urals." Andrei Malenkov* made a special announcement at the opening, which began: "The audience, perhaps, is not prepared to appreciate a new art. We must warn you that the viewer here will be a creator. As opposed to figurative art, where there is little left for the viewer to do, just absorb the mood, composition, colors. In abstract art the viewer is everything. If he has rich associations, he can enjoy what another viewer will see as mere daubs."

"Now lie down!" came the command.

There was a line for the benches. People moved from bench to bench. And looked up at the ceiling.

Then the jury made its decision. The Bison read it, along with his commentaries. There was general delight.

To this day, whenever anyone talks about that show, he smiles.

The biostation in Miassovo consisted of a few cottages by the lake, a meadow, a two-story wooden lab building. Twenty-one kilometers over the crest of the range to the nearest settlement. Miassovo is recalled as a paradise. Not because it was so beautiful, but because everything came together there, life was full and science was full.

"I went there for four years, I spent all my vacations there. It was the best time of my life. You felt you could do anything," recalled Andrei Malenkov.

The Bison was its spiritual center, its axis. He played volleyball, gave

---

* Son of G. M. Malenkov, longtime associate of Stalin, briefly premier after Stalin's death, removed from that office by N. S. Khrushchev in 1954, dismissed from the Politburo in 1957–ed.

lectures, sang, drank, dictated, drank black tea. His own age did not matter to him and he never paid attention to people's ages, only their work.

He could be ruthless. For instance, about the level of thought. He could interrupt a speaker, pointing out an unfounded conclusion, and shout: "Utter nonsense! Dirty work!"

Students, no matter how they loved their work, goofed off. Once the kids threw test tubes in the lake, they were too lazy to wash them. The Bison went swimming, saw the test tubes, and was so furious that if he had not remembered that he had been a similar "bastard" in his youth, he would have thrown them out. But he still shouted a lot.

The more they loved him, the more they feared him.

"I don't need you, but I can't live without you. I don't need you; because I love you, I love you and there is nothing that I want from you. The fact that I lived my last decades with people who are dearer to me than anyone is a consolation given to me in my old age," is what the Bison said on his seventieth birthday.

Vsevolod Borisov came to Miassovo out of curiosity. He came to biology from physics with the disdain of a practitioner of the exact sciences, universal laws of matter, magnified by the arrogance of youth. All biologists, including the Bison, were mired in specifics, while physicists had a general vision. I'll go and resolve their problems—that was approximately his attitude when he came down to their prehistoric science.

His first meetings with the Bison showed him how pathetic his concepts of living nature were and how complicated, mysterious, and rich nature was.

"If you keep holding on to your DNAs, you'll never understand the living organisms," the Bison taught.

All these new, fashionable sciences ornamented with fancy equipment receded before ancient zoology, which was infinitely varied. DNA, RNA, amino acids—all that was fine, but there are forests as well as trees, and the forests are more than the sum of the trees.

The Bison's words were outrageous in those days, and a meeting with him was an astonishing event. No one managed to maintain a cool irony. A relic? An original? A natural man? What was his secret? His effect was not limited to young people and students. Major scientists visited Miassovo and went away stunned. In 1956 the Bison came to P. L. Kapitsa's institute and gave a lecture at one of his so-called *kapichniks*. He astonished everyone there, including Kapitsa himself. In that stormy year of 1956, filled with many events, his appearance made a strong impression. Older people had forgotten free behavior and the young had simply never seen it.

And who else could have come up with the idea of having the entire seminar—doctors of science and students alike—sit naked in the water and listen to the lecturer standing on the shore?

I must note that in those days only the atomic physicists had managed to liberate themselves; some wore their shirts outside their trousers, without ties, played Ping-Pong at work, sheltered geneticists, and argued with the bosses. But they were physicists, the reigning family of science, they could do anything then, they were pampered, because they were "forging an atomic shield," as they used to say in those days.

The Bison, once he left the laboratory in the Urals, turned into an ordinary biologist. He had no protection—no high titles, no benefactors. Except for his name, which needed no prefixes or titles before it. What mattered was that it was the Bison's opinion or judgment, his words, his evaluation.

A name is greater than any title. There are many doctors of science, and enough academicians, whereas you have only one name. But in the Bison's case, there were particulars and problems, not the least of which was that very few people knew him. Even among biologists. Thirty years' absence had done its work. Everyone read Schrödinger's famous book *What Is Life from a Physicist's Point of View?* In it the physicist referred to Timofeyev-Resovsky as the one who got him started in this work. But few people realized it was the same Timofeyev. He didn't fit their image of a classic, an idol.

Now historians believe that Schrödinger's book inspired Watson and Crick and thereby led to the discovery of the double helix. That is why the history of molecular biology pays homage to Timofeyev as a catalyst of that new science. Nonetheless, historians did not study him. Compared with his surviving classmates, his college friends, now respected, honored, quoted, he seemed wild, untamed, prehistoric, and at the same time outrageously young. They were ready for History, but young people saw them as weary and scared. Their voices were hushed. Next to the Bison they blended into one indistinguishable mass.

That was not to the Bison's credit, nor was it the fault of our biologists. There were sufficiently serious and powerful circumstantial reasons for it.

"To see him against that background, a man who had preserved everything that was our heritage—artistic, multifaceted, personal—was a miracle," said one who had been among the young people around him. "Here was a man who had preserved everything. It was important for us to see him, more important than for him to see us. It was a historic time. Thanks to him we could join the broken chain of time, which we could not have done alone. Even the most courageous and decent people were forced to keep quiet all those years. Or else they were in prison or exile. Dubinin, Astaurov, Efroimson—so many of our marvelous biologists were forced into silence in various ways. Except for Vladimir Vladimirovich Sakharov, of the pharmaceutical institute, who taught genetics at home secretly. But that wasn't the same thing. A tribune was necessary. And here was a man who brought time together."

That's what he said at the Bison's birthday party.

His students Tolya Banin and Andrei Malenkov also spoke then. They talked about the Bison's two principles: first, good people have to multiply; second, our generation has to try to pass on to the next one all that is the best, and then it's up to them.

He broke the rules, he terrorized his students, he was savage, and they liked that. He was like a bison among placid oxen in a domestic herd; an animal of the 1920s, a period they knew less well than they did the 1820s.

He was a living link with the celebrated scientists of Europe and America. People they knew from textbooks and encyclopedias were his friends and acquaintances, his co-authors, his opponents. That alone was incomprehensible. He himself was part of that world. He belonged simultaneously to Western science and Russian, he joined them. He was proud of Russian scientists and did everything he could to make them better known in the West, but inside science, in the kitchen of some problem, he didn't care who solved it, we or the Americans. Questions of priority simply did not worry him. Competition between countries did not touch him.

He was not stifled by dogma, "bourgeois idealism" was not a bugbear for him. He wasn't afraid to praise Western scientists, he bowed before some of them, and he berated Russia and Russians for their laziness and ignorance. He respected Germans for their punctuality. He would not deal with the fact that his name was odious because he had lived in Germany during the war and had worked there under the Nazis. The worst kinds of rumors were spread about him (by D., among others). He should have kept quiet. But in the very years that Lysenko was back in favor he shouted that Lysenko was a Rasputin.

It was clear that he had not changed his manner: he complained about whatever he felt like and behaved the way he always had–in Germany, in the camps, in exile in the Urals, and here, in freedom. "Liberty" is a word that suits him better than "freedom." Liberty demands space, expanse, fields, open skies and an open soul. It is a more Russian concept than freedom.

He still had that fire of the twenties, that intoxicating air of the flourishing of Russian culture. It had been a holiday, a festival in the arts, music, poetry, and science, a renaissance which unexpectedly lifts a nation on its crest.

He cannot be considered a fighter. He did not fight for his convictions, he simply followed them in all situations. He managed always to be himself. Nothing external could interfere with that.

His approach to scientific problems was heretical.

"The wise Lord taught us: everything complicated is unnecessary, and everything necessary is simple."

"Unimportant problems in science require as much labor as important problems, so why the hell waste time on unimportant things?"

"When is the last time you called yourself a fool? If it's less than a month ago, then you're all right."

"It's good to be able to do everything yourself, but not to do it all."

"You need not only to read but to think a lot while you're reading."

"For the time being there isn't a barely useful, logical concept, much less a strict or precise one, of progressive evolution. Biologists still have not been able to formulate what progressive evolution is. There still is no convincing answer to the question: which is more progressive, a plague bacillus or a human being?"

He thought scientists' pretensions to be studying mechanisms was foolish. He said, "You get facts, you get phenomenology. A mechanism is the product of your thoughts. You're just tying facts together. That's all."

He was an opponent of breakthroughs, discoveries, eurekas, sensations, and revolutions. He felt that the systematic development of science was more important, leading in a natural way to revolutions. One shouldn't chase after individual acts. You need the whole chain of events that leads to the big leap. He did have major discoveries, but he was not a discoverer, he was an understander. The first to understand and explain to the rest. A major talent for universalizing.

"The goal of scientific research in this ever-flowing and mysterious world is to find what is regular and what is systematic. That's what we are paid our salaries for."

"Science is a privilege for very healthy people. The weak can only catch a chill in it. Take Vavilov, for instance, and think how many expeditions he lived through."

He was asked, "What if you get sick?"

"Pay no attention. People who take medicine and complain can never be real workers!"

They sat in the Bison's small, chilly office in Miassovo. Everyone was wrapped in blankets, it was that cold. On the alcohol cooker, a pot of dark brown, extra-strong tea. The Bison was recounting why and how he got the idea for one of his works in radiobiology. About ten people were in the room. Listening avidly. The logic of science. Natasha Lyapunova tried to write it down but ended up with fragments; because it was so interesting, she listened instead of writing. That often happened to her: she knew she should be writing it down, a shame to miss it, but listening took all her attention, all her strength.

Miassovo . . . They recall it even now: "We all came out of Miassovo." "It was like a lyceum." On the Bison's birthday, they read a poem that said first there was the word, which they heard at Miassovo.

He did not know how to be great in life. He kept falling off the pedestal. Once the young geneticist Vargash G. came to visit the Bison. He came to Miassovo as if to Mecca, the way people came to Tolstoy's Yasnaya Polyana estate. To offer his work to the Bison's eyes. To have him look at it. The work, according to general opinion, was marvelous: he did a statistical analysis of an old genetic issue—when are more boys born, when more girls, what does it depend on? The results were fascinating. But were they accurate? The Bison, without delving deeply, attacked him as a charlatan. It was horrible to witness such a big animal screaming at and trampling on that young boy. It was not nice, it was ugly.

He flew off the handle, then he suffered and regretted it. So the Bison was like everyone.

He was free and not dependent on his fame.

Envying him the freedom of his actions, I often asked myself: where did it come from, why aren't we all like that? We're constrained, repressed, controlled. First I thought it was the independence that comes with talent. But not all talented people are that free. Talent, of course, builds self-confidence and dignity. However, he was free of his talent. He did not worry about priority or supremacy. His independence had hidden supports and deep roots. Every man dreams of independence, but does not always have the willpower for it, it's hard to free oneself of the desire for fame, success, money. As for the Bison, he got that strength from faith. He believed in justice, in the victory of good over evil, in absolute good.

His independence was tied to his family tree, to his ancestors, to a code of honor. He could stand alone. It explained his majesty, a sense of continuity with his past, his duty to defend its honor.

28

LIMBO

At the Ministry of Internal Affairs, Zavenyagin turned all the offices upside down, looking for the Bison. Some of the documents in the case were lost and it was not easy to find him. Zavenyagin persisted in the search. They told him the man did not exist, was not in the files, could not be found. Zavenyagin didn't believe them, a mammoth couldn't just disappear. And finally he found the Bison in the concentration camp at Karlaga. He was in a bad way, weakened, in the final stages of pellagra, a horrible camp disease, avitaminosis brought on by malnourishment, when you can no longer digest anything. His barracks mates dragged him to work in the pits, leaned him against the wall, and he sang. That was the only thing he had strength left for, singing. And that's why the other prisoners put up with him.

He was dying. You would think, with his health and strength, he could have put up with more deprivation. But it wasn't the deprivations that played the fatal role. He had nothing left for which to hold on.

The state of a scientist deprived of his work, his laboratory, his experiments, is so difficult that it's hard for a nonscientist to understand. Rutherford understood Kapitsa, who was in Moscow, living in normal conditions but not allowed to work, and who flew into rages and depressions. Worried about his condition, Rutherford wrote: "Take up scientific work a soon as possible (even if it's not epochal work!), and you'll feel much happier. The harder the work, the less time you'll have for other worries. As you know, every dog needs some fleas, but as it seems to me, you feel that you have received more than your quota of fleas."

And Kapitsa wrote to Bohr: "Our institute is in a stage of completion. We got our equipment, I hope to start up our scientific work again. You feel immense relief, approaching research after a two-year hiatus. I never thought that scientific work played such an essential role in a man's life, and being deprived of that work was tormentingly difficult."

The Bison's condition grew acute. He had lost the lust for life, his life had lost its beauty and meaning . . .

He was put on a sled and taken to the train station. Orders were orders, especially such a categoric one: get him to Moscow immediately. If it had to be immediately, they couldn't stop to treat him. He had to travel one hundred fifty kilometers in the hard frost. And in farewell, the criminals, the very ones who liked his voice and his robber songs, cut out the back of his coat with their razors. The professor was a goner anyway, why let the fabric go to waste, they could make warm pants out of it. Corpses don't bear grudges . . .

The sled traveled through the icy haze, a pink fog filled his eyes. It was wonderful, he felt no anxiety at all.

At the station he was sent into the delouser, he couldn't stand up, they pulled him through. The train to Moscow crossed all of Russia, jolting him along the war-torn tracks. He couldn't digest food, it went straight through him. He no longer felt pain, everything that could have hurt had hurt before, now he felt empty, he didn't have enough strength to groan. He was unconscious most of the time. He barely heard noises, but the vibrating floor let him know he was still traveling. There seemed no end to that trip. Once in a while he would regain consciousness and he could not understand what thin sinew of life was still there, holding on to him. A miracle. Every time he became conscious he was amazed at the independent vitality of his organism. The flickering consciousness turned into flickering oblivion, with rarer bursts of consciousness, and the ebbing of life did not make him sad.

Once he saw women in white above him, washing his weightless body with warm water. He realized that they were angels and therefore he was dead and in limbo. The angels smiled at him, he barely felt their touch.

Everything was white, the walls shone with flawless whiteness, water was flowing, he was floating somewhere. His gray crumpled skin was like sackcloth, and his bones rattled inside. He didn't need the body anymore, but for some reason the angels were fussing with that obsolete shell. He couldn't see their wings behind their backs.

He recalled how his friend J. B. S. Haldane had once calculated what kind of muscles an angel would need to be able to fly. The angel's body ended up having thin, birdlike legs and a chest with such muscles that it stuck out like a coffin. These real angels were slender and beautiful. Haldane's thoughts, which had once seemed amusing, now seemed blasphemous. Life, which had been large and colorful, was compressed into a tiny, scribbled-over sheet, like a rough draft. Warm sunny light filled him and carried him away, like a mote of dust. He tried looking around. The river Styx, Charon the ferryman, all that must have been left behind. But then he thought that this passion to observe was left over from his former life, he should just give in to the warm light and be carried off . . .

The next time he opened his eyes he saw white plasterwork above him, faces appeared and vanished, men's faces in white starched caps. It took him a while to realize he was in the hospital. Winking and chuckling, he admitted to me that he was in no hurry to understand and proclaim himself alive. Later he learned what had happened to him. They brought him to the Ministry of Internal Affairs hospital from the station and worked on bringing him out of the coma. They had developed a system for intravenous feeding, not just glucose, but all the necessary amino acids, because in the last stages of pellagra protein synthesis is destroyed, which means that food is not nourishing. The treating physician slept in the cot next to him. Apparently, they had been given strict orders: do whatever is necessary, but save him!

From time to time he saw colonels and other officers with white robes tossed over their uniforms. They stood over him, waiting to see if he wanted anything. They brought mountains of butter, chocolates, fruit, they got ham and other delicacies.

A month later he spoke. The chef would come in the morning and ask what he would like for lunch and dinner. He discussed the menu readily, it reminded him of the times his mother planned menus with their chef.

The Bison did not eat much yet and secretly gave his former angels food, those nurses and aides.

"They started blood transfusions. They made a mess of it and I got an infection. Our people can't leave well enough alone, they always have to spoil things. There was a big scandal, I thought they were going to arrest the chief surgeon, he barely got out of it . . . I got over it and then began growing stronger and stronger."

His recovery was considered a miracle. Besides his great health he also had what you could call the strength of predestination. It was clear that his life was unfinished, that fate could not let him leave this world.

There were consequences, of course: his vision deteriorated and he could not read without a loupe.

There were spiritual repercussions, too. He began worrying about the immortality of the soul. He continued building his faith. Good was absolute, that was clear. Evil was relative. The world was stable because it was built on good, that was the spiritual essence of the world. Evil was transitory and random . . .

When he got better, he began teaching church songs to the hospital staff. The authorities sighed, but they weren't allowed to argue with him.

29

STALIN'S
RASPUTIN

In Miassovo they set up the first practicum in genetics in the country since 1948–that's how biologists referred to the fateful session of the Academy of Agricultural Sciences. They did so despite the fact that Lysenkoism was gaining strength again. Fears were returning to their usual places. Too many people had suffered and died in the last few years. The lives of everyone who had struggled against Lysenko were ruined. They had to take whatever work they could–translations, accounting, jobs in dreary agrostations. Z. S. Nikoro worked as a ballroom pianist at a club. Yu. Ya. Kerkis become a zoo technologist on a state farm. N. Sokolov went to work in Yakutia. A. A. Malinovsky became a doctor. B. A. Vasin went to Sakhalin. They were all first-class scientists. Their years of experience were wasted. Those who had not struggled against Lysenko were successful. They had titles, awards, positions. The young generation received a good lesson in adaptation and accommodation.

The Bison began to understand Lysenkoism only in Miassovo, as he met its living victims and opponents. The scope of the damage was not clear at first. Not only genetics had suffered, but also, and for a long time, agronomy, plant selection, animal husbandry, physiology, medicine, and people's way of thinking.

It was not easy to convince those who had surrendered to Lysenkoism. The absence of real results did not discourage his adherents. When the experiments failed, Lysenko explained, "You didn't believe. You have to believe, then it works."

Biology was undermined. Biologists themselves knew they could not win back freedom of scientific work, too much was broken, chopped down, science was dispirited. And here physicists and mathematicians came to their aid. Academician S. V. Vonsovsky came to Miassovo with his theoreticians from Sverdlovsk, as did a group of cyberneticists headed by A. A. Lyapunov. They got letters from I. Ye. Tamm, G. M. Frank, P. L. Kapitsa.

In October 1955, Igor Yevgenyevich Tamm invited the Bison to lecture on genetics in Moscow at Kapitsa's Institute of Physical Problems. A lecture like that was unthinkable at any biology institute. They were all under the control of Lysenkoists. Only the physicists were autonomous. They had their own fortress, and inside the fortress they organized a public appearance for the Bison. Tamm would also participate. He was interested in the newly formulated concepts of Watson and Crick on the double helix as the basic structure in the reproduction of chromosomes. The structure of DNA was the sensation of those years, and he was going to talk about it. He asked the Bison to talk about radiation genetics and the mechanism of mutation. Kapitsa approved the topics and both lectures were put on the schedule for the year.

The news upset Moscow's scientists. It was no joke, holding public lectures on genetics, which was still banned. Lectures on genetics were not permitted. Many people were afraid that these would be canceled at the last moment. In essence, it was a challenge, a public challenge to the monopoly of the Lysenkoists. The fact that the Bison would appear in Moscow, a man about whom there were so many rumors, was also generating interest. Kapitsa asked for announcements to be posted everywhere, at the institute and in the physics department of the Academy of Sciences, so that it would all be done openly. Three days before the session someone in authority called the institute and gave orders to remove the notices for the genetics lectures because they were "not in accordance with the resolution of the VASKhNIL session." That someone tried to reach Kapitsa himself, but could not and had to deal with his assistant. Hearing out his assistant, Kapitsa calmly said that the VASKhNIL resolution could have no effect on the Institute of Physical Problems. The next day the telephone call was repeated. This time the voice on the phone categorically referred to the directives of

THE BISON

Nikita Khrushchev. Then Kapitsa decided to clear up the issue with Khrushchev himself.

Kapitsa had always enjoyed special respect. When he was brought in to work on the atomic bomb, he ran into Beria. Beria was crude, unceremonious, and ignorantly interfered with the work of the scientists, shouting at Kapitsa. After one of these sharp encounters, Kapitsa wrote an indignant letter to Stalin, not afraid of open conflict with the all-powerful minister. Complaining about Beria was an irrational action in those days. Moreover, with his usual openness, Kapitsa asked Stalin to show the letter to Beria. Naturally, this had repercussions, and soon afterward Kapitsa was taken off the work and removed from his position as director of the institute he created. He went off to his dacha and continued experimenting in a shed, setting up a primitive lab there. That was a truly heroic period, which continued until the fall of Beria in 1953.

In 1937-38, at the height of Stalin's purges, Kapitsa was not afraid to intercede for the unjustly arrested Academician Vladimir Alexandrovich Fok, the marvelous theoretical physicist, and he got him out of prison. He later saved L. D. Landau.

They were fearless. Kapitsa, Pryanishnikov, and Timofeyev. Courage of thought was combined with civic courage. That was the wholeness of their natures.

Kapitsa had to be taken into account, his behavior created an aura of insubordination, that quality which always confuses bureaucratic souls.

Thus Kapitsa telephoned Khrushchev. He was put through. Was it true that Khrushchev had banned the seminar? Not at all! Did Krushchev know about the call to the institute? He was assured that Khrushchev knew nothing about it; if it had been necessary, he would have called Kapitsa himself. The seminar schedule was their internal business and depended only on Kapitsa.

The next day, February 8, 1956, at 7 P.M., as usual, the 304th session of *kapichniks* opened. The hall was packed, as were the corridors and stairs leading to the hall. The physicists had to set up loudspeakers for the overflow. They had expected a crowd, but nothing like this. Everyone was there, from academicians to students. Natasha and Elena Lyapunova, students then, still remember the details of the meeting, even though they only heard the voices over the loudspeakers. In science as well as in politics there are historic reports. Everyone knew that this was a breakthrough in the blockade, the beginning of the restoration of regular biology.

The lectures were not militant. The lecturers did not attack, polemicize, or denounce. Tamm reviewed the work involved in the discovery of the double helix. The Bison painted a picture of the development of radiation genetics and the mechanism of mutations.

Their success, the Bison later told me, was not due to the "lecturers' artistry," it was just that the audience, especially young people, were starved for modern genetics. For the first time in many years they saw the brilliant world of new ideas, the movement of world thought, everything that had been hidden for so long. The genetic *kapichnik* was an event not only for Moscow, it was seen throughout the country as the escape of scientific genetics from imprisonment, a precedent, a good sign.

After the success of this "duet," Tamm went into genetics with re-newed vigor. It was in genetics that he expected the most important discov-eries of the near future. He said that the struggle for knowledge was impor-tant, not the victory. After every victory—that is, each conquered peak—there comes a "twilight of the gods," and the concept of victory dissolves at the very moment it is achieved.

The Bison was not protected, as Tamm was, by a title or by being a physicist. And the epithet "odious" still followed him. The daring of his appearance was acknowledged, whereas for him there was no daring about it, just an opportunity to correct the situation in biology, an opportunity he had to take. What did "not allowed" mean, when it was possible? He did not feel the limits of "allowed." And after his lecture people suddenly discovered that it was possible to talk about genetics, about Mendel's laws, about the new work being done by the Americans. This inspired the young. Of course, one swallow doesn't bring spring, but it would come!

The more the Bison learned about Lysenkoism, where it came from and how it grew, the less he understood how it could have happened. He called Lysenko a Rasputin, who was the only analogy in history for this absurdity.

Heredity as result of environment! Oats turning into wild oats, pines into firs, sunflowers into zinnias! Animal cells turning into plant cells and vice versa! "How can there be hereditary diseases in a socialist society?" "From the nonliving will come the living!" All this was served up officially as late as 1963! The Bison tore his hair and howled in anger. He could not imagine how widespread this nonsense was, how this medieval malarkey had become part of people's thinking, especially among the young. Even those disposed to be critical said, "Well, there's something to it."

Fiction reigned, that which had not existed, which could not exist. Mirages were declared reality, mystifications affirmed. And what had existed, that which the whole world was working on, was declared nonexistent. Genes did not exist. Chromosomes did not exist. The enlightened were banished from the temples of science. Those who did not reject the truth were branded charlatans. Facts obtained with great difficulty were thrown away like garbage. Idols were pulled from pedestals. Demons frolicked among the ruins. They played pipes and horns glorifying their leader. They raised up pictures of him—an ascetic, elongated face with a crooked lock of hair and piercing eyes. The bureaucrats liked the fact that he, without finishing any academies, a self-taught man, had managed to expose world luminaries, and also they liked the fact that his teaching was accessible to any ignoramus, everyone could be enlightened. It did not require knowledge or talent to teach and correct any specialist. All it required was faith. Faith created miracles, made experiments successful. If it did not work, you did not believe. Faith affected harvests, tree plantings. The frenzied cries of Himself encouraged the believers. He promised a miracle, and not just sometime, but soon, next year, in two years. Trusting souls were attracted to him, they were tired of the exhausted earth's abortions, of reforms, unful-filled plans, resolutions, officials. They greeted him with ovations and booed those who disagreed with him. He knew how to promise. Those who make promises are always followed.

There were skeptics, of course, who said, "The king is naked!" There were those who demanded tests, referred to foreign studies. They were seized, bound, and gagged.

There is a phrase in scientific folklore that comes from a magazine of those years: "He showed a total lack of principle, refusing to admit the erroneousness of his views."

Yuri Ivanovich Polyansky, the famous geneticist, was removed from his position as prorector of Leningrad University right after the VASKhNIL session. Professor Strelkov was fired because he said that he was and would remain a friend of Polyansky's. Then Polyansky was expelled from the Party for methodological mistakes in genetics. He told me what happened later.

"I was called before the regional Party committee. They read out the report: 'Unanimously expelled by his organization! Any opinions?' A lieutenant general took the floor. He was a member of the Party committee's bureau. My former commander in the army. I did not say hello to him, so as not to embarrass him. But he said, 'Who? Polyansky? What does this mean? The man who was at the front with me? Are you crazy? He was with me for four years! . . . Are you . . . ? What is this?' And everyone got so confused, and he kept on shouting . . . And just imagine, they rescinded the decision! They simply gave me a chewing-out. That was unexpected. I went home. My wife was waiting on the stairs, and there I was walking along, singing a song. She said, 'Are you crazy?' So there I was, fired. I lived in institute housing. They couldn't evict me. No one touched me, not a word. I was there a month. Three months. Nothing to eat. I had no savings. No one hired me. I had one phone call, a disgusting call! I was sitting one evening translating Mechnikov for Classical Sciences. It seems some of his works had not been translated into Russian. So I was translating an article about jelly fish from a German journal. Suddenly the phone rings. From Moscow.

" 'Who's this?'

" 'Deputy Minister Svetlov. How are you feeling, Yuri Ivanovich?'

" 'How do you think I feel?'

" 'Would you like everything to be back to normal?'

" 'Naturally! But how?'

" 'You are considered one of the leaders of Weismannism-Morganism. We need a major article in the central press denouncing this direction and fully supporting Lysenko. Well, what do you say?'

"I couldn't express myself fully because my wife was in the room. But I used a strong enough word. And then I said, 'Who do you think you are dealing with? You are dealing with a fundamentally decent man. What are you suggesting? Total betrayal!' And I hung up. What else could I say? So vile! I'll never forget that call."

Every faith finds adherents. And if it triumphs, then it develops many fierce zealots. A scientist once said to Lysenko, "It's shameful to guard a theory not with facts but with police!" Aware of the guards and political support, the zealots took over departments, institutes, publishing houses, laboratories, and journals. The pseudo-professors began teaching the pseudo-science, did pseudo-experiments, published pseudo-textbooks, and young scholars on the make wrote pseudo-dissertations.

THE BISON

Falsehood was taking on scientific legitimacy. Instead of results it produced promises, outfitted them with numbers and graphs. The promises grew, and the unfulfilled promises were replaced with new ones, even more tempting, more colorful.

Falsehood looked permanent and all-powerful.

Despite the fear, brave people appeared here and there to challenge it to a duel, throwing their lecture notes and letters in its face. A. A. Lyubishchev wrote a whole volume of research, *The Damage Wrought by Lysenko*. He demonstrated the damage done to crops and to the productivity of animal husbandry, how plant selection and the development of seed varieties were ruined. The volume was read, people sighed sympathetically and hid it in their safes. One day the history of the resistance will be written, with heroes like Astaurov, Sukachev, Khadzhinov, Sakharov, Formozov, Efroimson, Baranov, Dubinin, Rapoport, Polyansky, Alexandrov, and Zherbak. There are many I still don't know, their names are lost. These are glorious pages that speak not of our science's shame but of its dignity. The resistance worked without hope of success, but it did not give up. This Resistance deserves to be capitalized. At a meeting at Leningrad University a Lysenkoist lecturer asked straight out, "Could it be that there are no Morganists among you?" Lebedev rose and said, "Why not, we have some, I'm a Morganist!" There were many who did not deny it, who stood up to be counted.

Too many of the Bison's colleagues and friends had changed, beyond recognition. Changed inside. Something had happened to them. They were hushed, they weighed every word. The ones who did not avoid the Bison listened to him nervously. Said nothing in response. P. used to whisper and squirm. The guilty smile did not suit his large florid face. The Bison had remembered him as a congenial fellow, daring, with a good war record. He was a specialist in animal selection, a few of his works were internationally known. But now, and especially among strangers, he approved of Lysenkoism: ". . . they're basically right . . . you have to take the philosophical side . . . and the practical . . ." The Bison shook him, demanded proof, shouted that they had destroyed farming. Potatoes, corn, citrus fruits—wherever Lysenko interfered, things went bad. P. would shiver and look around, beg him to shut up. "You don't know what it is, you haven't experienced it," he maintained. P. did not believe in sticking his neck out.

When the opponents of Lysenko began exposing Boshyan's faked experiments and mocking Lepeshinskaya's delirious theory, he still kept quiet.

Everyone had his own fear. K.T. stood firm for a long time but gave up and went over to the service of the Lysenkoists. He went to them and offered a truce. They snatched him up. He was a brilliant polemicist and wrote well. He included a chapter on Michurin's agrobiology in his monograph, ornamented it with a portrait of Lysenko, criticized Darwin's "flat evolution," and the book came out without a hitch. He was not ashamed and in fact bragged that he had been let off lightly. He cynically proposed a similar switch to the Bison, with attractive conditions: "I can guarantee you'll be made an academician, and they might give you an institute! Otherwise you'll just waste your time being angry."

The daughter of an old friend, the famous evolutionist S-ov, denounced her father publicly after the VASKhNIL session that branded him a Weismannist. The father went to the Far East, got a job tending animals on a state farm. The daughter, a clever woman, became a director at the Ministry of Agriculture. She tried to talk to the Bison several times, but he refused. In the sixties her father returned to Moscow, he was reinstated at the institute, he came to see the Bison, they embraced and kissed.

"You shouldn't condemn my daughter," S-ov said. "I don't, and you shouldn't. She fed the whole family, saved the apartment and the library. I am grateful to her, she sacrificed her honor."

The Bison snorted and shook his head.

"Saved the library! What about her soul? Can such sacrifices be made!"

He could forgive, but he refused to understand.

"You're a European, you didn't live through all that."

They had a difficult discussion. S-ov used their mutual friend Mikhail Mikhailovich Zavadovsky as an example.

"You blame him for that business in Askania-Nova, but he fought Lysenko in the most terrible years, when it took courage, maybe more than in the Civil War. He didn't tell you how he was thrown out of the university? He, Shmalfausen, and Sabinin were thrown out in '38. Everyone was outraged in a whisper and no one defended them. No one quit in solidarity, the way they did at the same university back in 1911. Zavadovsky had a heart attack, Sabinin shot himself. It wasn't just a verbal war. There was bloodshed."

The Bison was prepared to give their due to Zavadovsky and Sabinin, to everyone who stood up, but examples had no effect on him. There were too many justifications. No one noticed how science had changed. Russian science, the Soviet science which he had left in full flower, which he was used to being proud of and which he had publicized in the West . . . It was now full of weeds, it had shamed itself with medieval blather. Scientific journals published instances of transformations, found witnesses to confirm them. They weren't ashamed to swear to it. And academicians obediently said yes, it's so . . .

Lysenko himself outstripped all his students: he had a chiffchaff lay an egg with a cuckoo.

It was an easy way to get ahead. You get jobs and titles! Grab them! No time for honor. Now is the time to get all those empty places. Denounce anyone who is against the great scientist, denounce non-Michurinian genetics. The more vociferous got the better jobs.

The Bison saw destinies crumpled, characters destroyed. Young people saw that independence was not valued; obedience was. Talent was suspect. Newspapers and magazines glorified the new teaching. How could you doubt it? All the textbooks were redone. Embryology, seed studies, physiology, forestry, medicine, ichthyology, cytology, botany–wherever you looked, in all the sciences, theoretical or practical, there were energetic young people ready to look at things "in light of the VASKhNIL session." Bureaucrats supported the innovator, he supported them; the system worked.

Quite a few people made their careers in those years. A solid career in science. Took their places in scientific councils, in college departments, institutes, editorial departments. Developed reputations as fighters. They did not have heart attacks or doubts. Lysenkoism led to people falsifying data, forging citations, stealing ideas. They did it well.

30

A FALLEN ANGEL;
THE BERLIN
UNDERGROUND

The Bison's open appearance against Lysenkoism could not go unpunished. They sensed a dangerous opponent in him, one with a world-famous name. Not a physicist, but a pure-blooded biologist, a geneticist, and not a frightened one, not one who had been through the mill . . . In 1948 they would have gotten rid of him quickly, but the times were different. They couldn't use the old labels "bourgeois science," "fly lovers are man haters," or "genetics is the whore of imperialism." After all, it was 1957. They had to get the attacking bison some other way, scare him off. They spread a rumor that he had worked for the Nazis in Germany, doing experiments on humans, on Soviet prisoners of war. Anonymous letters were sent to the Central Committee, to the Academy of Sciences. There were no facts; slander does not need facts: "As you know, he was Hitler's main adviser in biology." "He was close to Bormann." They were not lacking in imagination. A man who had lived in Germany during the war was already regarded with hostility. More so if he worked there. More so if he was Russian . . .

In 1957, when I first was invited by a publishing house in the GDR, my friends criticized me: how can you go to Germany? Official propaganda persistently separated Germans from Nazis, but there was still great hatred among the people for the sorrow and grief they had caused, without distinction between Nazi and non-Nazi.

It wasn't enough that he had stayed in Germany, he was attacking

Soviet science . . . The lies worked. Even his close friends avoided questions about his life in Germany. And the Bison did not rush to justify himself or protest. Much later, without him, the facts about the help he gave to Soviet prisoners and the details of his son's arrest came to light. He kept silent. The silence increased suspicion. The slander spread. Formally no one accused him of anything, but the chill of alienation accompanied him. People whispered when he made an appearance. Strangers meeting him were hostile. There was nothing more shameful in those years than being a Nazi collaborator.

It was a clever revenge. And not dangerous. No one caught the butchers red-handed, and they added lie to lie.

"Let him prove his innocence!" they demanded, using a trick from the years of repression.

Fate had taken away his son, tossed him in the camps, and now deprived him of his honor. It looked as though there was fate at work in the randomness of his life. Didn't Job think the punishment with which God tested him was merely random? His children died. His cattle died . . . But that was the Lord testing his faith. Sooner or later Job figured it out. Perhaps providence was testing the Bison? And now, with the slander, the lies sticking to him. But the question was: for what was he being tested? He couldn't find the answer. The skies fell, he was under an avalanche, humiliatingly helpless, stifling a cry of pain. The rocks should have crushed him, flattened him, he was too big an animal to survive. Fate had deprived him of his homeland, his son, his freedom, and at last, his good name. Any one of these could have killed him, crushing his soul and mind. Why? What for? he asked, as man through the ages has asked, not understanding his guilt. What for, O Lord?–losing faith, staring into the blue sky. All evil came from politics, which he avoided, protecting his life with science. He wanted to work only in science, live in its wonderful world, where he felt his strength. But politics kept finding him behind his beloved barriers, behind the institute's walls. He couldn't hide from politics anywhere.

People avoided him: he was a fallen angel. But humiliation did not satisfy his enemies. Humiliation is a subjective perception, as D. said. The point was to render him harmless. For that they had to break his independence and block his way upward. But a mysterious force which always brought him up when he was down interfered. When he was almost dead, had been given up for dead, one little sinew remained alive, and that was enough to save him. Another power stood up to his evil fate. What was it? Luck, fortune? Whatever it was, that power raised him up from the ruins. Luck and fate fought, and the battleground was his destiny.

Did he have his own God? I could never work it out to the end. Dostoyevsky felt that if there was no God, everything was permitted, and if there was, then you could fall into despair. But man is a mystery, a mystery to himself. He does not believe in devils or demons, yet something stops him. Does not let him. There is no God, there is no fear, but . . . it's not allowed. Those who commit sins do it believing in God, saying prayers, and they still sin. When religious faith weakened, people thought that it would be a matter of "anything goes." But it didn't happen. There are still things that an unbelieving soul cannot do. The taboos were always there, in all times; they are what bring people and generations together, everyone who ever wept and laughed on this earth.

What is it, this power that stops man and does not allow him to give in to evil, fall into insignificance, lose his self-respect, does not let him become vile and low?

That is the question of questions. The question that I tried to understand through the Bison's fate.

As for God and faith, I never did clear up whether or not he was a believer, whether or not he had a God. Some said he did; others insisted he did not, that he was a materialist, an atheist. One does not ask such questions directly, and it was absolutely impossible to ask him. He did not allow people to get too close to him uninvited, he would become haughty, develop an aristocratic manner that was disconcerting.

Actually, I did learn a few things from various people who had had frank discussions with him. We shall return to that later.

When this work was published in the journal *Novy Mir*, I began getting letters from readers, mostly from people who had known my hero. There were dozens of them, soon there were over a hundred. Of those who responded, each treasured his meeting with the Bison, giving me details, wanting to help fill in the blanks.

If I were writing now, I could use the new material and probably the character of my narrative would change. But the work was constructed, completed, and I could not add to it. When you write, you measure, seek a rhythm, avoiding pauses and longueurs, and whether you like it or not, an interpolation is disruptive. An inserted passage usually remains just that.

Once a letter came from Kharkov, from Vladimir Grigorievich Kucheryavy. He wrote that if I was interested in more complete information on Foma Timofeyev, he could tell me, since he knew him from their underground work in Germany. While in the Grunewald camp, Kucheryavy worked in the underground Berlin Committee of the All-Union Communist Party (b). The link to the committee was Foma Timofeyev. One of the leaders was Yevgeny Vasilyevich Indutnov, who had known Foma well, and who, after the organization collapsed, had seen him in the transit prison. The man had died. Kucheryavy had Indutnov's memoirs.

Naturally, I wrote Vladimir Grigorievich that I would like to have those memoirs. There soon arrived a bulky manuscript, over seventy pages, written four years before Indutnov's death in 1976. An excerpt was published in 1985 in the Kharkov journal *Prapor*. No sooner had I started working on those reminiscences than I received a letter from Arkhangelsk containing the detailed recollections of Mikhail Ivanovich Ikonnikov, who also had known Foma in the underground. Ikonnikov had belonged to an anti-Fascist group and had been connected to the Berlin Committee through Foma. The Berlin Committee did not encompass all of the city, only the southern districts. Not much is known about its activities—a few newspaper items in Indutnov's archive memoirs and the evidence of Bushmanov, Numerov, and a few others.

After the Berlin Committee collapsed in late 1943, a few people survived the Gestapo chambers, the torture, and the camps, but most died in the postwar period. But two survivors read my book and sent me their memoirs. Even the first reading astonished me. What I had only guessed at and had written about on the basis of rumors and fragments of third-hand evidence was confirmed, became real. Some of the stories, I admit, had seemed exaggerated to me. People who had told them to me were not eyewitnesses, not one had worked with Foma in the anti-Fascist underground. So I had listened disbelievingly, and I had omitted some material, afraid of overdoing it.

In Indutnov's notes, Foma Timofeyev is only an episodic hero. He is mentioned in passing, and I think that he is described objectively. Clearly Indutnov is much more interested in his fellow prisoners of war. But Ikonnikov had written to me especially about Foma. My image of him began to be filled out by knowledge of his action, the fearless work of an underground worker. It revealed much about the atmosphere which ruled the Timofeyev house during the war years.

And then Nikolai Vladimirovich Numerov appeared, a Muscovite, the third member of the anti-Fascist Berlin underground and the first person from that legendary life whom I met. Numerov also told me many curious, sad, and strange things. I ended up with an extraordinary amount of material on Foma. So I decided to insert information on Foma's work for the Berlin Committee. Perhaps this story will remain a patch, but I cannot reject this felicitous find, this belated present from fate, this astounding story of the brief life of the Timofeyevs' older son, things that neither the Bison nor Elena Alexandrovna knew.

In 1941 Yevgeny Vasilyevich Indutnov did not succeed in being evacuated along with his factory from Kharkov, so he stayed behind in the city, was captured by the Germans, and was sent to Germany in a convoy. In the camp he received an armband that said "OST" and he became an Eastern worker (*Ostarbeiter*). He was sent to Grunewald, a town near Berlin and now part of the city, to a plant where he was given the job of warehouse loader. In 1942 he began forming an underground group of Eastern workers. This is approximately where his memoirs begin. The group carried out anti-Fascist propaganda and sabotage. In repairing railroad cars, they overheated the metal when welding, made bad joints, and damaged the axles. Indutnov learned that somewhere in Berlin there was an underground organization of POWs and decided to get in touch with them. One of the plant foremen, a German, brought him civilian clothes, an old jacket and trousers, and in the evenings Indutnov began going into the city. He learned conversational German and tried to make the connection in Berlin. This is where Foma Timofeyev first appears.

"In a few days, during my evening walks not far from the camp, I met a Russian fellow who lived in Berlin with his parents. In conversation he asked about our camp life, working conditions at the plant. He was interested in how we got to Germany and what I had done before the war. He was sympathetic to my story about the horrible quarantine camp in Dabendorf. I felt that he was interested in me, that he was feeling me out, probing for my evaluation of the situation, my reactions to events. What was this? A police provocation or something else? We set a date to meet in the nearby woods. Grunewald cut into the city line from the west with a lovely forest. At our next meeting Foma Timofeyev told me a lot about himself. It was unusual and very interesting. His father, Professor Timofeyev, a noted Soviet biologist, had gone on a long business trip to Germany in the thirties. [Clearly, Indutnov got the date wrong, but that's typical. –D.G.] His wife and son, Foma, had traveled with the professor. Living in Berlin, the professor worked in one of the biological institutes and Foma became a student at Berlin University. Foma felt that he could not find real friends among Germans brought up by the Hitler Youth in a nationalistic, chauvinistic, and anti-Semitic spirit.

"Soon the Germans treacherously attacked the U.S.S.R., and the second imperialistic war began. Now it seemed that all the bridges were burned, and the only consolation was that Foma was not a German citizen and could not be drafted. He tried to help his homeland as best he could, thinking of his childhood friends defending Russia from the barbaric invasion of the crazed Fascists. But how? What could he do? Tormented in the search for ways and means, according to him he met people who were organizing an active struggle against Fascism in Berlin. And now, when he was part of that struggle, he felt that he had found himself again. Foma said that when he met me he felt that I was seeking a way to join the struggle actively. At the time he did not tell me that he had come to Grunewald on the orders of N. V. Kazban, who had not managed to get me to speak frankly, but he sensed that perhaps with my help they could work with the Russians at the plant in Grunewald. Could I believe everything Foma Timofeyev told me? Could it be a clever Gestapo provocation? How did Foma find me, the leader and organizer of the underground in Grunewald? Maybe I had been found out and now I was being trapped? These thoughts gave me no peace. I began looking closely at the situation at the plant. Everything was normal, the lads were still ruining the railroad cars, stealing food from them, sabotaging whenever possible. The work was continuing.

"If the Gestapo did have suspicions they would have arrested me immediately, tortured me into naming the other saboteurs, and put an end to our work. Apparently, Foma was not from the Gestapo. I concluded, therefore, that I should agree to participate in the Berlin underground organization, without telling him about our Grunewald group's work. That way, I would risk only my own life.

"At our next meeting I agreed to join the underground organization. Foma told me that he and Kazban had talked to the leaders of the organization about me and that they had decided to accept me. Foma told me that the organization was called the Berlin Committee ACP (b).* It had only Soviet citizens, many POWs. Thanks to the system of underground groups organized at factories, construction sites, and camps, Russian workers were doing a great deal to keep up the patriotic spirit of the Soviet combatants. The organization provided accurate information on the situation at the front. They organized sabotage, formed military units that could strike small but damaging blows in the rear, gathered valuable military and industrial information to be passed to Soviet organs, agitated against joining Vlasov's army and the Russian Liberation Army. At the end of our talk, Foma took from the lining of his jacket several leaflets printed on cigarette paper. The leaflets had the latest news from the Soviet Supreme Command as well as an appeal from the Berlin Committee to Russian workers temporarily in German custody. Brief but very warm phrases were written in simple, understandable language. The organization called on all Soviet people in Fascist camps to remember their civic duty and to continue to struggle against the Nazi occupiers. The leaflet was signed: Berlin Committee ACP (b).

"I brought the leaflets into the camp as something particularly valuable. In the barracks, I hid them well. Then I met with my best comrades, Vasili Polyakov and Nikolai Mikhno, and told them my news, without, of course, naming my connection."

Thus, by late 1942, the Berlin Committee was already in existence. It had a developed network. Therefore, it had been organized much earlier. Judging by their printed materials, the committee must have been formed in early 1942, which is confirmed by other data.

The leaflet had information about the defeat of the German army at Stalingrad. The POWs were astonished that a committee of the Communist Party was active in Berlin.

"People were in shock from that leaflet."

Through Foma and Fedya Chichvikov they sent out leaflets regularly. Act of sabotage increased. They didn't have enough leaflets. Then, as Indutnov writes, and this struck me strongly, they began printing leaflets in Foma's room in his parents' apartment in Buch. They removed the glass door from the wardrobe, placed it across chairs, wrote the text on the glass, and then printed the leaflets. "The press run was determined by the amount of

* All-union Communist Party (bolsheviks)—ed.

paper we had and by the length of time that Foma's parents were out of the house."

Indutnov visited the apartment several times to pick up leaflets. He did not meet the leaders of the committee. Once they had a meeting set up outside of town, but when he got to the station, he saw Foma with a red shopping bag. That meant: get out immediately. He knew from Foma that the leaders of the organization were Colonel Nikolai Stepanovich Bushmanov and Andrei Dmitrievich Rubalchenko, the political commissar. They wrote the leaflets. Foma also told him that he had made contact with Resistance organizations of Czechs, Poles, and Frenchmen.

On July 31, 1943, Indutnov was arrested. The provocateur Vladimir Keppen had turned in the entire leadership. Interrogations and beatings followed. In late October, Indutnov was sentenced to life imprisonment in a harsh-regime camp for "dissemination of Communist ideas." Ernst Kaltenbrunner signed the papers.

On November 10, in a transit prison, Indutnov met Foma Timofeyev and told him about Keppen's treachery.

Foma was amazingly staunch during Gestapo questioning. The newly arrested people knew about it. Mikhail Ivanovich Ikonnikov wrote to me that he learned about Foma's behavior in prison on the Prinz-Albrecht-Strasse and in the Tegel Fortress. Foma's bravery was important, since he knew everyone, all the leaders and all the representatives. Ikonnikov made his acquaintance in 1943 and regularly met him at the Berlin Zoo. "It was not customary to know details about one another in the underground. So I knew little about him then, especially since our suspiciousness toward former White émigrés kept us from getting closer."

At first Foma told his comrades that his parents were apolitical and asked them to be careful what they said around them. Apparently he did everything he could to keep his family out of his dangerous work. If anything happened, the underground had to know they were not part of it. Moreover, he hinted that his father had refused to return to the U.S.S.R. Of course, some of the leaders of the committee guessed at his parents' real feelings, because it was impossible to hide the constant meetings at the apartment, printing the leaflets, and storing them there.

When he met Ikonnikov, Foma was head of a group of Russian émigré youths. They were part of the famous youth organization NORMA (National Organization of Russian Youth).

Fedor Chichvikov was the first POW to meet Foma Timofeyev. It happened in a café on Alexanderplatz where foreigners gathered. Chichvikov liked the "handsome intelligent young man who was born in Russia but had grown up in Berlin. . . . The important thing was that his father was not a White émigré, but a professor who came to Germany to work," wrote Ikonnikov. "We knew that there had been an exchange of specialists. Usually we did not trust White émigrés, but here was an exception.

"Chichvikov reported about Foma to Colonel Bushmanov, who suggested he feel him out carefully, and if it seemed that he could be trusted, make contact with him. A number of us were assigned that task, including me. I was introduced to Foma by Nikolai Antipin. We former students soon found a common language. Foma had a command of French, German, and English. His knowledge helped us translate leaflets from Russian into those languages. Chichvikov was convinced that Foma was a dependable comrade and introduced him to Colonel Bushmanov. Foma responded eagerly to Bushmanov's invitation to participate in the underground work. In May 1943, Foma Timofeyev was inducted into the executive board of the Berlin Committee ACP (b). That's how they signed the leaflets printed by Bulgarian anti-fascists in the secret printing house of the German Communist Eva Kamlein-Stein."

Ikonnikov remembered Foma as a sociable young man, intelligent in conversation. Foma had many ideas and plans, he was prepared to obey all orders, and even though he was three years younger than Ikonnikov and did not know war, "I bowed to his mind and pure heart. He was sometimes childishly naïve and too frank, he did not know how to hide his thoughts."

In many ways he was like his father, the Bison, who was also too frank, sometimes naïve, but naturally, in the underground Foma kept a grip on himself.

The group was betrayed by Vladimir Keppen, the son of a White émigré. "On the basis of his denunciation (he had ties to the Abwehr officer Erwin von Schultz) people were arrested, including Foma, Alexander Romanov, and Nikolai Kapustin." (Kapustin's letter to Foma's parents has been quoted earlier in this book.)

In 1944, Ikonnikov met Fedor Chichvikov in the Tegel prison, and Chichvikov confirmed that Foma had behaved courageously, telling the

Gestapo nothing. Chichvikov admitted that he had not expected such staunchness from him.

After the war Ikonnikov met Bushmanov in Moscow and he told him about Foma's major role in the Berlin underground. Before his death in 1976, Bushmanov asked them to continue seeking information on their lost comrades. He did not know that Foma had died in Mauthausen.

Indutnov learned from Foma back in 1943 that the interrogation had continued for a long time. The Gestapo officers realized that Foma had important information, they beat him, brought him face to face with other underground members, and finally they condemned Chichvikov and Timofeyev to execution. "After his parents' efforts on his behalf, his sentence was commuted to life imprisonment in a concentration camp. We hoped that perhaps we would be sent to the same camp. But in the morning they took Foma first and then came for me." They were separated in November 1943.

Eight members of the Berlin underground perished along with Foma Timofeyev. The fate of the others varied; some escaped, others formed new underground groups. Ikonnikov met Musa Dzhalil in the spring of 1944 in the Tegel prison . . . The postwar life in the U.S.S.R. of former German prisoners was difficult. They were pursued by suspicion and doubts. Take Nikolai Vladimirovich Numerov, who was expelled from the Party and put in prison. But no matter what befell these people later, they all preserved a touching image of the Soviet youth in Berlin, Foma Timofeyev, and they retained their gratitude to him.

The Bison kept silent. It would have been no trouble to get testimony from prisoners of war he had saved in Germany, given refuge in his house. Birulya and Borisov were still alive, as was Lutz Rozenketter, of whom we know only that he had escaped from Dresden and hid with Foma in Buch. There was Welt, whose mother died in a camp, there was a Georgian, an Italian . . . He could get testimony from the Buch Germans, co-workers at the Kaiser Wilhelm Institute, the many German scientists who were still in the GDR or who had gone to West Germany–they were all alive and corresponded with him: Melhers, Charlotte Auerbach, Boris Raevsky, the Peroux brothers. He could have gathered letters, evidence from people he had saved, the ones he had helped in the Nazi years. The Buch workers would have disproved the rumors about human experimentation and other lies. Laue, Heisenberg, and Pauli would have given testimonials. The Bison could have shamed the slanderers and would have appeared as one of the heroes of the Resistance. It was a glorious story about a Soviet scientist who rejected his safe existence and entered the fray against Fascism in the middle of Germany. The story of how, once he lost his son, he did not give up and continued . . . Supported by documents, names, photographs, it would have been exceptional.

But he didn't do any of it, and now I have to be an archaeologist, looking for shards. No wonder journalists buzzed around the Bison then. Their instinct told them there was a hidden treasure there.

The rumors did their work. People close to him knew that they were not credible. Strangers believed them.

The rehabilitation of the illegally convicted was underway, people came back from the camps and were now considered martyrs. But the Bison's arrest and exile was presented by the liars as a just punishment for collaboration . . . No one asked why the investigators did not charge him with that, why the sentence didn't mention it. No one credited him with 1945. Suspicion surrounded him with a noose and it was getting tighter.

Without bowing his shaggy, hoar-touched mane, he walked through the malevolent glances and did not wish to respond to the accusations. Once I saw this happen. And not from a scoundrel, but from a respectable, decent man. I rushed to the Bison's defense, shouting indignantly, while the Bison said nothing, just pouted with distaste, puffed, and silently left the room.

31

OLD-FASHIONED
KNIGHTS OF
THE TRUTH

The end of the fifties blazed with happy expectations of new changes. Besides the general hopes there were the special scientific ones: the creation of Akademgonodok, an Academy of Sciences town near Novosibirsk, with a boarding school for children gifted in physics and mathematics. People gathered in Moscow apartments and discussed passionately how to educate children in closed schools and who should be raised there. A. A. Lyapunov lured linguists and people in the humanities to teach these wunderkinder, established a syllabus for reading fiction, created curricula for future mathematicians. They seriously believed that under the aegis of mathematics the arts would flourish. They had an exhibit at Akademgorodok of paintings by Pavel Filonov, who had never been shown anywhere, and then a show of the works of Falk.

The febrile, crooked graph of the dreams of the scientific brotherhood of those years shot up, then dropped sharply. Cybernetics, which was supported by Lyapunov, one of the great mathematicians of the country, was declared "a pseudo-science conceived by imperialism." It was not the specialists who attacked cybernetics but philosophers like V. Koblanovsky. His profession was fighting "for Soviet science against its ideological foes." He attacked the geneticists I. Agola, S. Levit, and N. Vavilov until they were arrested. Then he fought O. Yu. Shmidt. He joined Lysenko. He went from one battle to another. Not a day without a fight. He was a philosopher who did not know how to do anything but fight. He opened up his own front against cybernetics, he was the commander and devoted all his efforts to holding up the development of that science. He got what he wanted, and had it not been for the activity of Alexei Andreyevich Lyapunov, who went all out in the defense of cybernetics, he would have achieved more.

The first thing you perceived when you met Lyapunov was his inexhaustible kindness. Nonetheless, this kindest of men was ruthless, steadfast, and clever in his defense of cybernetics. He got Academician Aksel Ivanovich Berg on his side, got the anthology *Problems of Cybernetics* published, and tried to set up a base of mathematical research for cybernetics.

Lyapunov and the Bison hit it off immediately, as if they had been friends since childhood. They understood each other perfectly. The same thing had happened between the Bison and Tamm and Kapitsa. None of them worried about the fact that the Bison wasn't an academician, and the Bison didn't care about their titles. Lyapunov and the Bison were particularly close. Lyapunov was projecting an eight-hundred-hour math course for biologists. "The idea for this course," he wrote to the Bison, "came up in Miassovo under your influence."

The Bison replied, "I went and wrote *Microevolution* for you cyberneticists. I tried, on the one hand, to put down everything essential and, on the other, to express myself simply. I ended up with thirty-two paragraphs in an aphoristic style, different from all other writing on evolution."

No one wanted to give cybernetics a home. Lyapunov met with his students at his apartment, they heard lectures and discussed them. In the summer they all went to Miassovo. The scientists knew that no matter how the authorities might put down cybernetics, staff had to be trained, theory had to be formulated, mathematical apparatus made ready.

Home meetings were forbidden, but Lyapunov continued lecturing in his apartment on the theory of programming. He used the slightest excuse to lecture on cybernetics to engineering, military, and medical personnel. In his home circle he taught the theory of probability to his biology students, showing that their statistical illiteracy led certain agrobiologists to absurd conclusions. He was the link between mathematicians, physicists, and biologists. He fought for the rehabilitation of persecuted cybernetics and genetics. He elicited petitions from physicists to the Central Committee describing the terrible situation of genetics. The war had spared Lyapunov any fear for himself. He had been in combat as early as December 1941 and reached Königsberg as a senior lieutenant.

THE BISON

He and the Bison were quiet different, yet Lyapunov complemented the moral climate of Miassovo. Lyapunov, for instance, had never published jointly with anyone. The Bison always published jointly. And they operated from the same lofty principles. The Bison felt that since he had to use interlocutors, opponents, they should be co-authors. Lyapunov was an infinitely kind man who could refuse no one. The Bison could refuse, but he also was capable of helping without being asked.

They first met at a train station in 1955. They had never seen each other but had heard a lot. They were on their way to visit mutual friends at their dacha, where they were to be introduced. They were standing in line for tickets. And suddenly the Bison came over to him: "Are you Lyapunov?" They found each other.

I asked what had attracted Lyapunov to the Bison. I was told it was his stormy nature, the breadth of his scientific view, his desire for accuracy in scientific formulation, his desire to separate individuals in the biological process. But there was nothing of that when they were on the ticket line. People are attracted not by their similar views on elementary particles. There is a hidden magnetic force that attracts us to some and repels us from other, equally unfamiliar people. They were both active volcanoes, and in their rumble and flame you could sense the fire of underground forces. Old-fashioned knights of decency, they recognized each other.

How much disillusionment we have seen since then, how many hopes mocked. Just legalize cybernetics and things will be fine. Restore genetics and abundance will come. Science will flourish in the Akademgorodoks, and talent will be appreciated . . .

The history of disillusionment is the most useful history, if the knowledge of history can teach anything at all. Yet the fifties are still recalled with tenderness.

The combination of the Bison with Lyapunov and with others produced an unexpected effect. Academician Lev Alexandrovich Zenkevich was older than the Bison and remembered him as a student. "The two huge hulks walked around in almost total silence, understanding each other without words," S. Shnol recalled. "They reminded me of two ancient lizards. I slipped between them carefully. They were like the two philosophers in

Nesterov's paintings, the course of their thoughts tied to the universe, to faith, and to consciousness, walking, plunged in silent argument."

The Bison and Zenkevich sat at a table at his birthday party and discussed loudly why so many people nowadays were having heart attacks. They decided that earlier, in their own childhood, in taverns and inns bedbugs sucked off excess blood and introduced anticoagulants into the circulation, thus reducing heart attacks. You could never understand what the Bison's jokes meant, nonsense apparently, but there was something to them . . .

Boris Stepanovich Matveyev, one of the Bison's teachers, came to the Bison's birthday party. The young people were amazed to see a living teacher of their teacher. Boris Stepanovich ran the practicum on vertebrates for Koltsov. Suddenly he asked the Bison, in front of everyone, "Kolyusha, did we teach you well?"

"You did, Boris Stepanovich."

"Then tell me, Kolyusha, please, what are the rudimentary veins in mammals left over from reptiles?"

Everyone froze. It was the Bison's seventieth birthday. Boris Stepanovich was in his eighties, but for the young people they were equally ancient elders.

The Bison huffed and puffed and burst out, "Vena azygos and vena hemiazygos!"

That choked up Boris Stepanovich and made him weep, and the Bison was touched, too.

Sukachev, Pryanishnikov, Astaurov, Vavilov, Koltsov, Zenkevich . . . Those people created a mountain range. They created a scale of height. They were the measure of decency. People feared them—what would they say? A real, constant public opinion did not exist, there was no public or scientific community to determine moral criteria, to condemn plagiarism, exploitation of students, dishonest acts, or to praise civic courage, decency. Public opinion was replaced by a few individual scientists who happily combined moral and scientific authority. But, as they say, their days were numbered, the giants were receding into darkness, and no one was taking their place. At least it seemed that way to us.

There were fewer and fewer people whose word was feared. There was no one to shame us. Some died, others were exiled, still others grew quiet or despaired. Their rules of honesty were too difficult, and they were branded old-fashioned. They went off into the realm of legend—Prophets, Knights of the Truth, Protectors of Honor.

The theories and works created by the Bison's comrades grew so that the original trunk could no longer be made out. The discoveries that once had elicited delight and wonder had turned into the self-evident, and the hard to understand into naïve talk. The mammoths who were still alive did not understand or accept much of the new in science. As they say, scientists don't change their views, they simply die out. New generations learn new views at their school desks: two or three decades later they have to be changed again.

Everything changes—interpretation, explanations, connections, the concept of the gene, the cell, the laws of heredity. But there are things that remain behind the departed scientists: their moral acts, their moral laws, the rules of their decency. These things live on, among biologists, for instance, for an amazingly long time, passed from students to the students of students, constituting the basis of every "guild." The seeds of honor grow through the generations, pushing apart rocks and tombstones.

When people talked about Sukachev, the first thing they said was how he had defended the forests against the predatory lumber industry of those years, when such conservationist views were considered harmful to the state and were dangerous to hold.

What, for instance, did people recall at the meeting dedicated to the centennial of the major histologist Alexei Alexeyevich Zavarzin? His kindness, his tireless solicitude, his noisy cheerfulness, and his intolerance of evil. How after a report by O. Lepeshinskaya, filled with unscientific garbage, Zavarzin went up to the lectern and said, "If a student of mine displayed exhibits like yours, I would have kicked him out!" He went back into the audience, laughing.

Sometimes these people's approach to ordinary things astounded us. Once I asked Simon Shnol if people had stolen from the Bison, taking his ideas, which he tossed around so insouciantly. Shnol was glad to talk about it.

"Steal? You can steal a watch from a piano, but you can't steal the piano. The Bison sometimes begged people to steal! But no one would. They said it's too heavy. A stolen thing has to be introduced. In technology they steal the obvious, which can be used right away. You can't steal mutagenesis.

Delbrück, for instance, when he came here, kept insisting that the main author of his discovery was Timofeyev-Resovsky, that it was his idea . . . Of course, when Delbrück received the Nobel Prize in Stockholm, for some reason he did not say that. Must have forgotten. But I'm certain that Nikolai Vladimirovich didn't pay any attention to that, he was glad that his idea had taken off."

For Shnol, this implied a different problem: why didn't people steal, why didn't they notice, why were great discoveries going to waste?

"We discover, then forget, then resurrect. First we bury, then we exhume, and then a new life begins. Madness! Wastefulness! Perhaps we shouldn't bury things? There's a regularity to new knowledge. The labor pains of thought are connected to the sum of views on the world. Darwin gave us the theory of evolution. That theory could have been created fifty years before him. Why did we have to wait half a century? The great biochemist David Kailin discovered what the Scots physicist MacMoon had discovered forty years earlier. He looked at a moth wing through a spectro-scope and came to the conclusion that hemoglobin-like substances exist everywhere; he was crushed by the great Austrian biochemist Komozani. And so Kailin got the Nobel Prize, making himself and MacMoon famous. But why had MacMoon been crushed? Just confidence in himself on the part of Komozani, confidence that the rest were fools."

Reflections of the Bison's volcanic flames flickered on Shnol's angular face. When Shnol, Molchanov, or Ivanov talked about the Bison, they began to glow. They tried to be objective and mentioned every moral lapse, his sarcasm and gruffness. Nikolai Vorontsov recalled how the Bison used to attack him and Yablokov.

"He was difficult to talk to, the bruises stayed with you a long time. He was infuriated because I spent time on civic work."

But Vorontsov's face is still warm with that glow.

The Bison's moral level was not revealed right away. At first one noticed his manner of speech, his erudition, the power of his thought.

In his presence young people learned a difficult lesson: valor lay not in proving the superiority of your idea but in rejecting your mistakes, allowing yourself to be proved wrong, giving in to the truth. That can be bitter, but it is the only way to stay in line.

Goethe wrote in *Faust:* "You are equal to him whom you understand." Vladimir Pavlovich Efroimson once told me in another connection, "N.V.

was higher than me because I did not understand him. But the point was in *how* I didn't understand. I didn't understand that he was two heads higher than I. I was stunned by his capacity for work and his energy. He still didn't have time to do many things, but he did have time to connect us with those Western and Soviet scientists with whom the chain of time had been broken."

I said to Valeri Ivanov, "Try to talk about him in a way that is detached from your personal interest. Science, as you know, knows no borders, it doesn't care where the gene was discovered, in Canada or in Japan; the important thing is when. Science is international in its essence. What does it matter to science where the Bison worked, in our country or in the United States, where he was invited after the war? If he had gone from Berlin to the West he would have worked just as successfully, but he would have avoided a lot of unpleasantness and insults, while the benefit to science would have been the same."

"Just a minute, I can't imagine him not staying in our country. My personal interest in him is the interest of a whole scientific school. Not many people manage to create a school. A hundred people, perhaps more, are directly in his debt. It's not a question of a professor's teaching. This was an upbringing. No, no, it does matter to science. He could not have worked like this anywhere but at home. His very presence gave out science . . . How can I put it? . . . It's enough to have several major scientists to bring about a flourishing of science. Ten major scientists left Nazi Germany and poof, that let all the air out. Physics, then mathematics and biology went into a decline. The same thing happened in Italy. You need a critical mass. Lavrentyev took eight or ten major scientists with him to Siberia and they created a real scientific center . . ."

The Bison had no inclination to philosophize. Biology, however, forced him to think about eternal questions of death, the soul, and consequently about religion. His thoughts came not from books but from life. Young people turned to him with these eternal questions. Here is one of those conversations.

"You and I are both deeply religious," the Bison said. "But the difference between us is that I believe in the existence of higher powers and you believe in their nonexistence. Neither of us can prove his thesis, no one can."

"But I keep seeing the absence of these higher powers, their uselessness.

The world manages without them and functions on the basis of other powers which are comprehensible and logical."

"By definition, those higher powers are unprovable. They are higher, incomprehensible. You cannot prove their existence. Otherwise they lose their attributes as higher powers. I feel that my system is simpler and more convenient for human life. While you have to keep admitting your faith in nonexistence."

"Now you separate science from religion, but science studies existence."

"Science can establish the connection between phenomena, but it cannot answer the fundamental questions of philosophy and is not responsible for doing so."

"Any religion is simply erroneous science, because real science is capable of describing facts on the basis of its postulates and logic and often predicts the actions of the material world . . ."

It was not an argument, but a conversation, not between philosophers but between naturalists, discussing problems on their level, in particular the problem of the soul and its immortality, a matter which worried the Bison then. They were discussing the fact that a scientific discussion of the soul was pointless. Whether the soul exists or not cannot be examined scientifically. It is given to everyone directly, and you cannot prove anything to anyone else. Science cannot disprove immortality of the soul. But religion also cannot prove its dogma on life after the death of the body.

"Unfortunately, there is only one way to check by experiment whether your soul lives on, and that is death," the Bison concluded.

And once again everything was suspended between a joke and seriousness.

32

AN ACCIDENTALLY
SURVIVING
BISON

It was awkward that he still was
not a member of the Academy of Sciences. Not for him. He wasn't the type
to feel overlooked. The other biologists and laureates, though, felt awkward.
His students thought the situation was unjust and absurd. They decided to do
something about it without telling him. Nikolai Nikolayevich Vorontsov
took charge, and he was joined by Alexei Vladimirovich Yablokov. First they
had to clear a path, clear up the story of his life in Germany, do away with
false accusations. Beginning in the late sixties, Vorontsov and Yablokov sent
out queries, collected testimony and documents, raided archives, compiled
notes. Now both men are famous biologists, with their own students and
schools: Vorontsov is a doctor of biological sciences, Yablokov a corresponding member of the Academy of Sciences of the U.S.S.R. They no longer
remember that back then, working to clear the Bison, they were endangering
their own careers. They were warned, but nothing stopped them: they lived
in the happy conviction that if they were defending a just cause, they had
nothing to fear. They managed to get in to see all kinds of big shots. They
showed their materials, they explained, they persuaded. They were supported by the academicians who knew the Bison's work. I am astonished by
the energy and sacrifice of Vorontsov and Yablokov, as well as of Lyapunov
and Volkenshtein. In their voluminous file I found letters from Academicians
A. Yanshin, L. Zenkevich, V. Menner, A. Prokofieva-Belgovskaya . . . I

won't hide the pleasure I felt in listing the people who supported Timofeyev's candidacy.

The value of those documents lies in the fact that they officially and finally did away with all formal objections and rumors that were floating around at the time. I found a remarkable letter from Hans Stubbe, president of the GDR Academy of Agricultural Sciences, to Academician Engelhardt.

I have known Nikolai Vladimirovich since 1929, when he was department head at the Kaiser Wilhelm Institute in Berlin-Buch. We had common scientific problems at the time. In discussing these problems and during evening walks that followed, it was convenient to chat about the increasingly acute political issues. H. Muller, an American Nobel laureate, was invited to Buch then, and his presence precipitated arguments with the National Socialists of the Buch institute. I assure you that Timofeyev-Resovsky was constantly on the side of the anti-Fascists. This can be confirmed by other witnesses, such as Professor Melhers (Tübingen) and Professor Dr. Bauer. Our conversations gradually created a small circle of scientists who turned into an active group of the Resistance. These scientists, who in subsequent years were repressed by the Fascist authorities, were able to speak freely at the meetings in Buch and were given instructions on more expedient behavior. I was persecuted in 1936 for anti-Fascist activity and was fired from the Hybridization Institute. Timofeyev was a model adviser for me then. His young colleagues restrained him from excessive activity, which permitted him to continue his scientific work in relative peace. Some of his colleagues did anti-Fascist work outside the institute and, if I'm not mistaken, some of them went into illegal situations to avoid arrest.

Further on in his letter he writes about Foma's death, and he ends this way:

From the beginning of my acquaintance with Timofeyev until the end of the war, not only was he my teacher in science but his noble human qualities led to a close friendship which exists to this day.

I knew Hans Stubbe, he and the Bison once visited me in Leningrad. We spent a whole evening together, but it never occurred to me to ask Stubbe about the anti-Fascist group in Buch. However, the Bison didn't bring it up

234

either, didn't make use of Stubbe's visit to the U.S.S.R., didn't get a statement from him.

It would be incorrect to suppose that he was not concerned with his own reputation. He was! But why then did he keep silent? I persisted in questioning Vorontsov and Yablokov about that. With some reservations, they both agreed that his honor would not let him speak out. He did not wish to justify himself, to have to prove his honesty, decency, and love of his homeland. He did not wish to defend himself with his son's death. His pride would not let him.

Justify himself to whom? Slanderers, thugs, people without conscience? The blood of a hereditary Russian noble forced him to be silent. *He* knew that he was innocent, and that was enough for him. His honor said, if you don't believe me, I won't stoop to explanations. His self-respect freed him from the opinions of others. He was responsible first to his ancestors, the family honor. But not to you, kind sirs, oh no.

Few understood this, it was too archaic.

Aristocracy reared its head in him. That happened to him sometimes. That's why the biophysicists for their anniversary selected a photograph of him standing on the steps wrapped in a blanket, like a Roman patrician on the Senate steps. From time to time that patrician blew up before us. But that same aristocratic feeling made him respect the workingman. He could destroy anyone with a casual phrase, a look, a word, but it was always done without crudeness. There was a difference in background, talent, upbringing, the difference between marble and cobblestone, thoroughbred and dray horse . . .

Even to his friends he said nothing, which was not wise. It was high-handed and insulting. Now, looking back, we can understand the Bison, but we cannot justify him. He allowed people to love him and nothing more. He did not allow them to see him miserable, insulted, in need of consoling. This was not fair, it was based on the secret superiority of a man with other strengths, rights, and duties.

He didn't even ride the trolley. Only taxis. He paid in paper money. He didn't believe in coins–plebeian! Yablokov tirelessly went to government offices, working to clear him. But once he burst out, "Why the hell don't you go yourself and ask to have your sentence removed?" He replied, "I never asked anyone for anything and I won't start now." If he had been just a bit flexible, written a good review, mentioned someone favorably–there were so

235

many possibilities. And that would have helped with the Academy of Sciences. But he would make no move.

It is interesting that Yablokov accepted his response and did not consider it snobbery. Yablokov realized that his attitude came from another century, from the mores of his ancestors. In some ways the Bison was closer to Alexander Nevsky than to his contemporaries.

He was an accidentally surviving bison. Once they had been the largest animals in Russia, its elephants. A heavy thing, poorly adapted to the crowding and speed of today's life . . .

"The disappearance of the bisons is an irreversible loss of part of the experience of adaptation to changing living conditions. Life had preserved that experience for millions of years," I read in a work on bisons.

Of course, we don't know how that "part" kept its equilibrium, how it helped the development of man, but it did function. Without bisons something will change in man.

Job was more human: "I cry 'insult!' and no one hears; I cry and there is no judgment." Job called on God for an answer, sought justice, demanding a meeting with God to prove his innocence. He was not afraid of a duel. He bitterly complained to his friends about God's unfairness, his ruthlessness; he justified himself before them, asked for their attention and pity: "Hear now my reasoning and listen to the pleadings of my lips."

In Job's place the Bison would probably have kept silent, disdaining complaints and justifications. His independence and freedom ran from all rulers right up to the Almighty. His personal dignity was more important. Let others determine the truth, especially since truth discovered by others was more convincing.

And so he never revealed anything about the anti-Fascist resistance in Buch, about what Foma and his friends were doing.

The loss was irreparable.

But deep in my heart, through all the judgments and complaints, I envy his limitless freedom.

It did not work out with the Academy. His candidacy for election was not approved. The administration was afraid. And the others were afraid to argue. He seemed totally indifferent. It didn't work, well, all right. Maybe it was a defeat, and maybe it was the way things should be. Everything was relative, and yesterday's mistake could turn into a victory. Just turn the switch, and the past is illuminated differently. Click: everything's fine. Click: everything's bad. Click: the past is a line of losses. Click: it is a line of good fortune. And really, there had been so many threats of inexorable disaster, and yet he had survived, he was alive. He could have been depressed over losing his homeland, over how unfairly it had received him. He could have been happy over returning to his homeland and being received boisterously.

Several lives lay behind him. Three? Five? He did not add them up. Somewhere the smoking volcanoes of his dampened enthusiasms still glowed. Rivers flowed. Their waters were lower in the riverbeds. Groves rustled. Valleys lay open where he had once passed. Fog crept through crevices we did not know.

His trip to America: marble tables in Greek restaurants, tall glasses with murky retsina, Italianate courtyards and olive trees, the halls of Congress . . . Some of his lives remained hidden, I didn't have full knowledge of them, I merely followed the outlines I knew, the broken lines of life, joining the dots with gaping abysses in between. There were unknown women, passion and lust, brawls and drinking sprees.

The Bison's archives are gone. The letters and documents. I had to put his life together from fragments. Sometimes I would find things I simply could not fit in, damned if I knew where they came from. Who would ever think that obedience to the law would be one of his qualities! Just like heresy. For instance, he accepted his court sentence, took it for granted. Wasn't there a law about nonreturners? There was. Did he break that law? He did. Fine.

He loved poetry more than his science. He esteemed poetry as highly as he did music. Deep in his heart he recognized the talent of the painter and the poet as a gift from God, like a good voice. Something sent from above. Science was different for him. A scientist has the ability to ask precise questions of nature, to find, catch, understand the answer. There was nothing exceptional about that. Since I, Timofeyev, can do it, it follows that others can, too. But I am incapable of writing real poetry (though I have read so much of it!), I cannot draw, I cannot compose music. Whereas anyone can do anything in science.

What did his world of dreams look like? Where did he go in his dreams—to the stars, the grasses, the bugs? What did he suppress in himself, what passions and desires? What do we know about the inner workings of a man's life that do not resemble his speeches and actions at all? What do we know about his secret fears, his unaccomplished deeds, his pangs of conscience? . . . What do we know about people we seem to know everything about, what went on in the soul of Pushkin or Gogol? Can poems exhaust the spiritual life of a poet? Can you understand what happens inside a cloud from examining a drop of rain?

In 1965 the Bison was given the Kimber Genetics Award and gold medal for outstanding contributions to genetics (United States). Before that he had been awarded the Darwin Medal (GDR), the Mendel Medal (Czechoslovakia), the Lazaro Scalanzani Prize (Italy). He was an active member of the East German Academy of Sciences, an honorary member of the American Academy of Arts and Sciences (1973), the Italian Association of Biologists, the Mendel Society in Sweden, the Genetics Society of Britain, the Max Planck Scientific Society in the Federal Republic of Germany. And a member of many other organizations he tired of listing. Such titles were naturally pleasant, but he attached no great significance to them. The Kimber Medal is the greatest award in genetics; it is the Nobel Prize in that field, since there is no Nobel Prize in biology. It is the recognition of serious achievements, international recognition. The Bison gladly showed the large golden disc and the bronze copy to everyone. His pride was satisfied. He particularly liked the bronze copy.

"That's in case you have to pawn the golden original for food money. Obviously they foresee the future neediness and unemployment of their recipients. The very essence of glory is its ephemeral nature . . ."

33

REVISITING AN ANCESTRAL DOMAIN IN KALUGA

O ne of the Bison's late students was Anatoli Nikoforovich Tyuryukanov. A tall peasant-like man, with a crude face, a dumb look, and a workingman's speech, he did not look like the scientist and the sensitive, cultured man he was. It's not that he created this image on purpose (though that does happen!). Nature had intended him for one thing and at the last moment put in a soul and mind for another, showing that all correlation of form and content was nonsense, that you couldn't judge a book by its cover, and that no matter how much we studied physiognomy, man would still remain a mystery. Fortunately.

He was a soil specialist. He had walked over every inch of Kaluga Oblast and in his spare time told the Bison stories about the region.

"In general, he didn't like listening to people, but he listened to Anatoli . . ."

This was in Obninsk, where the Timofeyevs moved in the sixties. Kaluga Province was the Bison's home territory. Listening to Tyuryukanov, the Bison sighed and rumbled, "Hmmm, yes . . ." Something nostalgic was happening to his soul.

In the 1890s, the Bison's father, a respectable road engineer in his late forties–no joking matter!–was building a railroad there from Sukhinichi. One fine day, he broke his leg. The workmen carried him to the nearest estate. He had to stay in bed three weeks. The daughter of the family, a sweet, quiet, and shy maiden, took care of him and they fell in love. Their love affair followed the traditions established in the days of Pushkin's stationmaster. Of course, the hero was neither hussar nor officer, but in the nineties a road engineer was a fashionable figure, no less romantic than a hussar. Something like a cosmonaut today. He wasn't very young, either, but the maiden was getting long in the tooth by their standards, twenty-nine. Their love exploded without reference to age, without any concern for the bride's despotic mother. The Timofeyevs' fading lineage did not suit the Vsevolozhskys, who were proud of being descendants of the Scandinavian Ruriks who settled Russia.

"Today people check the parents, their education and social position," Tyuryukanov noted, "but back then grandparents and great-grandparents were taken into account, your genetic background."

To rise up to their level somehow, Timofeyev bought three nearby villages on the Ressa River. He had the money for it. He became part of the Kaluga nobility. The Ressa River made him Timofeyev-Resovsky. The river still flows, and according to Tyuryukanov, is the cleanest he knows. You can drink the water.

"It survived by accident, since it has no industrial or strategic importance."

The Russian Geographical Society could give a person an additional surname for some great act. For instance, Semenov-Tian-Shansky or Muravyov-Amursky.* Timofeyev was given the surname Resovsky in view of his engineering work on the national railway system.

The Bison's move to Obninsk was a return to his Kaluga childhood, a gift at a time in life when childhood memories revive with a sweet sadness. The Bison's favorite theme was the province's heroic past. Fifteen kilometers from Obninsk was Tarutino, where Kutuzov's army had marched against Napoleon. Further along the Protva River stood a gem of a church erected by Boyar Lykov to commemorate the expulsion of the Poles from Moscow and the ascension of Mikhail Romanov in 1613. He talked about Judge Savva Belyaev in the war of 1812. Who could stop the French cannons? Savva Belyaev decided to let out the water from weirs and dams. There were many mills on the river: in Peter the Great's day there were over a hundred mills on small rivers in the Kozelsky district alone. Savva dismantled the first dam,

---

* For their respective explorations of the Tian Shan Range and the Amur River—ed.

flooded some of the French cannons. The French had to withdraw to the old Smolensk road.

As he told this story, the Bison got very excited. At one such moment, in agitation, he grabbed a sheet of paper and drew a map of the Timofeyev estate. He drew the kitchen, the gallery by the house, the lime tree lane, the weir, the village streets.

Tyuryukanov said, "Why don't we go see what's left?"

The Bison snorted and waved his arms, but people begged and pleaded. What was there to be afraid of? Of course, they had nothing to fear. But later Tyuryukanov admitted that he had touched on something very deep and private in the Bison.

They talked him into it. They got a car and drove off. Just before they left, the Bison suddenly recalled a local store owner, a thief, a scoundrel. He got very angry, no one knew why and no one cared, since they didn't know this fellow, and soon this burst of indignation was forgotten.

Several of his students accompanied the Bison. He sat in the front seat, agitated, recognizing and enjoying the landscape, or rather its spirit, since many years had passed (this was in 1967) and much had changed.

They passed Meshchovsk, an ancient city where the best bass singers lived, according to the Bison. Then Tyuryukanov got mixed up and made a wrong turn but he didn't mention it, he didn't want to spoil his teacher's good mood, they would end up in the right place eventually. When they got to Serpeisk, Tyuryukanov decided to double-check the route. He saw a sweet old lady with a samovar sitting on a porch. He went over to her and she gave him directions. Then he asked if she had ever heard of the Timofeyev-Resovskys. That's where they were going.

She replied, "Of course I've heard of them. I was nanny to their youngest son, Viktor."

Viktor was the Bison's brother. A specialist in sables. And the complete opposite of the Bison. Unhurried, quiet, shy. He restored the sable population in the country. It is his achievement that there are more sables in Russia now than there were in Ivan the Terrible's day.

"I knew Nikolai, too."

Tyuryukanov went back to the car.

"Just imagine, Nikolai Vladimirovich, that woman was Viktor's nanny."

"What?"

He jumped out of the car, ran to her, kissed and hugged her, almost weeping.

He sent her parcels from Obninsk after that and took care of her.

They went on and came out of the forest into a field. There was a little house. A ruin. An old man came out from the house. Tyuryukanov asked him if they were going the right way. The old man muttered something. Inspired by the meeting with the nanny, Tyuryukanov asked if he had heard of the Timofeyev-Resovskys. The old man grimaced, shook his fists, and started yelling: damn those sons of bitches, who exploited the masses . . . It turned out he was that same storekeeper whom the Bison had recalled before setting out.

Naturally, Tyuryukanov didn't mention this to the Bison, but he was amazed. What were the odds of two people who had not seen each other in so many years meeting on a forest road? And if you were to add to that the meeting with the nanny, then no theory of probability could handle it. This was the devil's work.

When they reached the estate they saw that the old birch lane had survived.

"Mother Catherine gave the orders," the Bison explained, "to plant birches along the roads, so that travelers would not get lost. You can see birches in the dark."

The birches formed a white colonnade. The brick manor house was in ruins, with only the moss-covered foundation stones left; everything else had been stolen. A few lime trees remained from the old park. The path down to the river was still there. Nature is wiser than man—it does not change good for bad without a reason. It takes the best and keeps it, like the rookery that the rooks had used generation after generation in those trees.

They all got out of the car, except the Bison, who did not respond to their urging. He sat in silence. They pulled him out of the car.

He went down to the brook, took a few steps; everyone waited for his oohs and aahs, or at least expecting the scene from the opera *Rusalka*: "Here's the old mill, it's in ruins . . ." Everything was in ruins. But his memory should have been reconstructing it for him. He just stood there, stunned.

They were cleaning out the pond just then. The water was drained, revealing the bottom—muck with rusty cans, wheels, a rotten boat, a spring mattress. The Bison hunched his shoulders, as if he were cold. His face darkened. They suggested that he go to the park, to see how things were. Maybe something had survived. He said nothing.

There was a lopsided brick building on the bank, with a sign: "Village Library." For Tyuryukanov and the others it was just a little house. But for the Bison . . . He panted, not budging from the spot, not hearing any imprecations. Then he rushed for the car. Sat down, without looking at anyone, and demanded in a hoarse voice, "Home! Let's go home!"

And not another word. He shut them out. I know from my own bitter experience that it's better not to return to childhood sites. They never look better. For the Bison, that little building was an ink blot on the childish picture he kept in his memory. The water was gone . . . Everything was gone, leaving only the horrible pond bottom.

A few days later, he grumbled, "Tyuryukanov, why don't you go out to the estate by yourself, then you can tell me about the soils."

"I went. I tried to talk to old-timers there. No one knew anything, who used to own the land, who built what. The people who lived there didn't remember any history. But I know that in every godforsaken hole there's a local specialist. Usually a teacher. And I was right. There was a schoolteacher who had been taking oral history from the old folks. About the local land-owners the Vsevolozhskys, their neighbors the Timofeyevs, and the cheese-making place. They had brought in a Swiss consultant to set up the equip-ment and they made excellent cheeses. They sent the cheese to Moscow. They were nobility who worked from dawn till dusk. Interestingly, they also delivered milk to Moscow, to stores in the Arbat. They were so well organized. They had the milk in jugs, the evening milking, they carted it twelve kilometers to the train station, where it was loaded on the train. In Sukhinichi, the car was coupled to the Kiev train and early in the morning the milk was in the Arbat. Overnight. With two transfers! The schoolteacher had all this in his notebooks. He interviewed people who gave an interesting picture of the Bison's grandmother, who had a fiery temper and even spilled boiling water on the serf girls when she was angry with them. But she was also a modern businesswoman. If she had lived a few more years, she would have surpassed her Swiss consultant in cheese making, she was so industrious . . . Naturally, I didn't tell the Bison anything about her. I just spoke about the nitrogen in the soil and so on, the usual analysis, to confuse him."

34

THE OBNINSK SEMINARS—
AT THE WHIRLWIND'S
CENTER

He gave away his money without counting it. While his wife, Elena Alexandrovna, was alive the finances were in her hands. Sometimes he shouted, "Lelka, give Tyuryukanov some money for books!" After her death, he gave money to whoever asked. The students came, so did neighbors and workers. They borrowed, but they soon learned that this was a man who didn't notice, and few paid him back. He thought it improper not to give. If they asked for a five, say, he would pull out a bill from his pocket and say, I don't have a five, take a ten. Beggars began going to him, first to beg and then to demand. There were days when he pulled out the last coins from his pockets for them.

It got to the point where a policeman came to him one day and said, "Nikolai Vladimirovich, please, don't give money to all these bums. They've started rumors that you keep cash in a box. You never know what people might do."

"He always lived as if he were on a village square," one of his Obninsk co-workers said. "He needed to be surrounded by people, by an audience."

He liked many people, but settled for a few friends. He could orate happily in a cell, to his guards, to the cleaning woman. When he was in the hospital in Leningrad, I visited him. There were about twelve people in his ward. They wanted to transfer him to a smaller room. He resisted. He had an audience. Curious people always sat near him, even doctors came by to listen. They still remember him there. What he said stayed with them forever, there was so much force in his words. He nailed them in.

A. A. Yarilen said this about the Bison's attitude toward the poor: he felt obliged to give. Not because he saw it as his Christian duty, as charity cleansing him of sin. Their work, he felt, was to ask, and his was to give. Nothing to discuss. That's the way things were.

"We have three categories of people who work well," he used to say, either jokingly or seriously. "Ballet dancers, circus performers, and taxi drivers. And there are those who work so-so, better than scientific personnel at least, and that's beggars."

They robbed him shamelessly. Took books and didn't return them. Yarilen and other friends had to force more persistent visitors to leave.

He had paroxysms of giving.

"He might be going through his books or records. And he'd start giving them away. Couldn't stop himself. He liked giving more than taking. We had to put a stop to these sessions."

We returned to the problem of beggars: how to treat them? Personally, the Bison's position is incomprehensible to me and I'm not too eager to accept it. It did not interest Yarilen at all: the idea may be wrong, but he took the Bison as a total package. He liked the Bison just the way he was.

But I was just discussing these theories separately as theories. They were part of his character, his behavior; without them he would have been a different person. Do I want him to be different, even better? No, not at all. You don't need only good qualities to love someone.

The days of book reorganizing were holidays. Tyuryukanov, for instance, felt no greater joy. They could fuss the whole day. The Bison would pick up a book, leaf through it, recall the memories associated with it, his agreements, his objections. "No, this isn't the Fomin who . . . This is another one, don't mix them up, he did this in that year, while his brother . . ." And he'd start a story about the author. He liked talking about the authors more than about the books. And he'd go on and on, book after book.

The Bison considered love of books an inherited trait.

Tyuryukanov recalled how they wrote an article together. "Naturally, a fundamental work, we didn't write any other kind. About twenty typed pages—biosphere, soils, this and that. Twenty pages, without references. I said, it's awkward, we should have some quotes, references. Naturally, N.V. got mad. Why should we! 'Didn't you and I get this on our own? Why should we saddle ourselves with other people?' He yelled and yelled and then muttered, 'Well, who's written most about this and understands nothing? They always have long references.' I got out a book and found an enormous list of references. We went down the list alphabetically. I was supposed to read the authors' names. Abolin. He said, 'Abolin, Abolin, I think he was persecuted. Well, put a check mark then. Go on . . .' 'Berg . . .' I said. 'Lev Semyonovich? He should be mentioned, he's a fine man. How many titles of his are there? . . . Six? Too many, pick four. Go on . . . Vernadsky . . . Vernadsky is a dear man . . . Sixteen titles? A lot. With all respect, let's leave nine.' And that's how we went down the list: 'That's a decent man, this is a civilized gentleman, this is a scoundrel, this is a fool.' We chose about two hundred references out of six hundred. He found many worthy people. It was an education for me. Then we culled the list further, with detailed analysis of the authors' views, until we got down to fifty. And then he said, 'Where are we going to cite this motley crew? Oh, Lord Jesus, read our article.' I read the first sentence: 'In recent years much has been done in modern natural sciences in . . .' 'There,' he said. 'Put in a parenthesis here, throw in the lot from one to fifty, and be done with it.' That's what we did, everyone was happy, no one had to read anything."

All his co-authors were amazed by his style of work. Nikolai Vorontsov told me a colorful story about how he and Alexei Yablokov would take the commuter train to Obninsk to work with the Bison.

"Elena Alexandrovna fed us and went off to work. N.V. demanded that she feed us well, otherwise we would starve and not write anything. 'Let's start. What did we have last time?' He dictated the entire book. He paced fast from corner to corner and dictated. Alyosha, with the agility of a monkey, managed to write it down. Suddenly, a roar. 'Wait a minute, wait a minute. What have you written there?' He'd read it. 'Drop it. That's not it, this is. This is better.' Once Alyosha lost a chapter. He showed up guiltily and apologized to N.V. What could he do? He dictated it over again. Then they found the chapter. We compared them. They matched word for word, that's how carefully he had thought things through. There were sections we wrote. We read them to him. 'That's good,' he would say. 'And here we'll write a preamble.' "

Yablokov talked to me about this, too. I liked juxtaposing stories from several sources.

"I did all the reading research for the next chapter during the week. I made notes and an outline of how I would write it. I would come to him and read it. He'd start boiling. 'How is that possible? What are you using for your basis? You're a fool!' And he'd start dictating, not letting me talk. I'd talk anyway. Sometimes after an explosion of fury he'd change his mind: 'Damn you, write!' And he would dictate, incorporating my point of view. It was miraculous. His dictated text required no correcting. It was a burst of genius. Sometimes I would come the next day and say, 'Even though we mentioned something, it's not clear enough for fools.' He'd shout, 'The hell with them if it's not clear! . . . Well, all right, write.' And he'd give me what I asked for, but not in the form I asked. He spent a lot of time on the organization of the book. This was his method: The first outline was one page long. Then a more detailed version, ten or fifteen pages long, would lay out the approach to the book, each chapter summarized in at least a half page, everything clearly planned. I began using that method myself, it takes a long time doing the general outline, expanding it step by step . . ."

He was incapable of working alone. For instance, all his works on molecular biology were done with Delbrück. Delbrück was a young physicist then. He worked with the Bison just the way Vorontsov and Yablokov had.

The oldest art in human culture is the art of socializing. When there was no theater, no painting, no music, there was socializing. All the arts sprang from it.

It is hard to determine what the art of the Bison's socializing was or whether it could even be called an art. He did not impose himself, did not hog the floor, but he was quite capable of interrupting any conversation, scattering interlocutors. He won out because he was interesting to listen to. Everything grew animated in his presence, became intense. He was asked to give talks, people wanted to hear him.

He went off to lecture as if to a party. It was a better form of self-expression than writing articles. He was happy to have an opportunity to communicate, and people were attracted to him, sensing that live contact was important to him.

His charm and influence were so strong that people took on his expressions and mannerisms without noticing it.

"For years I spoke in a manner imitative of N.V.," Molchanov admitted to me. "I didn't even try not to do it, I actively played the role."

He was not bothered by it, he didn't develop the Demochkin complex. He imitated him eagerly, like the rest.

"I wasn't worried about aping him," he continued. "There were periods when I imitated N.V., and then I got over it.

"The important part was getting his thoughts. I took an imprint of them at such a deep level that even decades later I could recall his words, his expressions, how he used to jump up, running back and forth, getting angry, getting kind . . ."

In Miassovo most people did not understand the lecturers. That's the situation in most schools and symposia. Especially if mathematicians and physicists are involved. The Bison usually nodded off, lower lip protruding, during the talks. When they were over, he would open his eyes and sum up. Everything then became clear. He had a talent for extracting the point. He could unite discrete, seemingly disparate parts of a subject and explain why this point or that was necessary in the fifth place. That was one of his favorite questions: "Why is this important in the fifth place?" Often, the sad conclusion that followed was: "In the fifth place, this is not important at all."

His excellent memory was a help. Memory alone is not talent, but talent together with memory succeeds much better than either by itself. Anna Benediktovna Getseva told me that when she first came to Miassovo and met the Bison, telling him she was from the Zoology Institute, he asked who was head of her department. Ah, Popov? The Vladimir Veniaminovich Popov who published an article in 1921 in such and such a journal about those cockroaches? Yes, I know him! . . . She had never heard of her chief's article.

The young people from his lab bubbled around him in Obninsk, as well as young people from Moscow and those who were still attached to him since the days of Miassovo and those who got stuck after each biology session he taught.

They met in his apartment in Obninsk (where else?), an ordinary three-room apartment with low ceilings in a standard high-rise building. The dented samovar gurgled, Lelka poured tea, he paced the dining room, his study, full of energy. It was impossible to understand how he managed to get through that crowd, the tangle of arms, legs, and heads.

THE BISON

Nothing had changed. If you don't count what had changed in genetics, radiology, biophysics, and other sciences. Ever since the days of the Drozsoor, the routine was the same, everything took place the way it had in Berlin and in the Urals. Unshakable, no matter what.

Once we came to Obninsk for New Year's. The Bison and Lelka did not differ very much from their graduate students and young friends who had come from Moscow and farther afield. They sang louder, knew the words better, and he danced and joked like the rest. They read poetry. The Bison was at the center of a whirlwind, and no one was jealous or competitive.

In the morning, after sleeping late, we went cross-country skiing (though he didn't like it), and from lunchtime on we sat at the table again, finishing off the food and drink, and started talking about science, about which I knew nothing. Out of curiosity I jotted down a few phrases, his and those of others provoked by him.

"Engineers forget that the biosphere is necessary for more than food."

"We can't get rid of fools, we can only slow down their activity."

"The upper part of the forest determines the lower part, the shade-loving plants. Radiation damages the upper part, freeing the lower to form its own upper layer."

"I think we'll suffocate long before we starve to death."

"In nature there are the oppressed and the oppressors."

"The apostle Peter denied Christ three times, but that didn't stop him from becoming a major apostle."

When they got tired, they played Georgian music.

Music was part of the procedure of their socializing. The Bison didn't have enough arguments at work, he organized them at home (again, where else?), seminars on the history of music and other arts. They met every two or three weeks, taking turns reporting. A humanities education had ended for his lads at grade school. He himself hadn't had music education since seventh grade. And since then his students had become more ignorant: there was no humanitarian nutrition in the hard-science departments. Despite their college degrees, they could not be considered civilized people. And yet they hoped to become professors and mentors. Which would be the greatest shame of our intelligentsia.

These speeches were accompanied by a demonstration of the mediocrity if not total ignorance of those who tried to defend themselves. His tests broke their spirit.

Then the seminars began. Brand-new food for the young people's minds. Georgian music and instruments. Haydn. Roerich. A. A. Yarilen was assigned to lecture on ancient polyphony. They played old records for demonstration.

Twenty to thirty people would pile in for these lectures. They sat in the hallway, on the floor, under the table. Then they had tea and cookies. Some got as close as they could to their hostess, to make sure their tea was strong. They gathered at eight and broke up around midnight.

"The best part was the spirit, not the information," Yarilen told me. "We weren't great specialists, but he made us feel comfortable. He argued, he'd come up with a line like: 'I know of four great artists in the nineteenth century—Alexander Ivanov, Delacroix, Van Gogh, and Vrubel.' That was it. No arguing. No way to insert Surikov in there. But his formulas were memorable. 'Leonardo is a serious genius. A real genius is a healthy man. There can be a personality so huge that you can't tell if it's a man or a god.' "

Yarilen recalled his battle for Scriabin, whom he liked. He managed to get an acknowledgment that Scriabin was a good pianist, that he had successful piano works—but his symphonies were nonsense.

"And I agreed, I couldn't defend my position." Yarilen was not embarrassed by his defeat, he laughed as he recalled his losses to the Bison. "But he revealed Rimsky-Korsakov to me. I adored Stravinsky and learned that he liked him, too. We were very happy and embraced. He considered Mahler unbearably boring. The best part was when he lectured. Everything seemed marvelous. What he didn't know, he guessed, and that was interesting, too. He prepared his lectures. If you came early, he'd be pacing and muttering. He was like that when schoolchildren from Moscow came to see him, eighth-graders. He also prepared, got special material. He didn't care whether he was lecturing academicians or schoolchildren—he took his responsibility seriously."

These seminars continued for a year and a half, and were enormously popular. They had conducted over forty of them when the storm broke. A new person arrived in town, a new Party boss. He held the firm conviction that the greatest evil came from the intelligentsia.

Hearing about the at-home seminars, he found out that they had not been approved, and therefore were illegal meetings, not seminars. Who was in charge? A scientist who had worked for the Nazis during the war! Besides, what did it mean, a scientist without degrees? Not a professor, not a docent. Had served time. Not a very dependable type.

Strangers began coming to the seminars. Silently took notes. Then the boss gave an angry speech, with quotes. There was nothing special in the quotes, but at the same time they were apolitical, non-Marxist. There was a "stink" about these meetings, he said. What was society thinking about? How did they allow this? What about our young people?

With his pride, the Bison wouldn't have lifted a finger in his defense. But he wanted to save the seminars, and the Bison decided to talk with the authorities. People tried to dissuade him. No terms were possible with that Person, why get involved? But the Bison was convinced that he could explain, clear the air, prove to anyone at all that the seminars were useful.

He showed up for his appointment. He sat quietly in the waiting room. One hour, two. He was getting angry but he waited. By lunchtime, the secretary opened the door and said, "Go see the Party instructor, He won't see you." Her voice was full of awe at the might and power of her boss.

His students, wet behind the ears, to whom he explained Rubens and Stravinsky, had a much better understanding of the mores of that office.

The seminar was closed down. Nothing helped. And once they were shut down, the guilty party could be found. The leader was guilty. A suggestion was made to fire him from the institute.

His work was interrupted. His students left one after another. The Bison was invited by Academician Oleg Grigorievich Gazenko to work at his Moscow institute, and that's where he worked to the end of his days.

At Cambridge, a picture of a crocodile hangs in what used to be Rutherford's lab. That was the great physicist's nickname. In Obninsk perhaps they will hang a picture of a bison someday. But back then, in the early seventies, the city authorities wanted to get rid of that man and they had no idea that his memory would be revered.

In September, before going into the hospital, the Bison gathered his friends, old and young. He was eighty-one. Lelka's death had hurt him, the weight of the world was now his burden alone. His lower lip protruded even more. His pale features showed his noble lineage. He didn't look like an old man, though, just tired.

His mind was clear and fresh. Recently he had dictated an article for *Nature* about what should be studied in biology. The article made a big splash. He would have lasted a century if Lelka had remained by his side.

Everyone knew he had a reason for gathering them. They tried to joke and behave as usual. It didn't work.

He said that his life had been happy thanks to the good people who had surrounded Lelka and him. That was the truth. He was not bitter or angry over what he had had to put up with, the slander, the unfair blows . . . Much dearer to him than titles and awards was the fact that many people had loved him and helped him. They came to read to him, kept him up to date, took care of his household. The number of people around him did not diminish. Young people, unknowns, stuck to him in herds, even though he was no longer in a position of authority. They came to listen, to learn, and that was good.

The word "farewell" was not spoken. But people understood this was a farewell. The ancient Romans did it this way—the one who was departing called his friends in to say goodbye. Calmly and bravely they discussed death. For instance, could there be a glorious death, or was death indifferent? "No one praises death, they praise the one whose soul death took without excitement."

He was still with them, but in some other time. Perhaps the past? Sometimes he looked at them foggily from a distance where there was no time at all. Everyone realized that it was important to reach that place and there was no need to return. From there death was not an event or a mystery —merely the end of life; you could unroll the piece of paper and look at the picture of the life that had been, for life by itself is neither good nor bad, as the Romans had known, merely the vessel for good and bad.

He did not grieve parting from them, from life. Perhaps because he dreamed of meeting Lelka. Not that he believed in an afterlife, but the soul remained. He was counting on that. The soul exists as a psychic spot, and that meant that their souls could meet. It was his private faith. Faith which he did not confuse with his knowledge.

He gave each of them some advice, in passing, without solemnity. He told Yarilen about immunity. "He had never studied the field, but I'll never forget what he said, it got right to the essence of the matter."

He did not speak of his own work. Sooner or later it would become a "historical stage." People would discover errors, flaws, what he took for one process would turn out to be three–that's progress. New explanations for the same things . . .

He was leaving like an animal sensing the approach of death. Animals hide in secret places. People go off into themselves, down in the valleys of memory.

35

PASSING ON THE BEST TO THE NEXT GENERATION

Biophysicists from all over the country had gathered. Formally, it was a holiday, but using the banquets and parties as an excuse, they held a symposium. I had never seen so many biophysicists at once. They all looked young in the same way. Twenty, thirty, forty–all looked young. Fresh, tanned faces. Men with mustaches, beards, balding, and very young women. They all partied the same way, used the same words, told the same jokes, laughed the same way. The resemblance was due to the fact that they had the same set of "parents," they came from one nest, the biophysics department at Moscow State University, and they were celebrating its twenty-fifth anniversary. I was there by accident. I had been planning to go to Pushchino for a long time. S. Shnol had tapes of the Bison there. My visit corresponded with the anniversary party for the department, which the Bison had known well. I was lucky with the Bison, fortune dogged my steps.

The invitation for the party was ingenious, with poetry and caricatures of the current heads of the department. Inside was an honor roll of the founders, the mentors of Soviet biophysics at the university. The busts resembled Roman emperors. They were all academicians–Petrovsky, Tamm, Semyonov, Lyapunov–all except the Bison, whose bust was drawn in the center. And in the meeting room, where they had large photographs, his was the biggest, the one with him standing on the steps wrapped in a plaid blanket. It looked like a toga and he could have passed for Caesar.

254

He had been dead a long time, but that didn't seem to matter to anyone there. It felt like one of his seminars in Miassovo. His spirit reigned.

People came out onstage. They talked about themselves, what they had done after graduation. They spoke simply, so that even I understood a few things. The audience heckled. But the speakers mocked themselves even more. They preferred irony to exaggerating the importance of their work. That was the tradition—no seriousness. Judging from their reports, biophysics was comparable to chasing sneaky demons, playing hide-and-seek. It didn't seem to afford them much pleasure, however.

People think that scientific work gives man his highest satisfaction. Scientific discovery is supposed to be real happiness, altruistic, and an example for all who wish to be happy; generations were brought up believing this, novelists promised this, and the patriarchs of science said so when they addressed the young.

"I'm afraid that working in science is pathological," Lev Alexandrovich Blumenfeld said. As head of the department, he was the last to speak. He did not want to seem different from his students. "Many of us are convinced that pleasure from science is bait for the uninitiated. The joy from success beckoning in the distance comes so rarely that there is no point in counting on it. Besides which, pleasure is not in proportion to achievement. Science reminds me of drug addiction or alcoholism. You drink because you cannot not drink. You don't have the strength to resist. You drink, and you feel disgust, as a wino used to say, but not drinking is even more disgusting."

Lev Alexandrovich recalled his own moments of such pleasure over the last quarter century. He came up with five. And one of the cases was a mistake. They later found their error and had to retract the results. That left four. The fourth time had taken place ten years earlier, when, in order to understand something about unstable states of matter, he had to write a book about them. Before that, Lev Alexandrovich had given a few lectures that no one had understood. He himself understood no more than his audiences. By the time he got halfway through the book, he realized what was what. It became clear, and that gave him pleasure.

Another instance came when he was hospitalized after a heart attack. He wasn't allowed to read or write. That left thinking, "an unusual pastime for a scientific worker." He began thinking and worked out the problem of weak interactions in biology.

Successes and failures play hide-and-seek with the researcher. He was head of a project that discovered new magnetic properties in cells. They found them, were happy, published their work. Then they had doubts, got scared, double-checked, found a mess, and rejected their own work. It was a shame, of course. But honor was more important. However, someone continued the work and later found that their doubts had been groundless and that the ferromagnetic substances did in fact exist. That was a most luxurious failure. The rest of the time is spent on routine experiments, on boring detail work, on reports no one needs . . .

I wondered why he wasn't sparing himself, why he was showing his sore spots to this herd of youths who had no pity.

"Sometimes I write papers by myself, without co-authors," he continued.

A ripple of laughter went through the audience. They appreciated that. Not that they were paying great attention. He was in no way superior to them. On the contrary, his age was a disadvantage. His only advantage was the distance he had covered. He could warn them about a thing or two.

It was not easy competing with young people. They regarded the classics with pitying smiles. They knew more than the deceased laureates of the Nobel and other prizes. They knew their mistakes, the failures of their methods. Their equipment was primitive, inadequate. To them the classics meant old hat. Science wasn't music or literature, it didn't need classics.

The young were right, and there was something sad in their righteousness, in their ruthlessness. The great names were duly respected, revered, but they had no real feelings for them. Everyone remembered the Bison, but he was going off into the past, so filled with errors. Yet they were afraid of picking on him. They circled him carefully. He continued to be active, and one fine day it might turn out that he was right and not they. Some of them had already been burned that way.

One could remain a leader among them only by treating them as equals. The directors of the departments stayed in shape because no one made any allowances for them—not for L. A. Blumenfeld, not for Shnol, who had lived in Pushchino so long. They didn't need anything from their former students, just as they didn't need anything from their former teachers.

I asked a fellow from Riga why he had come, taking three days without pay to attend.

"I missed the guys," he said right off the bat. Then he added, "I wanted to check out my ideas, talk them through." He furrowed his brow. He needed another reason. "Maybe because here you can express any stupid idea you want. You can't do that at work . . ."

I felt there was still more. None of them could explain exactly why they had to come back to the nest periodically.

The graduates sat with their classes. Over two hundred people around long tables in the restaurant. They made toasts, reminisced. For recent graduates, the Bison was a legend. I sat down with the first graduating class, where everyone knew him. They still used the nicknames he had given them. Here was Tractor, there was Chromosome. They had worked with the Bison in Miassovo. They were brainwashed there, set straight, wised up. They still used the jokes of those years, the folklore passed from generation to generation: "There are two points of view—mine and the wrong one." "Don't ask how it's happening, ask how it can happen."

They were all on a first-name basis, these grown-ups who had become boys and girls again. If I had talked with Andrei Malenkov at his institute, I would have dealt with a solid, respectable scientist. Here I was talking to a boy, a fan of the Bison's.

"I'm a physicist by training. The directors of our department are not biologists. We got our real genetic education from Nikolai Vladimirovich. I was very lucky with my teachers. Lyapunov taught me how to think mathematically. Lately I've been thinking about it, because I have to determine the strategy of my works. A school is important. Timofeyev is the main link. He determined my fate in many ways. He taught me to regard biology in an evolutionary way. Teaching someone to think biologically is the hardest. The connection between physics and biology, the principle of complementing, of mutation, all that became part of me. He was egotistical enough and put his priorities first. But he was critical toward his own work, more critical than other scholars . . . He was distinguished by his optimism. I studied gerontology and I am convinced that longevity is impossible without optimism. It's genetic. You can't develop it easily. Despite his extraordinary life, Nikolai Vladimirovich was the most consistent and energetic optimist . . . He treated us mercilessly. It was hard to get his approval and you had to use every effort to get him to take an interest, to listen attentively. He was very demanding, and if someone said something boring or unfounded, he'd interrupt with 'Nonsense! Murk!' "

Someone joins the conversation, as if we were talking about a hot issue.

"He wasn't as interested in older people. That's why he liked our department so much. Naturally, he added the gloss of the twenties to our young people, making them better than they were, but that was all right. He had two basic principles: one, good people must multiply, and two, our generation has to pass on the best to the next and then let them handle it."

They were repeating things I knew, but I didn't stop them.

"I never heard better lectures than his," another young person added. "In genetics, population genetics, and art: Chekhov, Vrubel, and Serov. He had only six lectures on art."

The next morning Andrei went on with his story before the symposium.

"From the point of view of science, N.V. was heads above the rest in the breadth of his thought. At first you noticed his temper, his manner, his erudition, and it was only much later that I could appreciate the depth of his thought. We had even agreed to write a work on Russia. He felt that Russia was not a country, but something bigger–a world. There is an Arab-Persian world, there is the Far East, there is the Latin American world, and there is Russia–a continent with its fate, path, and predestination. Each continent has its own meaning . . . In his late years he was concerned by the question of the immortal soul. If good is absolute, he felt, then that is God. Evil was relative, but good was absolute–that was the source of his optimism. It was distinguished by concrete thought. He never discussed things in general. A Westerner in many ways, he was rational. The culture of his thought would not allow him to chase chimeras. He was a Russian Westernizer, a character like Peter the Great, who, however, valued people highly . . . We had our differences. For instance, I don't believe in the immortal soul. Immortality means retaining individuality. There is immortality in creative works, but the personality dissolves no matter how a person may want to preserve himself."

"He was a geographer, a geneticist, a botanist, and a zoologist," Shnol added. "But it's not a question of breadth but of extent. He felt close to Krashninnikov, who went off to Kamchatka to obey Peter the Great's wishes . . ."

"What do you think," one of the youngsters asked me, "after the Lysenkoists were exposed, why did none of them commit suicide?"

The question gets everyone's attention and the Bison is forgotten.

The past does not hold them for long. They have their own battles. Lysenkoism is such an absurd story for them that they cannot understand the triumph of their elders, their still hot anger.

THE BISON

The Bison is more interesting for them. Everyone has a memory and offers it to me like a souvenir.

Soon the conversation moves to whether Pushkins *The Queen of Spades* can be seen as a tragedy of Newtonian science: I do this, and I should get this result, but I don't! That can drive you mad.

Listening to them, I hear words and turns of phrase taken from the Bison. They adopted his manner of thought without noticing it. He will live on in at least one more generation. We all consist of someone's advice and example, follow someone, repeat someone. There is much of the Bison left. It seemed that he gave of himself extravagantly. Nothing of the sort! It was the best way to pass himself along to others . . . As he said, our generation has to pass on the best to the next and then let them handle it.

Life has one marvelous quality: like bread, life is something you never get tired of. Obninsk was more than a new place to live for the Bison, a new job at the Institute of Medical Radiology. It was a return to Kaluga, to his childhood. Homeland is always childhood: the old wooden house that lives in your memory—enormous, with creaks and sighs, and dry sunny dust, the aroma of dried mushrooms, the green moss on the well, and the smell, the damp smell of the river, and the grove with its scary owls and snakes, and the steep staircase going down to the green pond.

The promised land was given to him at the end of his road. He would not leave here, he would not leave the land of his ancestors. The end of his pilgrimage had come.

New students, new young people, new seminars, summer school on the shore of the Mozhaisk Sea. Everything was repeated, as it had been in Miassovo, on the next loop.

In the summer he and Lelka traveled by ship along the Enisei, the Amur, the Kama, the Ob, and the Belaya rivers and the Volga-Baltic Canal. He wanted to see new places. If he had not been a zoologist, he would have been a traveler. He sat on the deck staring by the hour at the slow movement of shores, villages, piers, and circling gulls. He was intoxicated by Russia. He sailed for a month, an entire epoch. He skipped the excursions, did not go into the towns, he wanted to be in the great outdoors. He looked, thought, worked.

His talent lay in finding what was important and dealing with it. Now, when he had so little time left, when the days grew shorter and the minute hands spun faster, he had to choose the last important thing.

I will note that his relationship with time was always respectful, he honored that silent flow which sometimes rushed and sometimes dragged. Everything in the world was made by time and out of time. Including human life. But time was not homogeneous and not equally valuable. You could take out the best from it, turning empty time into golden hours and minutes.

One evening I found him delighted: his family had gone to the movies, he decided not to go at the last minute, and he had gained two hours of precious time.

Yellow leaves floated on the smooth surface of the reservoir. In the middle of summer the remaining birches dropped their leaves. His heart ached at the sight of the sick rivers, filled with rotting logs, the empty forests, the lakes covered with oil spills. Russia's green cover was being torn into shreds. Better than others he understood the uniqueness of the miracle wrought by nature after millions of years of seeking. He knew what the fragile balance of the taiga, the steppes, the whole landscape had cost, what sustained the foxes and ravens, the lady bugs and moles, worms and butter-flies—two or three thousand components, a complex system. A self-regulating complex system, until man interfered.

He wondered where its stability came from. What were its limits? How did living things adapt to each other and maintain that stability from generation unto generation?

Nature's disease was man. Man did not see the earth as a living, suffering creature. How could we strengthen that creature? How could we improve the productivity of the earth's biosphere? He proposed the bases for analyzing the biosphere, its interaction with man.

Until recently people have seen nature as a collection of good parts, which they grabbed greedily, without thinking of the consequences. The alarm bells tolled too softly.

Nature preserves, small reservations granted to nature, were one thing, environmental protection was another.

In the seventies his views were rejected. Most people, even scientists, felt that the important things were productivity indexes in agriculture. Environmental protection was mere sentiment, the concern of intellectuals without practical knowledge. They felt that nature was boundless and that man's influence on it was insignificant. The Bison's persistent warnings only aroused their irritation. They accused him of sabotage: "Do you want to stop the work? We don't need concern for the environment if it hinders the development of industry." He was accused of political illiteracy: nature had to be protected from the rapacity of capitalism, not from the greed of a socialist economy. With a sad laugh he quoted Kapitsa: "This reminds me of the girl who wants to give in out of love, but they keep trying to rape her." Of course, Kapitsa was talking about his own problems. But a good comparison works like a proverb.

At the Institute of Medico-Biological Problems, Academician O. G. Gazenko took good care of the Bison, letting him work to the end of his days. He worked on problems of space medicine, setting up genetic research. Gazenko treated him with respect and tenderness. Luck struck once more!

Some scientists worried the Bison. They quietly endorsed barbaric projects to build destructive industrial enterprises beside lakes, to chop down forests, to erect dams, to dig canals. Others hid in their corners, avoiding conflicts. Science helped man live more comfortably at the expense of nature. Atomic technology, chemicals: there were always unexpected consequences, grave errors; science was losing its prestige. Sometimes it looked like a servile handmaiden.

In discussing science, he tried to find the reasons for its indifference to its impact upon nature. It was stupid to criticize wolves for eating deer or locusts for eating crops. Reason was the product of nature, it could not rise above it; what it did was part of a process we did not know . . . He was not justifying, he was looking for the best combination so that reason and the biosphere could coexist.

The beautiful firs stood tall, branches raised over the shimmering winter fog. The birches held the light, their crowns golden in the sunset; the firs were black, plunged in twilight.

His days were diminishing. His life on this earth was ending. Lelka was gone, and he never did figure out how to live without her. Science was left. Science had no end, and what he had achieved was no longer as valuable as it had been. The object of his life's work, the mysteries of the world he had unearthed, which he had devoured with insatiable appetite, all the while developing his talent—it all dimmed before the main mystery of life.

He did not want to change anything in his fate. He knew that no one would ever understand the main mystery, and that consoled him.

Once again he sat on the deck chair on the upper deck and gulls circled and cried above him. Once he had studied them. He esteemed ornithologists above all zoologists. He joked, but with pride, that he was the only zoologist who had been "shat upon by a pelican out in the field."

Birds behaved mysteriously. Just take their songs, their language. What did they talk about? Fledglings could fly across the ocean without their parents. How did they find their island in the ocean? Say it's in the genetic code—but how does that notation become orientation, a route to follow?

The river widened, majestically flowing to its mouth. His life was also approaching a terminus. There had been problems, insults, the business with the Academy of Sciences—things that had once upset him were left behind now and seemed petty. He felt he was a river flowing a long time and from far away. He carried waters from the mountains and from the source where everything began; in essence he had lived long before the time he was born, he came from the previous century. The Russia of Turgenev, Chekhov, the Russia of the Civil War, the Russia after the war, prewar Europe, Nazi Germany, the atomic world—all the epochs of our century came together in him, and they continued in him . . .

Sometimes it seems to me that he has not died. If he could come to us from the last century, he could have gone back there. An Indian legend speaks of the day when the bisons will come down from the pastures in the skies and thunder across the prairie. And the men of the tribe will run after them, to feel the earth trembling under the weight of the giants, to regain the feeling of fear and awe.